T0133248

Companion to the Papers of Donald Knuth

ALSO BY DONALD KNUTH
FROM CSLI PUBLICATIONS

Literate Programming
Selected Papers on Computer Science
Digital Typography
Selected Papers on Analysis of Algorithms
Selected Papers on Discrete Mathematics
Selected Papers on Computer Languages
Selected Papers on Design of Algorithms
Selected Papers on Fun and Games

CSLI Lecture Notes Number 202

Companion
to the
Papers of
Donald Knuth

CSLI Publications
Stanford, California

'TEX' is a trademark of the American Mathematical Society.
'METAFONT' is a trademark of Addison–Wesley.

Copyright ©2011
Center for the Study of Language and Information
Leland Stanford Junior University
17 16 15 14 13 12 11   5 4 3 2 1

Library of Congress Cataloging-in-Publication Data
Knuth, Donald Ervin, 1938–
  [Papers. Selections]
  Companion to the papers of Donald Knuth / Donald E. Knuth.
  xiii,441 p. 23 cm. -- (CSLI lecture notes ; no. 202)
  Includes bibliographical references and indexes.
  ISBN 978-1-57586-635-2 (cloth : alk. paper) --
  ISBN 978-1-57586-634-5 (pbk. : alk. paper)
  1. Computer algorithms. 2. Computer programming. I. Title.
  QA76.9.A43K5852 2011
  005.1--dc23
                                        2011029607

Internet page
   http://www-cs-faculty.stanford.edu/~knuth/cp.html
contains further information and links to related books.

to Dikran Karagueuzian, who conceived
and gave birth to this series of books

Contents

Preface

This book completes the series of volumes that contain archival forms of the papers that I've written during a period of more than fifty years. The first few chapters contain material that "slipped through the cracks" and did not appear in any of the previous eight volumes. The last few chapters contain complete lists of everything that I've ever published, together with finding aids by which individual items can readily be located. In the middle are several chapters of "table talk" that provide background for the entire collection; these chapters are transcriptions of informal lunchtime conversations that were recorded fifteen years ago. And everything is followed by the main reason for this book's existence, namely, a comprehensive index to all nine volumes of this series.

My attitude toward these volumes is identical to what Lars Ahlfors once expressed eloquently in the preface to his own works (1982):

> When first confronted with the prospect of having my collected papers published, I felt both awe and confusion, but I calmed down when I realized that the purpose was not to honor the author, but to be of service to the mathematical community. If young scholars of a future generation should desire to find out what some mathematicians of the twentieth century were up to, they would indeed have reason to be thankful if spared the need to seek this information from a multitude of sources.

Indeed, I look forward to seeing similar collections that bring together the works of my colleagues, including of course the 21st century as well as the 20th, and including computer science as well as mathematics.

Stanford's mathematics library presently contains the collected papers of more than 300 mathematicians, often in sets of ten or more volumes. Only 23 of those collections include an overall index to the contents of the papers that have been reprinted. (Well, probably I should say 24, because each of the eight volumes of John Tukey's papers does have its own index. But the number of indexed collections still remains less than 8% of the total.) Another 10 of the collections include an index of all the authors who are named, but lack a subject index. As a user of such collections, over a period of many years, I know that indexes have always been a great help, when they exist. Therefore I've done my best to make the indexes in the present book as useful as possible.

Most volumes of collected works simply reproduce original papers in facsimile. However, I decided from the outset that I wanted to have a last chance to apply spit and polish to what I've written, thereby achieving a more uniform style and typographic format, while striving to preserve the flavor of the original works. During the past twenty years, as these volumes of collected works have been taking shape, I've seized the opportunity to improve the wording of papers that were originally written before my publishers' copy editors taught me a thing or two about writing. Thus each paper has been reprinted in a form that I hope is worthy of being remembered. I've also included an Addendum with most of the papers, attempting to bring the material up to date with reports on subsequent developments. It seems to me that this "value-added" approach is far more useful than simply to copy the original documents verbatim; those originals can be found elsewhere.

Let me now discuss the contents of the present volume in more detail. Chapter 1 contains the texts of six dozen problems that I contributed to a variety of journals, beginning in 1965 and continuing to the present day. Some of the problems are, of course, more difficult than others. Some of them relate purely to mathematics, while others relate purely to computer science, but most of them involve a mixture of those two disciplines. In any case there is a lot of variety, and I still believe these problems are both instructive and interesting.

Solutions to nearly all of the problems in Chapter 1 have appeared elsewhere, and references to those solutions can be found in Chapter 20. But a few of the problems have not yet been solved in print; so I've filled that gap by presenting their solutions in Chapter 2.

The next four chapters are brief essays that I didn't want to leave out of my collection of publications, so I've sneaked them into the present book. Chapters 3 and 4 deal with undergraduate education; in fact, Chapter 4 was written when I myself was an undergraduate.

Chapters 7 through 17 are unique. They exist because of Dikran Karagueuzian, who is director of CSLI Publications and the publisher of all these books. In his words,

> Encouraged perhaps by the success of the first volumes of the *Selected Papers* series, I suggested to Don that we do a few

recorded interviews, in which he would be able to talk freely about matters that could not possibly be part of his professional writing. After some arm twisting, and some offers of free lunch, I convinced him to try this experiment. I was gratified at the end to see the transcripts take shape and become the basis of a narrative, which I hope will be appreciated by students as well as historians of computer science.

Those conversations explain the background for many of the papers, especially the earliest ones. Furthermore, 1996 was an interesting year from many points of view. For example, that was the year when I learned to use HTML, because the World Wide Web was growing so fast.

The index portions of this book begin with Chapter 18, which is sort of my "résumé." That chapter lists various activities that I've been involved in at various times. In particular, it mentions all of my students and their Ph.D. dissertations.

Chapter 19 is a complete list of all the books that I've written, together with all translations of those books into other languages. (Incidentally, I'd like to express here my heartfelt thanks to each of the translators, because I can perhaps appreciate the great difficulties they faced better than anyone else. When I wrote the original texts, I could say anything that I wanted; but they did not have such freedom. They also had to cope with my use of many strange American idioms that do not ordinarily appear in technical writing.) Logicians, please note: The present book is a member of the set of all books that cite themselves.

Chapter 20 is one of the most important, because it lists all of the papers together with their "opus numbers" like P1, P2, ..., Q1, Q2, ..., R1, R2, ..., which I've long been using for cross-references in my personal files. The original titles and journal citations are given here, as well as information about any translations or reprintings that have been brought to my attention—including, of course, the places where those papers have appeared within the nine volumes of collected works. Following Dikran's advice, I've also annotated each of the major papers with a sentence or two that should help to put it in context.

Chapter 21 is an alphabetical list of the titles of all the books and all the papers. Many of the books and many of the papers appear several times in this list, so that they will be easier to locate.

Finally comes the Big Index, which covers all nine volumes of collected papers in a combined index of names and index of subjects.

Perhaps the reader will indulge me if I take a minute now to express my own feelings about the completion of these nine volumes, even though

I know that I probably am mimicking Narcissus at this moment. I have always relished the concepts of completeness and "closure."

One way to express my sentiments is to tell a little story. When I first visited Norway in 1967, I was strongly impressed by the collection of sculptures in Frogner Park, one of the large public parks in the city of Oslo. Those bronze and granite statues represent the collected works of Gustav Vigeland, who had made a deal with Oslo's officials: If they would provide him with materials and a studio, he would donate all of his future output to the city, as a permanent collection for public viewing.

I was naturally impressed by the monumental scale of this collection. But most of all, I marveled that these hundreds of individual works, as they now exist, appear to be complete. During the decades when Vigeland was working on them, the project was unfinished and it must not have looked very satisfying. Yet he was able to live long enough to bring everything to a state that fulfilled his vision, providing a perpetual source of wonderment and inspiration. Therefore I've come back to the Vigeland Sculpture Park whenever I've had a chance.

Similarly, the completion of these nine volumes is, for me, a dream come true. In the 1960s, after having written a few dozen papers and acquired various piles of reprints from the journal publishers, I salivated at the prospect of some day having one copy of each reprint bound together in some sort of private book. Later I was extremely fortunate when Dikran approached me with plans to do something much better. What a tremendous luxury this has been, to have the opportunity to put my house in order! I'm enormously grateful that I've been able to live at a time and place in history when a project such as this could be brought to fruition.

What's left for me, now that I've written a complete collection of papers? God willing, I plan to devote full time to the completion of *The Art of Computer Programming*. That project not only allows me to teach readers about the beautiful results obtained by hundreds of brilliant computer scientists, it also allows ample opportunity for creative work, as explained in Chapter 13.

Once again I want to thank Dan Eilers and Udo Wermuth for their amazing proofreading skills. This book has been improved in several hundred small yet significant ways because of their diligence. My wife Jill has been of extraordinary help throughout the preparation of this series of books, especially when I needed to locate material in our family archives. Special thanks are also due to Miriam Palm, for helping to transcribe the (often nearly inaudible) tape recordings that Dikran and I made during our lunches in 1996.

I've tried to make these books as error-free as possible, but the number of opportunities to make mistakes has been vast. Therefore I will cheerfully award $2.56 to the first finder of every error that remains, in any of the nine volumes. An online list of all known errors in the present book can be found via the webpage

`http://www-cs-faculty.stanford.edu/~knuth/cp.html`

near the bottom. For other volumes, change 'cp' in that Internet address to 'lp' for *Literate Programming*, 'cs' for *Computer Science*, 'dt' for *Digital Typography*, 'aa' for *Analysis of Algorithms*, 'cl' for *Computer Languages*, 'dm' for *Discrete Mathematics*, 'da' for *Design of Algorithms*, or 'fg' for *Fun and Games*. Happy hunting!

Donald E. Knuth
Stanford, California
June 2011

Chapter 1

Problems

References to the original appearances of these problems, and to published solutions, can be found in Chapter 20.

Q16. Let V be a vector space over the real numbers, and let the operator $\|x\|$ be defined for all $x \in V$, satisfying the following conditions:

i) $\|x\|$ is a nonnegative real number.

ii) $\|x+y\|^2 + \|x-y\|^2 = 2\|x\|^2 + 2\|y\|^2$ (parallelogram law).

Prove that the triangle inequality holds:
$$\|x+y\| \leq \|x\| + \|y\|.$$

Q34. Prove that if m and n are any positive integers we can solve the congruence $F_x \equiv m$ (modulo 3^n) for some Fibonacci number F_x. Also prove that, if $\omega = e^{\pi i/n}$, the nth Lucas and Fibonacci numbers are

$$L_n = \prod_{k=1}^{\lfloor n/2 \rfloor} (\omega^{2k-1} + 3 + \omega^{1-2k}), \qquad F_n = \prod_{k=1}^{\lfloor n/2 \rfloor} (\omega^{2k} + 3 + \omega^{-2k}). \quad (*)$$

Q37. For natural numbers i and j, let "$i \bmod j$" denote the nonnegative remainder when i is divided by j; that is, $i \bmod j = i - j\lfloor i/j \rfloor$. Evaluate the following sum:

$$S_n = \sum_{k=1}^{2n^2} \binom{k \bmod n}{(2k+1) \bmod (2n+1)}.$$

Q38. What group is generated by the cyclic permutations $(1\ 2\ \ldots\ m)$ and $(1\ 2\ \ldots\ n)$, when $1 < m < n$?

Q39. Let X_1, X_2, Y_1, $\ldots$, Y_{m+n} be independent random variables, where X_1 and X_2 have common distribution F and $Y_1, \ldots, Y_{m+n}$ have common distribution G. Prove that

$$\frac{1}{2} \leq \Pr\big(X_1 + \max(Y_1, \ldots, Y_m) \leq X_2 + \max(Y_{m+1}, \ldots, Y_{m+n})\big) \leq \frac{n}{m+n}$$

when $m \leq n$ and G is differentiable.

1

Q42. Partition the real line into a countable union of compact subsets.

Q45. A recently discovered pair of microbes reproduces in a very peculiar way. The male microbe (a diphage) has two receptors on its surface, and the female (a triphage) has three receptors. When a culture of diphages and triphages is irradiated with a psi particle, exactly one of the receptors absorbs the particle (each receptor being equally likely). If it was a diphage, it changes to a triphage; but if it was a triphage, it splits into two diphages.

Give a simple formula for the average number of diphages present if we begin with a single diphage and irradiate the culture n times with psi particles.

Q56. Bentley's algorithm for inserting two-dimensional data points (x, y) into a 2D tree T can be expressed as follows in pidgin Pascal:

```
type node = record
    xcoord, ycoord: real;  leftson, rightson: ↑node
end;
var T = ↑node;
procedure insert0 (x, y: real; var p: ↑node);
        { insertion on even levels }
    begin if p = nil then newleaf (x, y, p)
    else if x < p↑.xcoord then insert1 (x, y, p↑.leftson)
    else insert1 (x, y, p↑.rightson);
    end;
procedure insert1 (x, y: real; var p: ↑node);
        { insertion on odd levels }
    begin if p = nil then newleaf (x, y, p)
    else if y < p↑.ycoord then insert0 (x, y, p↑.leftson)
    else insert0 (x, y, p↑.rightson);
    end;
procedure newleaf (x, y: real; var p: ↑node);
    begin new (p);
    with p do
        begin xcoord ← x; ycoord ← y; leftson ← nil; rightson ← nil;
        end;
    end;
```

We obtain a random 2D tree with n nodes by setting $T \leftarrow$ **nil** and then performing $insert0 (x[i], y[i], T)$ for $1 \leq i \leq n$, where the $x[i]$ and $y[i]$ are independent random real numbers, uniformly distributed between 0 and 1.

The following mutually recursive functions can be used to find the minimum x coordinate of all keys in the tree:

function $min0$ (p: ↑*node*): **real**;   { minimum on even levels }
  begin if p = **nil then** $min0 \leftarrow 1.0$
  else if $p{\uparrow}.leftson$ = **nil then** $min0 \leftarrow p{\uparrow}.xcoord$
  else $min0 \leftarrow min1$ ($p{\uparrow}.leftson$);
  end;

function $min1$ (p: ↑*node*): **real**;   { minimum on odd levels, $p \neq$ **nil** }
  var $xleft, xright, x$: **real**;
  begin $xleft \leftarrow min0$ ($p{\uparrow}.leftson$); $xright \leftarrow min0$ ($p{\uparrow}.rightson$);
  if $xleft < xright$ **then** $x \leftarrow xleft$ **else** $x \leftarrow xright$;
  if $x < p{\uparrow}.xcoord$ **then** $min1 \leftarrow x$ **else** $min1 \leftarrow p{\uparrow}.xcoord$;
  end;

The purpose of this problem is to analyze the average running time of such an algorithm, when it is applied to random 2D trees. If T points to the root of a random 2D tree with n nodes, and if we perform the function call $min0$ (T), let A_n be the average number of times the function $min0$ is invoked. Find a "closed form" expression for A_n, and determine its asymptotic behavior as $n \to \infty$ to an accuracy of $O(1/n)$.

Note that the values of A_n for small n are as follows:

$$n = 0 \quad 1 \quad 2 \quad 3;$$
$$A_n = 1 \quad 1 \quad 2 \quad 7/3.$$

Q57. Let T denote a binary tree. If v is an internal node, define its *inorder depth*, written $\text{ID}(v)$, to be the number of nodes on the path from the root r of T to v whose left link is on this path. The number $\text{ID}(v)$ reflects the stack depth while visiting v during a standard inorder traversal of T. Similarly define the *preorder depth*, written $\text{PD}(v)$, to be the number of nodes on the path from r to v whose left link is on the path *and* whose right subtree is nonempty. Again $\text{PD}(v)$ reflects the stack depth during a preorder traversal of T—where we avoid stacking a node if its right subtree is empty.

Show that there is a one-to-one correspondence π between binary trees of a given number of nodes, which extends to a node-wise correspondence, such that if v is any node of some tree T and if $\pi(v)$ denotes the corresponding node in $\pi(T)$, then

$$\text{PD}(\pi(v)) = \lfloor \text{ID}(v)/2 \rfloor.$$

Thus a preorder traversal of a tree requires just half the stack size of an inorder traversal, both in the worst case and also in the average case if all binary trees are assumed to be equally likely.

Q61. Consider the use of demand paging to support a virtual memory consisting of n pages on a computer with only two page frames of real memory. The pattern of references to the virtual memory can be thought of as a string over an n-letter alphabet. For each memory reference, the memory system first checks to see whether or not the referenced page is resident in one of the two page frames. If it is, the reference is called a *hit*. If it is not, we have a *miss*: One of the currently resident pages is chosen to be the *victim* and it is swapped out, while the newly referenced page is swapped in to take its place.

Analyze the performance of this system under the assumptions that

i) the reference pattern is an infinite random string on n letters;

ii) the page chosen as the victim when handling a miss is the one whose next reference is the furthest in the future.

This strategy for choosing victims is called *optimum paging*, since it is well known to yield the smallest possible number of misses.

Compute an exact formula for the probability of a hit under these assumptions, expressing your answer as a closed-form formula involving Ramanujan's function $Q(n) = 1 + (n-1)/n + (n-1)(n-2)/n^2 + \cdots$ [see Section 1.2.11.3 in D. E. Knuth, *Fundamental Algorithms*].

Q64. A student named J. H. Quick woke up one morning with an idea for a new kind of binary search tree. He had learned about the advantages of "late binding" in his studies of computer science, and he thought: *"Why should I use the first key to decide how the rest of the tree will be partitioned? I could do better by postponing that decision and letting further keys influence what happens."* Running to his interactive workstation, he hastily prepared a file containing a description of his new data structure, which he chose to call Late Binding Trees (LBTs); and then he ate breakfast.

Unfortunately there is not room here to describe the subsequent events in Quick's life; the story about his fateful encounters with the Chuvstvenni sisters in Gstaad, who vowed to stop at nothing until they had learned his secret, will probably never be told. Let us rather turn our attention to the specifics of LBTs, suppressing the details of how this information was learned.

There are two types of nodes: branch nodes and leaves. A *branch node* contains two keys a and b, where $a < b$, and it also contains two links l and r that point to subtrees. All keys in the l subtree are $\leq a$, and all keys in the r subtree are $\geq b$. Such a node can be represented by the notation '$(a \mathbin{..} b)$', having its subtrees drawn below. A *leaf node*, on the other hand, contains a full record, including a key a. Such a node can be represented by '$[a]$'.

LBTs are never empty; they start out with a single (leaf) node. One of the nodes in the left subtree of a branch node $(a \mathinner{.\,.} b)$ is the leaf node $[a]$; similarly, the right subtree of $(a \mathinner{.\,.} b)$ always contains $[b]$. If we want to insert a new record with key x into a given LBT, we proceed as follows, assuming that x is different from all keys already in the tree:

i) If the LBT is $[a]$, and if $a < x$, change the LBT to $(a \mathinner{.\,.} x)$, with left subtree $[a]$ and right subtree $[x]$. A similar construction with a and x interchanged is used if $x < a$.

ii) If the LBT has root $(a \mathinner{.\,.} b)$ and if $x < a$, insert the new record into the left subtree, using the same method recursively.

iii) If the LBT has root $(a \mathinner{.\,.} b)$ and if $x > b$, insert the new record into the right subtree, using the same method recursively.

iv) If the LBT has root $(a \mathinner{.\,.} b)$ and if $a < x < b$, flip a truly random coin. If it comes up heads, change the root to $(x \mathinner{.\,.} b)$ and insert the new record in the left subtree; otherwise change the root to $(a \mathinner{.\,.} x)$ and insert the new record in the right subtree.

The idea is therefore to keep track of a range of possible splitting keys in the root of the tree, instead of deciding prematurely on a particular one.

The purpose of this problem is to learn something about the analysis of algorithms by analyzing the average total external path length of LBTs, assuming that LBTs are created by inserting records in random order. The total external path length is the sum, over all leaves, of the distance from the root to the leaf. Let n be the number of leaves. Then if $n = 1$, the total external path length is always 0; if $n = 2$, it is always 2; if $n = 3$, it is always 5; and if $n = 4$, it is either 8 or 9.

(a) Let $x_1 \ldots x_n$ be a random permutation of $\{1, \ldots, n\}$, and consider the LBT obtained by starting with $[x_1]$ and proceeding to insert x_2, x_3, $\ldots$; there will be n leaves after x_n has been inserted. The root will then be $(k \mathinner{.\,.} k + 1)$ for some k. Furthermore the left subtree of the root will be the LBT formed by the permutation $y_1 \ldots y_k$ of $\{1, \ldots, k\}$ consisting of the x_i that are $\le k$; the right subtree will be the LBT formed by the permutation $z_1 \ldots z_{n-k}$ of $\{k+1, \ldots, n\}$ consisting of the remaining x_i.

Prove that the permutations $y_1 \ldots y_k$ are not uniformly distributed: If $y_1 \ldots y_k$ has t left-to-right maxima, it occurs with probability 2^{k-t} times the probability that the identity permutation $1 \ldots k$ occurs. Similarly, the permutations $z_1 \ldots z_{n-k}$ are not uniformly random; their distribution depends on left-to-right minima.

(b) Let p_{nk} be the probability that the root of an LBT will be $(k .. k+1)$, after inserting n keys that are in uniformly random order. Find a formula for p_{nk}.

(c) Let us say that permutations of $\{1, \ldots, n\}$ are U-distributed if all permutations are equally likely; they are L-distributed if they occur with probability proportional to 2^{-t}, where t is the number of left-to-right maxima; they are R-distributed if they occur with probability proportional to 2^{-s}, where s is the number of left-to-right minima; and they are X-distributed if they occur with probability proportional to 2^{-s-t}.

Subproblem (a) showed that the left and right subtrees of LBTs constructed from U-distributed permutations are respectively L- and R-distributed. Prove that if we start with L-, R-, or X-distributed permutations, the subtrees are constructed from (L, X)-, (X, R)-, or (X, X)-distributed permutations, respectively.

(d) Let U_n, L_n, R_n, and X_n be the average total external path length of the LBTs formed by distributions U, L, R, X. Prove that, for all $n \geq 2$, we have

$$U_n = n + \sum_{1 \leq k < n} p_{nk}(L_k + R_{n-k}),$$
$$L_n = n + \sum_{1 \leq k < n} q_{nk}(L_k + X_{n-k}),$$
$$R_n = n + \sum_{1 \leq k < n} q_{n(n-k)}(X_k + R_{n-k}),$$
$$X_n = n + \sum_{1 \leq k < n} r_{nk}(X_k + X_{n-k}),$$

where q_{nk} and r_{nk} are the respective probabilities that L- and X-distributed LBTs have $(k .. k+1)$ at the root.

(e) Prove that $q_{nk} = \binom{k-1/2}{k-1} / \binom{n-1/2}{n-2}$ and $r_{nk} = 1/(n-1)$, for $1 \leq k < n$.

(f) Prove that $X_n = 2nH_n - 2n$.

(g) Prove that

$$\sum_{1 \leq k < n} q_{nk}X_{n-k} = \tfrac{4}{5}(n + \tfrac{1}{2})(H_{n+1/2} - H_{5/2}).$$

(h) Solve the recurrence for L_n that appears in part (d), using the repertoire method to study recurrences of the form $x_n = a_n + \sum_{1 \leq k < n} q_{nk}x_k$. [The repertoire method is explained, for example, in pages 21–24 of D. H. Greene and D. E. Knuth, *Mathematics for the Analysis of Algorithms* (Birkhäuser Boston, 1981).]

(i) Prove that $U_n = (2n + \tfrac{1}{2})H_n - \tfrac{13}{6}n - \tfrac{5}{12}$.

Q65. Let $\|y\|$ denote the distance from the real number y to the nearest integer. Evaluate the doubly infinite sum

$$\cdots + 4\|x/4\|^2 + 2\|x/2\|^2 + \|x\|^2 + \|2x\|^2/2 + \|4x\|^2/4 + \cdots.$$

Q77. A positive integer is said to be "sorted" if the digits in its decimal notation are nondecreasing from left to right.

(a) Let x be any integer whose decimal notation consists of an arbitrary numbers of 3s followed by an arbitrary number of 6s followed by a single 7. Prove that x^2 is sorted. For example, $3336667^2 = 11133344666688889$.

(b) Which positive integers x are such that both x and x^2 are sorted?

Q81. A random knockout tournament of order $n > 0$ consists of 2^n players who are paired at random; the 2^{n-1} winners play a random knockout tournament of order $n - 1$. If $n = 0$ the sole player is declared the champion.

Suppose the players $x_1, \ldots, x_{2^n}$ have the property that x_i always beats x_j whenever $j > i + 1$; but x_i beats x_{i+1} with probability p, independent of the outcome of all other matches.

Show that x_1 will be the eventual champion with probability

$$1 + \sum_{m=1}^{n} (p-1)^m \prod_{j=1}^{m} \frac{2^n - 2^{j-1}}{(2^n - j)(2^j - 1)}.$$

Furthermore, if $q = 1 - p$, the limiting value as $n \to \infty$ is

$$(1 - q/2)(1 - q/4)(1 - q/8)(1 - q/16)\ldots.$$

Q83. Let $S(n)$ be the set of all positive integers k such that the fractional part of n/k is $1/2$ or more. For example,

$$S(17) = \{2, 3, 6, 9, 10, 11, 18, 19, 20, \ldots, 34\}.$$

Prove that

$$\sum_{k \in S(n)} \varphi(k) = n^2,$$

where φ is Euler's totient function.

Q101. Prove that

$$\left\lfloor \frac{m^2}{n} \right\rfloor + \sum_{k=0}^{m-1} \left(\left\lfloor \frac{k}{n} \right\rfloor - \left\lfloor \frac{m+k}{n} \right\rfloor \right) = \left\lfloor \frac{\min\big(m \bmod n, (-m) \bmod n\big)^2}{n} \right\rfloor$$

for all positive integers m and n.

Q105. Given a sequence $(x_1, x_2, \ldots, x_l)$ of nonnegative integers in which $x_k > 1$ for some k, where $1 < k < l$, let us say that a "k-move" is the operation of replacing the subsequence (x_{k-1}, x_k, x_{k+1}) by the subsequence $(x_{k-1} + 1, x_k - 2, x_{k+1} + 1)$.

(a) Prove that repeated application of such moves to the sequence $(0^m, 2m, 0^m)$, in any order, always leads to the sequence $(1^m, 0, 1^m)$ after exactly $(m+1)(m+1/2)m/3$ moves. Here 0^m and 1^m stand for sequences of m 0s and m 1s, respectively.

(b) Prove that, for sufficiently large m, the starting sequence $(0^m, a_1, \ldots, a_n, 0^m)$ leads inexorably to the sequence

$$(0^{m+p}, 1^q, 0, 1^r, 0^{m+n-p-q-r-1})$$

for some p, q, and r, if a_1, $\ldots$, a_n are positive integers. Furthermore, p, q, and r can be expressed in terms of $\sum_{j=1}^{n} a_j$ and $\sum_{j=1}^{n} j a_j$. How many moves does this transformation require?

Q106. Stirling's approximation leads to the asymptotic expansion

$$\binom{2n}{n} = \frac{4^n}{\sqrt{\pi n}} \left(1 - \frac{1}{8n} + \frac{1}{128n^2} + \frac{5}{1024n^3} - \frac{21}{32768n^4} + O\left(\frac{1}{n^5}\right) \right).$$

Prove that if this expansion is continued indefinitely, the coefficient of n^{-k} will be $2^{1-4k} m_k$, where m_k is an integer. What is the exact power of 2 that divides the denominator of this coefficient?

Q110. Solve the recurrence

$$x_0 = a, \quad x_1 = b, \quad x_{n+2} = x_{n+1} + x_n/(n+1) \quad \text{for } n \geq 0$$

both exactly (in terms of familiar functions of n) and asymptotically.

Q119. Find closed formulas for

$$\sum_{k_1 + k_2 + \cdots + k_n = m} \frac{1}{k_1! \, (k_1! + k_2!) \, \ldots \, (k_1! + k_2! + \cdots + k_n!)}$$

and

$$\sum_{k_1 + k_2 + \cdots + k_n = m} \frac{1}{2^{k_1} (2^{k_1} + 2^{k_2}) \, \ldots \, (2^{k_1} + 2^{k_2} + \cdots + 2^{k_n})},$$

where both sums are extended over all n-tuples of nonnegative integers with sum m.

Q120. Suppose m and n are positive integers. Find a closed-form expression for

$$\sum_{k=0}^{2^{mn}-1} \binom{k^m}{n} (-1)^{\nu(n)},$$

where $\nu(k)$ is the number of 1s in the binary representation for k.

Q121. Suppose a, b, and c are nonnegative integers with $b > a$. If $0 < \theta < 1$ and $0 \leq x \leq 1$, prove that

$$(-1)^{b-a-1} \sum_{k=0}^{c} \binom{c}{k} \binom{a+\theta}{b+k} x^k > 0.$$

Q122. Find the coefficient of $z_1^{k_1} z_2^{k_2} \ldots z_n^{k_n}$ in

$$(1-z_1)^{-a_1} (1-z_1-z_2)^{-a_2} \ldots (1-z_1-z_2-\cdots-z_n)^{-a_n}.$$

Q123. Let P be a monic polynomial of degree m with complex coefficients, and let ω be a primitive mth root of unity. Let A be the $m \times m$ matrix in which the element in row j and column k is

$$A_{jk} = \int_0^\infty (\omega^k t)^j e^{-P(\omega^k t)} \, dt$$

for $0 \leq j, k < m$. Prove that A is nonsingular.

Q124. A certain pill bottle initially contains m large pills and n small pills, where each large pill is equivalent to two small ones. Each day the patient chooses a pill at random. If a small pill is selected, (s)he eats it; otherwise (s)he breaks the selected pill and eats one half, replacing the other half, which thenceforth is considered to be a small pill.

(a) What is the expected number of small pills remaining when the last large pill is selected?

(b) On which day can we expect the last large pill to be selected?

Q125. Let S be a set of m distinct points on the unit circle such that no two are diametrically opposite. For a fixed integer $n \leq m/2$ suppose that we mark every point p in S such that fewer than n of the remaining points in S lie in the semicircle counterclockwise from p. Prove that at most n points are marked.

Q127. Any assignment of values to the 15 variables A, B, C, D, E, b, c, d, e, u, v, w, x, y, z in the matrices below yields a magic square in which all rows, columns, and main diagonals sum to a constant. Conversely, one of the two matrices is "universal" in the sense that there exist values of A, B, C, D, E, b, c, d, e, u, v, w, x, y, z for which any magic square will be attained. Identify the universal matrix, prove its universality, and find a magic square that the other matrix cannot produce.

$$\begin{pmatrix} A & B+b+u-v & C+c+v-w & D+d-u+w & E+e \\ D+c+x-y & E+d & A+e-x & B & C+b+y \\ B+e+y-z & C-u & D+b & E+c+u & A+d-y+z \\ E+b-x+z & A+c & B+d+x & C+e & D-z \\ C+d & D+e+v & E-v+w & A+b-w & B+c \end{pmatrix}$$

$$\begin{pmatrix} A & B+u-v & C+c+v-w & D+d-u+w & E+e \\ D+c+x-y & E+d & A+e-x & B & C+y \\ B+e+y-z & C-u & D & E+b+c+u & A-b+d-y+z \\ E-x+z & A+c & B+b+d+x & C-b+e & D-z \\ C+d & D+e+v & E-b-v+w & A-w & B+b+c \end{pmatrix}$$

Q134. Let $(a_1, \ldots, a_m)$ and $(b_1, \ldots, b_n)$ be sequences of real numbers. Also assume that $a_{m+1} = b_{n+1} = \infty$, where ∞ is larger than any real number. The following standard merging algorithm forms a sequence $(c_1, \ldots, c_{m+n})$ containing all the a_i and b_j, followed by $c_{m+n+1} = \infty$:

```
i ← 1;  j ← 1;  k ← 0;
repeat k ← k + 1;
    if aᵢ ≤ bⱼ then
        begin cₖ ← aᵢ;  i ← i + 1;
        end
    else begin cₖ ← bⱼ;  j ← j + 1;
        end;
    until cₖ = ∞.
```

It is well known that if $a_1 \leq \cdots \leq a_m$ and $b_1 \leq \cdots \leq b_n$, we will have $c_1 \leq \cdots \leq c_{m+n}$. However, suppose the arrays are only "half sorted," in the sense that $\lfloor a_1 \rfloor \leq \cdots \leq \lfloor a_m \rfloor$ and $\lfloor b_1 \rfloor \leq \cdots \leq \lfloor b_n \rfloor$. Will the output also be half sorted? (In other words, will it necessarily be true that $\lfloor c_1 \rfloor \leq \cdots \leq \lfloor c_{m+n} \rfloor$?)

Q135. An undirected graph with m edges on the vertices $\{1, \ldots, n\}$ can be represented in two arrays $e[1 \mathbin{. .} 2m]$ and $p[0 \mathbin{. .} n]$, by listing the vertices adjacent to k in $e[j]$ for $p[k-1] < j \leq p[k]$, in increasing order. (Thus $p[0] = 0$, $p[n] = 2m$, and in general $p[k]$ is the sum of the degrees of vertices 1 through k.) Let us call this the *sequential representation* of the graph.

A similar representation, the *short code* of the graph, uses only $e[1 \mathinner{\ldotp\ldotp} m]$ and $p[0 \mathinner{\ldotp\ldotp} n]$; it lists each edge only once by including only the vertices that are adjacent to k and strictly less than k, in the list $e[j]$ for $p[k-1] < j \le p[k]$. (Now $p[k]$ is the number of edges in the subgraph restricted to vertices $\{1, \ldots, k\}$.)

There is a simple algorithm to reduce a sequential representation to the corresponding short code, given $e[1 \mathinner{\ldotp\ldotp} 2m]$, $p[0 \mathinner{\ldotp\ldotp} n]$, and n:

$j \leftarrow 0$; $m \leftarrow 0$; $k \leftarrow 0$;
while $j < n$ **do**
  begin $j \leftarrow j + 1$;
  while $k < p[j]$ **and** $e[k+1] < j$ **do**
    begin $m \leftarrow m + 1$; $k \leftarrow k + 1$; $e[m] \leftarrow e[k]$
    end;
  $k \leftarrow p[j]$; $p[j] \leftarrow m$;
  end.

Show that there is also a simple algorithm that reverses this process, namely, an algorithm that expands the short code to the full sequential representation, given $e[1 \mathinner{\ldotp\ldotp} m]$, $p[0 \mathinner{\ldotp\ldotp} n]$, and n. Your algorithm should have running time $O(m + n)$, and it should work *in situ*, using no additional memory besides $e[1 \mathinner{\ldotp\ldotp} 2m]$, $p[0 \mathinner{\ldotp\ldotp} n]$, and a bounded number of pointer variables. The entire computation should be done with nonnegative integers whose values are $O(m + n)$.

Q136. Define a random binary operation $\star$ on the set $\{1, \ldots, n\}$ by choosing every value independently, so that each of the n^{n^2} possible binary operations is equally likely.

(a) Prove that the axiom

$$\big((x \star x) \star x\big) \star \big((x \star x) \star x\big) \;=\; x$$

holds for $1 \le x \le n$ with probability

$$\sum_{k=0}^{n} P_{n,k}/n^{2n-k},$$

where $P_{n,k}$ is the number of permutations of $\{1, \ldots, n\}$ with exactly k fixed elements.

(b) Prove that the probability in (a) is asymptotic to $\frac{1}{2}e^{n-1}n!/n^{2n}$ as $n \to \infty$.

Q137. Let $\left\{ {m+n \atop n} \right\}$ denote the number of ways to partition a set of $m+n$ elements into n nonempty subsets. Prove that

$$\frac{2^n 3^{\lfloor m/2 \rfloor} 4^{\lfloor m/3 \rfloor} 5^{\lfloor m/4 \rfloor} \cdots}{(n+1)(n+2)\ldots(n+m)} \left\{ {m+n \atop n} \right\}$$

is an integer.

Q138. A closed *knight's tour* of an $m \times n$ chessboard is a sequence $\langle (x_k, y_k) \rangle$ for $0 \le k < mn$ such that each pair of integers (x, y) with $0 \le x < m$ and $0 \le y < n$ occurs exactly once in the sequence, and such that $(x_{k+1} - x_k)^2 + (y_{k+1} - y_k)^2 = 5$ for all k (including $k = mn-1$ if we define $(x_{mn}, y_{mn}) = (x_0, y_0)$). Such a tour defines a closed *contour* C if we connect adjacent points (x_k, y_k) and (x_{k+1}, y_{k+1}) with straight line segments.

Let w_{ij} be the winding number of C about the point $(i - \frac{1}{2}, j - \frac{1}{2})$. Prove that

$$\sum_{k=0}^{mn-1} (x_k y_{k+1} - x_{k+1} y_k) = 2 \sum_{i=1}^{m-1} \sum_{j=1}^{n-1} w_{ij}.$$

Note: The winding number of a contour C about a point $z_0 \notin C$ is the net number of times C encircles z_0 in the counterclockwise direction. It can be defined using the complex variable $z = x + iy$ as $(2\pi i)^{-1} \oint_C dz/(z - z_0)$. The oldest known knight's tour (due to al-Adli in the ninth century) is illustrated below, together with the 49 winding numbers w_{ij} at the corner points between cells. In this example, $\sum w_{ij} = 49$ and $\sum (x_k y_{k+1} - x_{k+1} y_k) = 98$.

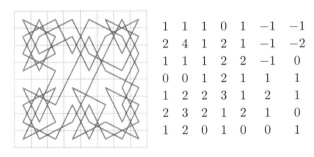

1	1	1	0	1	−1	−1
2	4	1	2	1	−1	−2
1	1	1	2	2	−1	0
0	0	1	2	1	1	1
1	2	2	3	1	2	1
2	3	2	1	2	1	0
1	2	0	1	0	0	1

Q142. Dominoes look different in China than they do in the West. In fact, we might well think of them as "trominoes," because their ratio of width to height is approximately 3 to 1 instead of 2 to 1. Each domino has two sets of spots, which range from 1 to 6; but eleven spot pairs are repeated, so that there are 32 dominoes, not 21, in a complete set:

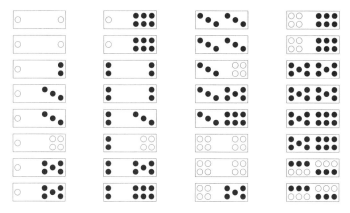

Some of the pieces also have colorful names; for example,

is called "earth,"   is called "plum flower,"

is called "bench,"   is called "redhead ten,"

is called "man,"   is called "heaven,"

and so on. [See Stewart Culin, *Games of the Orient*, page 115. A well-made set can be seen in *Games of the World* by Frederic V. Grunfeld (Holt, Rinehart and Winston, 1975), page 107.]

Is it possible to take a complete set of Chinese dominoes and pack them into an 8×12 box, in such a way that four dominoes never meet at their corners, and so that the spots total exactly 11 at every point where three dominoes come together? For example, on a smaller scale, the arrangement

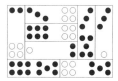

satisfies this condition: There are eight interior points where three dominoes touch, and the corresponding spot sums are $2 + 3 + 6 = 4 + 4 + 3 = 4 + 6 + 1 = 4 + 2 + 5 = 4 + 1 + 6 = 5 + 2 + 4 = 2 + 5 + 4 = 5 + 1 + 5 = 11$.

Warning: Once you start on this problem, you may find it addictive.

Q151. Call a matrix (a_{ij}) *special* if its entries satisfy

$$a_{ij} = \begin{cases} 0, & \text{if } j > i+1; \\ -1, & \text{if } j = i+1; \\ 0 \text{ or } 1, & \text{if } j \leq i. \end{cases}$$

Call a special matrix *minimal* if its determinant is zero, but the determinant becomes nonzero when any element on or below the diagonal is changed from 0 to 1. For example,

$$\begin{pmatrix} 1 & -1 & 0 & 0 \\ 0 & 0 & -1 & 0 \\ 1 & 1 & 1 & -1 \\ 0 & 0 & 1 & 0 \end{pmatrix}$$

is a minimal special matrix.

(a) Prove that there are exactly 2^{n-1} minimal special matrices of size $n \times n$.

(b) What is the largest number of zeros that a minimal special matrix can contain?

Q152. Let m_n be the maximum value of the quantity

$$\frac{x_1}{(1+x_1+x_2+\cdots+x_n)^2} + \frac{x_2}{(1+x_2+\cdots+x_n)^2} + \cdots + \frac{x_n}{(1+x_n)^2}$$

over all nonnegative sequences of real numbers $(x_1, x_2, \ldots, x_n)$. At what point or points does the maximum occur? Express m_n in terms of m_{n-1}, and find $\lim_{n\to\infty} m_n$.

Q157. Let m and n be integers with $n \geq m > 0$. Prove that, if q is any integer in the range $n - m < q \leq n$,

$$\sum_{k \equiv q \,(\text{modulo } 2)} \binom{(k+q)/2 - 1}{k-1}\binom{n - (k+q)/2}{m - k} \equiv \binom{n}{m} \quad (\text{modulo } 2).$$

Q158. Let n be a nonnegative integer. The sequence defined by $x_0 = n$ and $x_{k+1} = x_k - \lfloor \sqrt{x_k} \rfloor$ for $k \geq 0$ converges to 0.

Let $f(n)$ be the number of steps required; thus we have $x_{f(n)} = 0$ but $x_{f(n)-1} > 0$. Find a closed form for $f(n)$.

Q159. Alice and Bill have identical decks of 52 cards. Alice shuffles her deck and deals the cards face up into 26 piles of two cards each. Bill does the same with his deck. If any one of Alice's top cards exactly matches any of Bill's, the matching cards are removed. Play continues until none of the cards on top of Alice's piles matches any of the cards on top of Bill's piles. What is the probability that all 52 pairs of cards will be matched?

Q160. Prove that

$$\sum \frac{z - k_1 z^n}{(k_1 + 1)z^{(n-1)k_1}} \cdot \frac{z^2 - k_2 z^n}{(k_1 k_2 + k_2 + 1)z^{(n-2)k_2}} \cdots$$

$$\frac{z^{n-1} - k_{n-1} z^n}{(k_1 \ldots k_{n-1} + k_2 \ldots k_{n-1} + \cdots + k_{n-1} + 1)z^{k_{n-1}}}$$

$$= \frac{(1 - z)(1 - z^2) \ldots (1 - z^n)}{n! \, (1 - z)^n},$$

where the sum is over all 2^{n-1} choices $0 \le k_1, \ldots, k_{n-1} \le 1$; it reduces to the single term '1' when $n = 1$. The factors in the denominator reflect the lengths of carry propagation when powers of 2 are added to the binary number $(k_1 k_2 \ldots k_{n-1})_2$. For example, when $n = 3$ the left side is $z^3 + \frac{1}{2}(z^2 - z^3) + \frac{1}{2}(z - z^3) + \frac{1}{6}(1 - z^2)(1 - z)$.

Q167. Let m, n, and p be positive integers, and set

$$t_{m,p}(n) = \left\lceil \frac{\lfloor n/m \rfloor}{2p} \right\rceil; \quad s_{m,p}(n) = t_{m,p}(0) + t_{m,p}(1) + \cdots + t_{m,p}(n-1).$$

Prove that $s_{m,p}(n)$ is a multiple of $t_{m,p}(n)$.

Q168. Let p and q be positive numbers with $p + q = 1$, and suppose $0 < \epsilon < q$. Prove that

$$\left(\frac{p}{p + \epsilon}\right)^{p+\epsilon} \left(\frac{q}{q - \epsilon}\right)^{q-\epsilon} < e^{-2\epsilon^2}.$$

Q169. A certain matrix has m rows and $n = 1 + k^2$ columns. All entries of the matrix are ± 1, and the dot product of any two columns is less than or equal to 0. Prove that the total number of positive entries in the matrix is at most $\frac{1}{2}m(n + k)$, and construct a matrix that achieves this upper bound.

Q170. Let

$$a(l, m, n) = \sum_{k=0}^{l} \binom{n}{k} (l + m - k)^{n-k} (k - l)^k.$$

Prove that

$$\sum_{l=1}^{n} a(l, m, n) = \frac{m + n + 1}{2} a(n, m, n) - \frac{m + 1}{2} m^n.$$

Q177. Fix a real number $r > 0$. Let R be the ring of power series $\sum_{n=0}^{\infty} a_n x^n$ such that every a_n is an integer and $a_n = O(n^{-3/2} r^n)$. Also let I denote the ideal of R generated by $1 - 2x$.

(a) If $1 < r < 2$, prove that R/I is isomorphic to the field of real numbers.

(b) Does the same conclusion hold when $r = 2$?

Q178. Given positive integers m and n, what is

$$\max_{0 \le a_1, \ldots, a_m < n} \ \min_{0 \le k < n} \ \sum_{j=1}^{m} \big((a_j + k) \bmod n \big)?$$

Q180. A "binary maze" is a directed graph in which exactly two arcs lead from each vertex, one labeled 0 and one labeled 1. If $(b_1, b_2, \ldots, b_m)$ is any sequence of 0s and 1s and if v is any vertex, let $vb_1 b_2 \ldots b_m$ be the vertex reached after beginning at v and traversing the arcs labeled $b_1, b_2, \ldots, b_m$ in order.

A sequence $(b_1, b_2, \ldots, b_m)$ of 0s and 1s is a *universal exploration sequence* of order n if, for every strongly connected binary maze on n vertices and every vertex v, the sequence

$$v, \ vb_1, \ vb_1 b_2, \ \ldots, \ vb_1 b_2 \ldots b_m$$

includes every vertex of the maze at least once. For example, $(0, 1)$ is a universal exploration sequence of order 2, and it can be shown that $(0, 1, 1, 0, 1, 0, 0)$ is universal of order 3.

(a) Prove that universal exploration sequences of all orders exist.

(b) Find a good estimate for the asymptotic length of the shortest such sequence of order n.

[*Notes:* Sharp bounds for problem (b) are still unknown. The term "universal exploration sequence" has been given other meanings by other authors.]

Q181. Start in state 0. For every nonnegative integer k, stay in state k for X_k units of time, then go to state $k + 1$. What is the probability of being in state s after t units of time, assuming that X_k is distributed exponentially (a) with mean $1/(k + 1)$? (b) with mean $1/2^k$?

Q183. Evaluate

$$\sum_{k=1}^{\infty} \left(\frac{k^k}{k! \, e^k} - \frac{1}{\sqrt{2\pi k}} \right).$$

Q185. Let $a_0 = a_1 = 1$ and $a_{n+1} = a_n + e^{2\pi in/m} a_{n-1}$, where m is a positive integer.

(a) Prove that $a_{n+m} = a_n + a_{n-m}$ for all $n \geq m$.

(b) Find a simple formula for a_{mn}.

Q186. If a, b, and n are arbitrary nonnegative integers, prove that

$$\sum_{k=-\infty}^{\infty} \left(\binom{n}{a+5k} - \binom{n}{b+5k} \right)$$

is either a Fibonacci number or the negative of a Fibonacci number.

Q187. Say that an $n \times n$ matrix (a_{ij}) is a *balanced neighborhood square* if the set $\left\{ (a_{ij}, a_{(i+\delta)(j+\epsilon)}) \mid 1 \leq i, j \leq n \right\}$ equals $\left\{ (i, j) \mid 0 \leq i, j < n \right\}$ for all eight nonzero choices of (δ, ϵ) in $\{-1, 0, +1\}^2$; subscripts are periodic modulo n. For example, the matrix

$$\begin{pmatrix} 0 & 0 & 1 & 1 \\ 0 & 3 & 1 & 2 \\ 2 & 2 & 3 & 3 \\ 2 & 1 & 3 & 0 \end{pmatrix}$$

is a balanced neighborhood square.

(a) Construct an $n \times n$ balanced neighborhood square for every prime number $n > 4$.

(b) Do $n \times n$ balanced neighborhood squares exist for any nonprime numbers $n > 4$?

Q188. A polyomino *spans* a square if it can be embedded in the square touching all four sides. There are 6 pentominoes that span a 3×3 square:

How many polyominoes of $2n - 1$ cells span an $n \times n$ square?

Q190. For $n \geq 1$, let $\rho(n) = k$ if n is divisible by 2^k but not by 2^{k+1}. Prove that every nonnegative rational number occurs exactly once in the sequence x_0, x_1, x_2, ... defined by

$$x_0 = 0; \qquad x_{n+1} = 1/(2\rho(n+1) + 1 - x_n), \quad \text{for } n \geq 0.$$

Q192. Given a positive integer n, let a_k be the transposition

$$\big((k-1) \bmod (n+1), \ k \bmod (n+1) \big),$$

and let b_k be the transposition $(k \bmod n,\ n)$. Both sequences are periodic, but the periods are relatively prime. For example, when $n = 3$ we have

$$a_0, a_1, a_2, a_3, a_4, \ldots = (3,0),\ (0,1),\ (1,2),\ (2,3),\ (3,0),\ \ldots;$$
$$b_0, b_1, b_2, b_3, b_4, \ldots = (0,3),\ (1,3),\ (2,3),\ (0,3),\ (1,3),\ \ldots.$$

Prove that $a_0 a_1 \ldots a_k = b_k \ldots b_1 b_0$ for every $k \geq 0$.

Q199. Let $f(x)$ be a polynomial of the form $\sum_k a_k \binom{n}{k} x^k (1-x)^{n-k}$, where $0 \leq a_k \leq 1$ for $0 \leq k \leq n$. Prove for $0 < x < 1$ that

$$f'(x)^2 \leq n \frac{f(x)(1-f(x))}{x(1-x)}.$$

Q200. Find all solutions in positive integers (x, y, z) to the equations

$$xy \bmod z \ = \ yz \bmod x \ = \ zx \bmod y \ = \ 2.$$

Q203. A positive integer is *cube-free* if it is not divisible by the cube of any integer greater than 1. Let $\sum^*$ denote a summation restricted to the cube-free positive integers.
  (a) Evaluate $\sum^* n^{-2}$.
  (b) Prove that the sum $\sum^*_{n\,\mathrm{odd}} (-1)^{(n-1)/2} n^{-1}$ converges, and determine its value.

Q205. Let $\left[\begin{smallmatrix} n \\ m \end{smallmatrix}\right]$ be the number of permutations of n objects that have exactly m cycles. If n is a positive integer and $\max_{1 \leq k \leq n} \left[\begin{smallmatrix} n \\ k \end{smallmatrix}\right] n^k = \left[\begin{smallmatrix} n \\ m \end{smallmatrix}\right] n^m$, prove that

$$n \ln 2 - \frac{3}{4} \ < \ m \ < \ n \ln 2 + \frac{4}{3}.$$

Q206. Suppose n people are sitting at a circular table. Let $e_{m,n}$ denote the number of ways to partition them into m affinity groups with no two members of a group seated next to each other. (For example, $e_{3,4} = 2$, $e_{3,5} = 5$, and $e_{3,6} = 10$.)
  For $m \geq 2$ find the generating function $\sum_{n=0}^{\infty} e_{m,n} z^n$.

Q207. The *Fibonacci graphs*

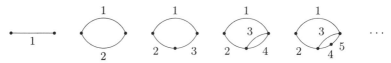

are defined by successively replacing the edge with maximum label n by two edges n and $n + 1$, in series if n is even, and in parallel if n is odd.

Prove that the Fibonacci graph with n edges has exactly F_{n+1} spanning trees, where $F_1 = F_2 = 1$ and $F_{n+1} = F_n + F_{n-1}$. Show also that these spanning trees can be listed in such a way that some edge k is replaced by $k \pm 1$ as we pass from one tree to the next. For example, when $n = 5$ the eight spanning trees can be listed as 125, 124, 134, 135, 145, 245, 235, 234.

Q208. A graph with n vertices $\{0, 1, \ldots, n-1\}$ and m edges can be specified by an array of $2m$ integers, where the edges join vertices $a[2k] — a[2k+1]$ for $0 \le k < m$.

Let v be a given vertex and assume that d is an integer array of size n. Find $\langle$ Statement 1 $\rangle$ and $\langle$ Statement 2 $\rangle$ such that the C-language subroutine `alldistances` shown below will set $d[u]$ to the distance from vertex v to vertex u, for $0 \le u < n$. (If u is unreachable from v, the "distance" between them is considered to be n.)

```
void alldistances(int m, int a[], int n, int d[], int v)
{
  register int i,j,k,l;
  int *b=(int*)malloc(n*sizeof(int));
  int *link=(int*)malloc(2*m*sizeof(int));
  for (j=0; j<n; j++) b[j]=-1, d[j]=n;
  for (k=0; k<m+m; k++) ⟨Statement 1⟩;
  d[v]=0, k=b[v], b[v]=-1, j=-1, l=1;
  while (k>=0) {
    v=a[k];
    if (b[v]>=0) {
      d[v]=l;
      for (i=b[v]; link[i]>=0; i=link[i]);
      ⟨Statement 2⟩;
    }
    k=link[k];
    if (k<0) l++, k=j, j=-1;
  }
}
```

$\langle$ Statement 1 $\rangle$ begins 'link[k]=' and $\langle$ Statement 2 $\rangle$ begins 'link[i]='. Does your program run in linear time?

Q209. Solve this additive alphametic:
```
   KNIFE
    FORK
   SPOON
    SOUP
  ──────
  SUPPER
```

Q211. An $m \times n$ matrix of 0s and 1s is a *parity pattern* if every 0 is adjacent (horizontally or vertically) to an even number of 1s and every 1 is adjacent to an odd number of 1s. It is *perfect* if no row or column is entirely zero. Thus,

$$
\begin{pmatrix} 1 & 1 \\ 0 & 0 \\ 1 & 1 \end{pmatrix}, \quad
\begin{pmatrix} 0 & 0 & 1 & 1 \\ 0 & 1 & 0 & 0 \\ 1 & 1 & 0 & 1 \\ 0 & 1 & 0 & 1 \end{pmatrix}, \quad
\begin{pmatrix} 0 & 1 & 0 & 1 & 0 \\ 1 & 1 & 0 & 1 & 1 \\ 0 & 1 & 0 & 1 & 0 \end{pmatrix}, \quad
\begin{pmatrix} 0 & 1 & 1 & 1 & 0 \\ 1 & 0 & 1 & 0 & 1 \\ 1 & 1 & 0 & 1 & 1 \\ 1 & 0 & 1 & 0 & 1 \\ 0 & 1 & 1 & 1 & 0 \end{pmatrix}
$$

are parity patterns of sizes 3×2, 4×4, 3×5, and 5×5, respectively; only the 4×4 and 5×5 patterns are perfect.

(a) Determine the number $c(n)$ of perfect parity patterns that have exactly n columns.

(b) The 5×5 parity pattern above has eightfold symmetry, in the sense that it is invariant under transposition and under rotation by 90 degrees. Prove that a perfect $n \times n$ parity pattern with eightfold symmetry exists for all n of the form $3 \cdot 2^k - 1$ with $k \geq 1$.

Q212. A "*d*-swap" changes a word by interchanging pairs of letters that are d positions apart; any number of such pairs may be interchanged in a single d-swap. Thus, the word `abcdef` can be changed into `fedcba` in two steps by first using a 4-swap to get `efcdab`, then finishing with a 1-swap. Let $s(n)$ be the minimum number of such swapping steps that will change an n-letter word into its reverse.

(a) Given $m \geq 0$, what is the largest n such that $s(n) = m$?

(b) Prove that $s(32) = s(41) = s(63) = 4$.

(c) Find the asymptotic behavior of $s(n)$ to within an absolute error that is bounded by a constant multiple of $\log \log n$.

(d) Find $s(23)$, $s(25)$, or $s(44)$. Better still, devise an efficient algorithm that determines exact values of $s(n)$.

Q213. Prove that, for nonnegative integers m and n,

$$
\sum_{k=0}^{m} 2^k \binom{2m-k}{m+n} = 4^m - \sum_{j=1}^{n} \binom{2m+1}{m+j}.
$$

Q217. Given a real number $\alpha > 1$, let

$$
a_1 = 1; \qquad a_n = \max_{1 \leq k \leq n/2} (\alpha a_k + a_{n-k}) \quad \text{for } n > 1.
$$

Prove that if $n = \sum_{j=0}^{t} 2^{e_j}$ with $t \geq 0$ and $e_0 > e_1 > \cdots > e_t \geq 0$, then

$$
a_n = (\alpha + 1)^{e_0} + \alpha(\alpha + 1)^{e_1} + \cdots + \alpha^t (\alpha + 1)^{e_t}.
$$

Q218. A *near-deBruijn cycle of order* d is a cyclic sequence of $2^d - 1$ zeros and ones in which all $2^d - 1$ substrings of length d are distinct. For all $d > 0$, construct a near-deBruijn cycle of order $d + 1$ such that the leading and trailing substrings of length $2^d - 1$ are both near-deBruijn cycles of order d. (Thus, for example, 1100010 is near-deBruijn of order 3, while 110 and 010 are both near-deBruijn of order 2.)

Q219. Prove that for all real t, and all $\alpha \geq 2$,

$$e^{\alpha t} + e^{-\alpha t} - 2 \leq (e^t + e^{-t})^\alpha - 2^\alpha.$$

Q221. Solve the alphametic SEVEN + TEN + ONE = THREE + NINE + SIX.

Q222. Solve the alphametic HOT × HOT = ONION.

Q226. Say that the permutations $a_1 a_2 \ldots a_k a_{k+1} \ldots a_n$ and $a_k \ldots a_2 a_1$ $a_{k+1} \ldots a_n$ are equivalent when $k = n$ or when a_{k+1} exceeds all of $\{a_1, \ldots, a_k\}$. Also say that two permutations are equivalent whenever they can be obtained from each other by a sequence of such flips. For example, $321 \equiv 123 \equiv 213 \equiv 312$ and $132 \equiv 231$. Show that the number of equivalence classes is equal to the Euler secant-and-tangent number E_n, for all n. (The nth secant-and-tangent number counts the number of "up-down" permutations of length n, namely the permutations like 25341 that alternately rise and fall, beginning with a rise.)

Q236. Remove the central $(n-2)^2$ squares from an $(n+2) \times (n+2)$ array of squares. In how many ways can the remaining squares be covered with $4n$ dominoes?

(For example, the problem for $n = 3$ is to cover all but the center square of a 5×5 array with dominoes, and there are 196 solutions.)

Q237. Pack the sixteen pentominoes below into an 8×10 box in such a way that the "tied together" unit cells are adjacent.

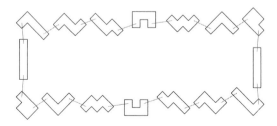

The pieces may be rotated, but not flipped over.

Chapter 2

Solutions

Four of the problems in the preceding chapter appeared in the Journal of Algorithms *without any corresponding solution. Solutions are therefore given here. (See Chapter 20 for the remaining solutions.)*

Q57. The desired correspondence can, for example, be defined by

$$\square' = \square; \qquad \left(\begin{array}{c} \begin{array}{c} \textcircled{0} \\ \textcircled{1} \quad \mathcal{T}_0 \\ \mathcal{T}_1 \quad \textcircled{2} \\ \mathcal{T}_2 \quad \ddots \\ \quad \textcircled{m} \\ \mathcal{T}_m \quad \square \end{array} \end{array} \right)' = \begin{array}{c} \textcircled{1} \\ \mathcal{T}_1' \quad \textcircled{2} \\ \mathcal{T}_2' \quad \ddots \\ \quad \textcircled{m} \\ \mathcal{T}_m' \quad \textcircled{0} \\ \mathcal{T}_0' \quad \square \end{array} .$$

[This transformation can be found in the book *Mathematics for the Analysis of Algorithms* by Daniel H. Greene and Donald E. Knuth, on page 104 of the first or second edition (1981 or 1982) or on page 100 of the third edition (1990).]

Q61. The "probability of a hit" keeps changing; for example, the first reference always triggers a miss, while the second is a hit with probability $1/n$. The person who posed the problem (me) was probably thinking of a limiting, steady-state situation in which the hit probability is essentially constant. But let's try for an exact analysis and see how far we can get.

Suppose page a is fetched at time 0; then a is the only page present, and we can call this state 1. At time 1, we remain in state 1 with probability $1/n$; otherwise we advance to state 2, in which we know that exactly two pages are present, a and b. We remain in state 2 with probability $2/n$; but if $n > 2$ we'll almost surely reach state 3, a new state in which things begin to get interesting. In state 3 a new page is present, page c; and we also have either page a or page b, whichever was not the "victim." For purposes of analysis, we can *postpone* the decision about who should be the victim; future events will reveal what we should have done.

Indeed, if we're in state 3 and if a reference is made to either a or b, we will consider it to be a hit; and then we'll be back in state 2. (If page b is referenced, for instance, we'll know that exactly two pages are present, b and c.) On the other hand if c is referenced in state 3, we stay in that state. And if a new page d is called for — this happens with probability $(n-3)/n$ — we enter state 4, in which page d is present and also one of the three pages $\{a, b, c\}$. Again, future events will tell us which of those pages will yield a hit when we next have a choice; we needn't commit ourselves. (Think about it. If c occurs before a or b, the earlier decision about whether to victimize a or b has turned out to be irrelevant and immaterial. Thus there is essential symmetry between a, b, and c in spite of the order in which those pages were encountered.)

And so on; there are n states. In state s, for $1 \le s \le n$, the probability of a hit is s/n. When $s > 2$, we go next to state 2 with probability $(s-1)/n$; we stay in state s with probability $1/n$; and we advance to state $s + 1$ with probability $(n-s)/n$.

In other words, the demand paging process with random page references and with optimum choice of victims is a Markov process, characterized by the $n \times n$ transition matrix $P = (p_{ij})$ where

$$p_{ij} = [j\,{=}\,2]\,\frac{i-1}{n} + [j\,{=}\,i]\,\frac{1}{n} + [j\,{=}\,i+1]\,\frac{n-i}{n}, \quad \text{for } 1 \le i, j \le n.$$

The matrix when $n = 5$, for example, is

$$P = \begin{pmatrix} 1/5 & 4/5 & 0 & 0 & 0 \\ 0 & 2/5 & 3/5 & 0 & 0 \\ 0 & 2/5 & 1/5 & 2/5 & 0 \\ 0 & 3/5 & 0 & 1/5 & 1/5 \\ 0 & 4/5 & 0 & 0 & 1/5 \end{pmatrix}.$$

The probability that we'll be in state s after making the first $k + 1$ references is the entry in row 1 and column s of the matrix P^k. Multiplying by z^k and summing on k tells us that this is the entry in row 1 and column s of

$$I + Pz + P^2z^2 + \cdots = (I - Pz)^{-1};$$

thus the probability of a hit at time $k + 1$ is the coefficient of z^k in

$$(1\ 0\ 0\ \ldots\ 0)(I - Pz)^{-1}(1/n\ 2/n\ 3/n\ \ldots\ n/n)^T.$$

For example, small values of n have the following generating functions:

$$n = 2 \qquad \frac{1}{1-z} - \frac{1}{2-z};$$

$$n = 3 \qquad \frac{7}{9}\frac{1}{1-z} + \frac{2}{9} - \frac{2}{3-z};$$

$$n = 4 \qquad \frac{11}{17}\frac{1}{1-z} + \frac{6}{17}\frac{16-z}{16+z^2} - \frac{3}{4-z};$$

$$n = 5 \qquad \frac{199}{355}\frac{1}{1-z} + \frac{12}{71}\frac{325-30z+9z^2}{125+15z^2+2z^3} - \frac{4}{5-z}.$$

In general, the theory of Markov processes tells us that the generating function for n-page hitting probabilities will have the form

$$\frac{p_n}{1-z} + q_n r_n(z) - \frac{n-1}{n-z},$$

where p_n is the steady-state probability, $q_n = 1 - p_n$, and $r_n(z)$ is a rational function that converges for $|z| \leq 1$ and has $r_n(0) = 1$. In particular, the coefficients of $r_n(z)$ always decrease exponentially to zero, making the overall probability very close to the steady state.

The case $n = 5$ already indicates that there probably is no simple expression for r_n. Indeed, the coefficient of z_k in r_5 is $O(\rho^{-k})$, where $\rho \approx 2.729633$ is equal to $\frac{5}{2}\frac{1-\alpha}{\alpha}\sqrt{1+\alpha+\alpha^2}$ with $\alpha = (3 - \sqrt{8})^{1/3}$.

We can, however, determine the steady-state probability p_n and express it in terms of Ramanujan's function, as stated in the original problem. To do this we seek a nonzero solution to the matrix equation $(x_1\, x_2\, \ldots\, x_n)P = (x_1\, x_2\, \ldots\, x_n)$; then the probability of being in state s during the paging process approaches the limiting value $x_s/(x_1 + x_2 + \cdots + x_n)$. In particular we must have $x_1/n = x_1$ and $(n-j)x_{j-1}/n + x_j/n = x_j$ for $3 \leq j \leq n$; and we can assume that $x_2 = 1$. Then $x_1 = 0$, $x_3 = (n-2)/(n-1)$, $x_4 = (n-2)(n-3)/(n-1)^2$, $x_5 = (n-2)(n-3)(n-4)/(n-1)^3$, etc., leading to $x_1+x_2+\cdots+x_n = Q(n-1)$. The steady-state hitting probability p_n is therefore

$$\frac{x_1 + 2x_2 + \cdots + nx_n}{nQ(n-1)} = \frac{Q(n-1) + x_2 + 2x_3 + \cdots + (n-1)x_n}{nQ(n-1)}$$

$$= \frac{Q(n-1) + (n-1)x_2}{nQ(n-1)} = \frac{1}{n} + \frac{n-1}{nQ(n-1)},$$

using the fact that $(2x_2 + 2x_3 + 3x_4 + \cdots + (n-1)x_n)/n = x_2 = 1$.

[For another solution, see Donald E. Knuth, "An analysis of optimum caching," *Journal of Algorithms* **6** (1985), 181–199, §3.]

Q134. Yes. We show, in fact, that if $c_k > c_{k+1}$ then c_k and c_{k+1} were adjacent elements in one of the two input arrays.

Otherwise we must have either (i) $c_k = a_i$ and $c_{k+1} = b_j$ for some i and j; or (ii) $c_k = b_j$ and $c_{k+1} = a_i$ for some i and j. In case (i), it follows that $a_i \leq b_j < a_{i+1}$; in case (ii), $b_j < a_i \leq b_{j+1}$. Therefore in both cases $c_k \leq c_{k+1}$.

Conversely if $a_i > a_{i+1}$ and $b_j > b_{j+1}$, these elements will be adjacent and out of order when they are copied to the c array. If there are α ascending runs in $(a_1, \ldots, a_m)$ and β ascending runs in $(b_1, \ldots, b_n)$, there will be $\alpha + \beta - 1$ ascending runs in $(c_1, \ldots, c_{m+n})$.

Q135. This interesting problem of *in situ* transformation can be solved in at least three instructive ways.

The solution *sol1* that I had in mind when I originally posed the problem is somewhat tricky. It first traverses and reformats the short code from left to right, then it produces the full sequential representation from right to left. After the left-to-right phase, the values of $e[1 .. m]$ and $p[0 .. n]$ will have been transformed in a slightly peculiar way: If the original appearances of vertex l in $e[1 .. m]$ were in the lists for vertices $(k_1, \ldots, k_r)$, then these appearances will have been replaced respectively by $(p[l-1], m+k_1, \ldots, m+k_{r-1})$, and $p[l-1]$ will have been replaced by $m + k_r$. This transformation gives just enough information for the right-to-left phase, which copies $e[t] \leftarrow e[s]$ for appropriate values of t decreasing from $2m$ to 1 and s decreasing from m to 1. The transformation is undone after the transformed e values have moved into their final resting place; the p values temporarily record the locations of untransformed e values.

```
sol1 : begin m ← p[n];  j ← 0;  k ← 0;
         while j < n do
            begin j ← j + 1;  u ← p[j];
            while k < u do
               begin k ← k+1;  l ← e[k];  e[k] ← p[l−1];  p[l−1] ← m+j;
               end;
            end;
         t ← 2 × m;  l ← n;  s ← m;  p[n] ← t;
         while l > 0 do
            begin u ← p[l − 1];
            while u > m do {untransform "high" neighbors of l}
               begin j ← u − m;  k ← p[j − 1];  u ← e[k];
               e[k] ← l;  p[j − 1] ← k − 1;  e[t] ← j;  t ← t − 1;
               end;
```

$l \leftarrow l - 1; \quad k \leftarrow u; \quad p[l] \leftarrow t;$
while $s > k$ **do** {copy transformed "low" neighbors of $l + 1$}
   begin $e[t] \leftarrow e[s]; \quad t \leftarrow t - 1; \quad s \leftarrow s - 1;$
   end;
  end;
 end.

Shortly after the problem had appeared in print, a completely different solution, let's call it *sol2*, was submitted by Mihaela Juganaru. Her solution was never published because the *Journal of Algorithms* problem section unfortunately became dormant in 1992. In *sol2* the final long-form edge table is filled in from right to left. For each edge $e_k \longrightarrow j$ with $e_k < j$, we move e_k to its final resting place, and reserve space for the eventual appearance of j; this is done for decreasing values of j and k. Reserved positions are flagged by adding n. Each original entry e_k is cleared to 0 when it has been used, or to n if position k is reserved. The p array keeps track of the largest edge-table entries that are yet to be filled in, for each j.

sol2: **begin** $m \leftarrow p[n]$;
  phase1: {construct the final p table}
    for $j \leftarrow n$ **downto** 1 **do** $p[j] \leftarrow p[j] - p[j - 1]$;
    for $k \leftarrow 1$ **upto** m **do** $p[e[k]] \leftarrow p[e[k]] + 1$;
    for $j \leftarrow 1$ **upto** n **do** $p[j] \leftarrow p[j] + p[j - 1]$;
  phase2: {move from short-form to long-form positions}
    for $k \leftarrow 1$ **upto** m **do** $e[k + m] \leftarrow 0$; {clear the second half}
    $j \leftarrow n$;
    for $k \leftarrow m$ **downto** 1 **do**
      begin $u \leftarrow p[j]$;
      while $u = p[j - 1]$ **or** $e[u] \neq 0$ **do**
        begin $j \leftarrow j - 1; \quad u \leftarrow p[j]$
        end; {determine the mate, j, of $e[k]$}
      $v \leftarrow e[k]$;
      if $v > n$ **then**
        begin $v \leftarrow v - n; \quad e[k] \leftarrow n$ {clear a reserved entry}
        end
      else $e[k] \leftarrow 0$; {clear a free entry}
      $e[u] \leftarrow v; \quad p[j] \leftarrow u - 1$; {do the move}
      $u \leftarrow p[v]; \quad e[u] \leftarrow e[u] + n; \quad p[v] \leftarrow u - 1$ {reserve position u}
      end;
  phase3: {construct the final p table again}
    for $j \leftarrow 1$ **upto** $n - 1$ **do** $p[j] \leftarrow p[j + 1]$;

$p[n] \leftarrow 2 \times m;$

phase4: {fill in the reserved places}
$\quad j \leftarrow n;$ **for** $k \leftarrow 2 \times m$ **downto** 1 **do**
$\quad\quad$ **begin while** $k \leq p[j-1]$ **do** $j \leftarrow j - 1;$
$\quad\quad v \leftarrow e[k];$
$\quad\quad$ **if** $v < j$ **then**
$\quad\quad\quad$ **begin** $e[p[v]] \leftarrow j; \; p[v] \leftarrow p[v] - 1$
$\quad\quad\quad$ **end**;
$\quad\quad$ **end**;

phase5: {and construct the final p table yet again}
$\quad$ **for** $j \leftarrow 1$ **upto** n **do** $p[j] \leftarrow 0;$
$\quad$ **for** $k \leftarrow 1$ **upto** $2 \times m$ **do** $p[e[k]] \leftarrow p[e[k]] + 1;$
$\quad$ **for** $j \leftarrow 1$ **upto** n **do** $p[j] \leftarrow p[j] + p[j-1];$
$\quad$ **end**.

Finally, I realized in 2007 that it would be possible to avoid tricky tagging altogether, if the short-code edge table were first expanded to a different long form in which we simply list all m pairs. As in *sol2*, the smaller vertex of each adjacent pair can then be moved into its final position, because one can show that the final long-form position always lies to the right of the expanded-form position. (More precisely, the condition $t > s - 1$ always holds when the statement $e[t] \leftarrow e[s-1]$ is performed in the following program.)

sol3: **begin** $m \leftarrow p[n]; \; s \leftarrow m;$
$\quad$ *phase1*: {expand to show both endpoints of each edge}
$\quad\quad$ **for** $j \leftarrow n$ **downto** 1 **do**
$\quad\quad\quad$ **begin** $p[j] \leftarrow 0; \; u \leftarrow p[j-1];$
$\quad\quad\quad$ **while** $s > u$ **do**
$\quad\quad\quad\quad$ **begin** $e[2 \times s] \leftarrow j; \; e[2 \times s - 1] \leftarrow e[s]; \; s \leftarrow s - 1$
$\quad\quad\quad\quad$ **end**;
$\quad\quad\quad$ **end**;
$\quad$ *phase2*: {compute "rightward degrees" in the p array}
$\quad\quad$ **for** $s \leftarrow 1$ **upto** m **do** $p[e[2 \times s - 1]] \leftarrow p[e[2 \times s - 1]] + 1;$
$\quad$ *phase3*: {move left part of each edge into final position}
$\quad\quad s \leftarrow 2 \times m; \; t \leftarrow s;$
$\quad\quad$ **for** $j \leftarrow n$ **downto** 1 **do**
$\quad\quad\quad$ **begin** $r \leftarrow p[j]; \; p[j] \leftarrow t; \; t \leftarrow t - r;$ {skip reserved slots}
$\quad\quad\quad$ **while** $s > 0$ **and** $e[s] = j$ **do**
$\quad\quad\quad\quad$ **begin** $e[t] \leftarrow e[s-1]; \; s \leftarrow s - 2; \; t \leftarrow t - 1$
$\quad\quad\quad\quad$ **end**;
$\quad\quad\quad$ **end**; {the p table now has its final form}

phase4: {move right part of each edge into final position}
  for $j \leftarrow n$ **downto** 1 **do**
    begin $t \leftarrow p[j]$; $u \leftarrow p[j-1]$;
    while $e[t] < j$ **and** $t > u$ **do**
      begin $s \leftarrow e[t]$; $t \leftarrow t-1$; $e[p[s]] \leftarrow j$; $p[s] \leftarrow p[s] - 1$
      end;
    end;
phase5: {reconstruct the final p table}
  for $j \leftarrow 1$ **upto** n **do** $p[j] \leftarrow 0$;
  for $k \leftarrow 1$ **upto** $2 \times m$ **do** $p[e[k]] \leftarrow p[e[k]] + 1$;
  for $j \leftarrow 1$ **upto** n **do** $p[j] \leftarrow p[j] + p[j-1]$;
  end.

The running time of *sol1* turns out to be $11m + 3n + 2$ mems, where a "mem" means an access to memory. (Nonarray variables like j, k, ... are considered to be registers, hence a statement such as $m \leftarrow p[n]$ costs one mem.) The other two solutions are notably less efficient; *sol2* takes between $28m + 10n + 1$ and $28m + 13n - 5$ mems, and *sol3* takes between $20m + 10n + 2$ and $20m + 11n + 1$. So this is a case where trickiness pays off rather handsomely.

All three solutions work with multigraphs, namely with graphs that have identical edges repeated any number of times, provided that there are no self-loops (no edges from a vertex to itself).

But self-loops present a problem. Indeed, the stated definition of short form precludes self-loops. And if we modify it to allow j in the list of vertex j's "prior" neighbors, we should really consider the edge $j \longrightarrow j$ to occupy *two* positions in the long sequential form, so that the long form is always twice the length of the short one. Thus a self-loop contributes 2 to the degree of its vertex. The original program to convert the full sequential representation to its short code should be patched by changing '$e[k+1] < j$' to '$e[k+1] \leq j$' and then '$e[m] \leftarrow e[k]$' to

$$\text{'}e[m] \leftarrow e[k]; \text{ if } e[m] = j \text{ then } k \leftarrow k+1;\text{'}.$$

None of the three solutions presented above will work reliably when self-loops are allowed. But some fairly simple patches to *sol3* will suffice: First we append the statement

$$\textbf{for } u \leftarrow p[j] \textbf{ downto } p[j] - r \textbf{ do } e[u] \leftarrow 0$$

at the end of the loop on j in *phase3*, so that all of the reserved slots are cleared to zero. Then we capture the self-loops by inserting the following instructions just after '$u \leftarrow p[j-1]$' in *phase4*:

```
if t > u then
  begin v ← t;
  while e[v] = 0 do
    begin e[v] ← j;  v ← v − 1
    end;
  t ← 2 × v − t;
  end;
```

(The key condition that $t > s - 1$ when $e[t] \leftarrow e[s - 1]$ is no longer true in the presence of self-loops. But one can show that $t < s$ can hold only when $e[t] = e[s - 1]$, hence there is no problem.) These patches add at most $m + n$ mems to the running time.

Similar, but trickier, patches to *sol1* will make it handle self-loops with even more efficiency; I leave this as an instructive exercise for the reader. But self-loops seem to defeat *sol2*, making it effectively unpatchable, because they cause it to reserve non-adjacent positions in array e.

Richard Bird ["Two in-situ algorithms for changing graph representations," to appear] has found an instructive solution to a similar problem, using Haskell as the programming language.

Chapter 3

Teach Calculus with Big O

*[Originally published in Notices of the American Mathematical Society **45**, 6 (June/July 1998), 687–688, in abridged form, as a letter to the editor.]*

I am pleased to see so much serious attention being given to improvements in the way calculus has traditionally been taught, but I'm surprised that nobody has been discussing the kinds of changes that I personally believe would be most valuable. If I were responsible for teaching calculus to college undergraduates and advanced high school students today, and if I had the opportunity to deviate from the existing textbooks, I would certainly make major changes by emphasizing several notational improvements that advanced mathematicians have been using for more than a hundred years.

The most important of these changes would be to introduce the O notation and related ideas at an early stage. This notation, first used by Bachmann in 1894 and later popularized by Landau, has the great virtue that it makes calculations simpler, so it simplifies many parts of the subject, yet it is highly intuitive and easily learned. The key idea is to be able to deal with quantities that are only partly specified, and to use them in the midst of formulas.

I would begin my ideal calculus course by introducing a simpler "A notation," which means "absolutely at most." For example, $A(2)$ stands for a quantity whose absolute value is less than or equal to 2. This notation has a natural connection with decimal numbers: Saying that π is approximately 3.14 is equivalent to saying that $\pi = 3.14 + A(.005)$. Students will easily discover how to calculate with A:

$$10^{A(2)} = A(100) \,;$$
$$\bigl(3.14 + A(.005)\bigr)\bigl(1 + A(0.01)\bigr)$$
$$= 3.14 + A(.005) + A(0.0314) + A(.00005)$$
$$= 3.14 + A(0.03645) = 3.14 + A(.04) \,.$$

I would of course explain that the equality sign is not symmetric with respect to such notations; we have $3 = A(5)$ and $4 = A(5)$ but not $3 = 4$, nor can we say that $A(5) = 4$. We can, however, say that $A(0) = 0$. As de Bruijn points out in [1, §1.2], mathematicians customarily use the '$=$' sign as they use the word "is" in English: Aristotle is a man, but a man isn't necessarily Aristotle.

The A notation applies to variable quantities as well as to constant ones. For example,

$$\sin x = A(1)\,;$$
$$x = A(x)\,;$$
$$A(x) = x A(1)\,;$$
$$A(x) + A(y) = A(x + y), \quad \text{if } x \ge 0 \text{ and } y \ge 0\,;$$
$$\bigl(1 + A(t)\bigr)^2 = 1 + 3A(t), \quad \text{if } t = A(1)\,.$$

Once students have caught on to the idea of A notation, they are ready for O notation, which is even less specific. In its simplest form, $O(x)$ stands for something that is $C A(x)$ for some constant C, but we don't say what C is. We also define side conditions on the variables that appear in the formulas. For example, if n is a positive integer we can say that any quadratic polynomial in n is $O(n^2)$. If n is sufficiently large, we can deduce that

$$\bigl(n + O(\sqrt{n}\,)\bigr)\bigl(\ln n + \gamma + O(1/n)\bigr)$$
$$= n \ln n + \gamma n + O(1)$$
$$\quad + O(\sqrt{n}\ln n) + O(\sqrt{n}\,) + O(1/\sqrt{n}\,)$$
$$= n \ln n + \gamma n + O(\sqrt{n}\ln n)\,.$$

I would define the derivative by first defining what might be called a "strong derivative": The function f has a strong derivative $f'(x)$ at point x if

$$f(x + \epsilon) = f(x) + f'(x)\epsilon + O(\epsilon^2)$$

whenever ϵ is sufficiently small. The vast majority of all functions that arise in practical work have strong derivatives, so I believe this definition best captures the intuition I want students to have about derivatives. We see immediately, for example, that if $f(x) = x^2$ we have

$$(x + \epsilon)^2 = x^2 + 2x\epsilon + \epsilon^2\,,$$

so the derivative of x^2 is $2x$. And if the derivative of x^n is $d_n(x)$, we have

$$(x + \epsilon)^{n+1} = (x + \epsilon)\bigl(x^n + d_n(x)\epsilon + O(\epsilon^2)\bigr)$$
$$= x^{n+1} + \bigl(x d_n(x) + x^n\bigr)\epsilon + O(\epsilon^2)\,;$$

hence the derivative of x^{n+1} is $x d_n(x) + x^n$ and we find by induction that $d_n(x) = n x^{n-1}$. Similarly if f and g have strong derivatives $f'(x)$ and $g'(x)$, we readily find

$$f(x + \epsilon)g(x + \epsilon) = f(x)g(x) + \big(f'(x)g(x) + f(x)g'(x)\big)\epsilon + O(\epsilon^2)$$

and this gives the strong derivative of the product. The chain rule

$$f\big(g(x + \epsilon)\big) = f\big(g(x)\big) + f'\big(g(x)\big)g'(x)\epsilon + O(\epsilon^2)$$

also follows when f has a strong derivative at point $g(x)$ and g has a strong derivative at x.

Once it is known that integration is the inverse of differentiation and related to the area under a curve, we can observe, for example, that if f and f' both have strong derivatives at x, then

$$
\begin{aligned}
f(x + \epsilon) - f(x) &= \int_0^\epsilon f'(x + t)\,dt \\
&= \int_0^\epsilon \big(f'(x) + f''(x)\,t + O(t^2)\big)\,dt \\
&= f'(x)\epsilon + f''(x)\epsilon^2/2 + O(\epsilon^3)\,.
\end{aligned}
$$

I'm sure it would be a pleasure for both students and teacher if calculus were taught in this way. The extra time needed to introduce O notation is amply repaid by the simplifications that occur later. In fact, there probably will be time to introduce the "o notation," which is equivalent to the taking of limits, and to give the general definition of a not-necessarily-strong derivative:

$$f(x + \epsilon) = f(x) + f'(x)\epsilon + o(\epsilon)\,.$$

The function f is continuous at x if

$$f(x + \epsilon) = f(x) + o(1)\,, \quad \text{as } \epsilon \to 0;$$

and so on. But I would not mind leaving a full exploration of such things to a more advanced course, when it will easily be picked up by anyone who has learned the basics with O alone. Indeed, I have not needed to use "o" in 2200 pages of *The Art of Computer Programming*, although many techniques of advanced calculus are applied throughout those books to a great variety of problems.

Students will be motivated to use O notation for two important reasons. First, it significantly simplifies calculations because it allows us to be sloppy—but in a satisfactorily controlled way. Second, it appears in the power series calculations of symbolic algebra systems like *Maple*® and *Mathematica*®, which today's students will surely be using.

For more than 20 years I have dreamed of writing a calculus text entitled *O Calculus*, in which the subject would be taught along the lines sketched above. More pressing projects, such as the development of the TEX system, have made that impossible, although I did try to write a good introduction to O notation for post-calculus students in [2, Chapter 9]. Perhaps my ideas are preposterous, but I'm hoping that this letter will catch the attention of people who are much more capable than I of writing calculus texts for the new millennium. And I hope that some of these now-classical ideas will prove to be at least half as fruitful for students of the next generation as they have been for me.

References

[1] N. G. de Bruijn, *Asymptotic Methods in Analysis* (Amsterdam: North-Holland, 1958).

[2] R. L. Graham, D. E. Knuth, and O. Patashnik, *Concrete Mathematics* (Reading, Mass.: Addison–Wesley, 1989).

Chapter 4

Writing

*[Originally published as an editorial in Engineering and Science Review, Case Institute of Technology, **2**, 3 (March 1959), 5.]*

If you were to ask a company executive what is the most serious fault with his engineering staff, chances are he would immediately bemoan their poor writing ability. A vast majority of today's engineers are highly skilled, but they just cannot communicate with each other or with upper management. The engineering profession faces the serious risk of drowning in its own technical knowledge.

Probably the best cure is to stop this deficiency at the college level. Yet today at Case there are warring forces at work, which only serve to make the situation worse. The sum total of a Case man's writing experience is usually 6,000 words of nontechnical writing every year for his humanities courses, plus his lab reports.

Lab reports should provide the student with the necessary experience in good technical writing. But so many professors use the lab report only as a grading mechanism for lab performance. To ease the task of grading reports, they require a fixed format ("Purpose: This experiment was performed to ..."; or "Abstract: The purpose of this report is ...") and encourage the use of the dull passive voice throughout ("It was next noticed that ...", "The data was taken by the observers in two steps ...", etc.)

To make matters worse, if the student tries to write a report using reasonably good English, so that it would be interesting and meaningful to a layman, he is graded down for it.

This is why we keep sending illiterate engineers into an already tongue-tied profession. This is why Western Civilization term papers sometimes end with a data sheet instead of a bibliography.

The truth of the matter is that technical writing is not hard to do at all; in fact it's quite easy. *All it takes is practice.* And now is the time to get that practice.

Naturally I would personally suggest that students practice by writing an article for *Engineering and Science Review,* or perhaps writing two. The experience gained in such a venture is of great value to each author.

But an even stronger plea of mine is for professors to encourage good technical writing in lab reports, and to reward such writing suitably. Such a change will improve the quality of Case engineers by one hundred per cent.

Chapter 5

Memories of Andrei Ershov

*[Originally published in Programmirovanie **16**, 1 (1990), 113–114.]*

The editors have asked me to note down a few of my personal reminiscences of Andrei Ershov. Although Andrei and I lived on opposite sides of the globe, with about 180° of longitude separating us, his life influenced my own in many positive ways.

Those influences began when I was an undergraduate student at Case Institute of Technology. Andrei's book on his Programming Program for the BESM had just appeared, and a bunch of us students were able to convince our Russian teacher to include it as one of the two texts for our course on understanding scientific Russian. This was an excellent experience for us because many of the technical words for computer terms were not in any of our dictionaries, nor had our teacher ever seen them before! (The English translation by Nadler had not yet appeared.) We got a feeling that we were seeing the "real" Russian language as actually used in science; this was much more exciting to us than the other text, which was about Sputnik and space exploration but at a very simple level.

Besides learning a bit of Russian from that book, I also learned interesting algorithms for compiler optimization. Indeed, Andrei's early work, which initiated this important subfield of computer science, is still of interest today. His method of exposition also turned out to be significant: The appealing flowchart illustrations in his book were a major influence on the way I later decided to illustrate program flow in my paper "Computer-drawn flowcharts" [*Communications of the ACM* **6** (1963), 555–563], and in my subsequent series of books on *The Art of Computer Programming*.

My first personal encounter with Andrei was at an IFIP Working Group meeting when a successor to ALGOL 60 was being planned. By then I had learned that he had been an independent co-discoverer (with

37

Gene Amdahl) of "hashing with linear probing" — an important algorithm that was a key turning point in my life because it led me to the field of algorithmic analysis. (See the footnote on page 529 of my book *Sorting and Searching*; this footnote appears on page 628 of the Russian translation.) And I had heard intriguing rumors about new techniques incorporated in Andrei's Alpha language project. So I was excited to meet him in person and to learn that he spoke English fluently. We spent about two hours talking about compilers and languages, while he was using the Xerox machine to copy numerous documents at that meeting.

Eventually I was able to see him more frequently, because he regularly came to see John McCarthy at Stanford University. During one of those visits a seed was planted for one of the most memorable events of my life, the conference on Algorithms in Modern Mathematics and Computer Science held in Urgench, 1979. That conference — a scientific pilgrimage to Khwārizm, the birthplace of algorithms — was a dream come true for me. Although Andrei and I were officially listed as co-chairmen of that meeting, the truth is that Andrei took care of 99% of the details, while I was able to relax and enjoy the proceedings and to learn important things from the many people I met there. Such an experience is a once-in-a-lifetime thing, and I hope it will be possible for many other computer scientists to participate in a similar event if someone else is inspired to follow Andrei's example. During that week I got to know him much better than ever before, and I was especially struck by the brilliant way he filled numerous roles as conference leader, organizer, philosopher, speaker, translator, and editor.

I have many other memories — including especially the night in 1983 when my wife and I took him to an American square-dance party and he was doing the Virginia reel and "do-si-do" — but the above should suffice to explain why Andrei has had such a special significance to me personally.

On his last visit to Stanford I learned of the great work he undertook during the final years of his life, a revolutionary improvement in computer science education for millions of students; this has justly been acclaimed throughout the world. We are all sad that his life was destined to end so prematurely, yet we are pleased to celebrate the many things he accomplished. And we know that the fruits of his life will continue to nourish the next generations of computer scientists everywhere.

Chapter 6

Theory and Practice and Fun

[Acceptance speech after receiving the 2010 Frontiers of Knowledge Award in Information and Communication Technologies from the BBVA Foundation, Madrid, 15 June 2011.]

Members of the Presidency, authorities, distinguished guests:

Of course I'm deeply honored to have been selected for this award, and deeply thankful to the distinguished computer scientists who have commented so favorably on my work. I'm also delighted to be receiving the award in Spain, since I've been a long-time fan of the concept of *siesta* ... and I love the Spanish language, especially the word *mañana*.

Occasionally in past years I've been asked to reflect on my life's work taken as a whole, and my response has always been to regard it as a mixture of two main themes: "theory" and "practice." I've devoted considerable time to humanity's ongoing quest for rigorous mathematical underpinnings, by which the fundamental ideas of computer science can be better understood and advanced. And I've also devoted roughly the same amount of time to the practical application of those theories, by writing computer programs that many people have found useful in their daily work.

The best theories are inspired by natural problems that arise in practice. The best practice is informed by theoretical results that quantify how much can be achieved by various methods. So there's a wonderful positive feedback loop, with theory grounded in practice and practice optimized by theory.

However, when I learned about the BBVA Foundation's award and was asked to prepare these brief remarks, it struck me that my life's work has in fact been characterized also by an important third dimension, namely "fun." My story is really best understood as a blend of theory, practice, and fun.

In fact my theoretical work has been driven by intellectual curiosity, by a compulsion to answer intriguing questions that seem to have begged for answers. And I've also experienced a thrill whenever I've been able to train a computer to produce beautiful patterns of numbers or images. It's enormously exciting to imagine how electrons dance inside a machine when it is performing computations. So it seems to me that the joy of such so-called "aha moments" is what really lies behind all scientific discoveries and advances in technology.

This realization came to me a few months ago when I completed a book called *Selected Papers on Fun and Games*, because I discovered to my surprise that that book meant more to me personally than any of the other volumes, which contain my papers on more traditional aspects of theory and practice.

Today I also want to highlight the continuous encouragement and joy that I've received from my wife, Jill: Nine days from now, she and I will in fact be celebrating our golden anniversary, after fifty years of wedded bliss. Those years have certainly been for me a magnificent mixture of theory, practice, and fun, for which I'm profoundly grateful.

Chapter 7

Conversations, 1996: Prizes and Choices

[This and the following ten chapters are transcripts of lunchtime conversations between Dikran Karagueuzian and Donald E. Knuth during the summer of 1996. Dikran's idea was to query Don about his life and work, so that loquacious Don would wind up doing most of the talking. We sometimes met in restaurants near the Stanford campus, but often had bag lunches on the campus itself, for example in the Stanford Barn or in the Rodin Sculpture Garden. The discussion below was recorded on 2 July 1996.]

DK: You recently received the Kyoto Prize. What was your immediate reaction?

DEK: How did I feel last Friday? It was wonderful: Phyllis* called me up at 7 o'clock in the morning at home to tell me that I had won the prize. She had just seen the fax from Japan, and I'm really glad that I could learn about it from her. She too was very happy about the news. She's been working for me for a long time. She's read more of my papers than anybody else in the world. She's typed them all. It was like she was receiving the prize vicariously. It was a prize for her as well.

Earlier I had received a book about the Kyoto Prize, but I didn't want to bother to deal with it or show it to Jill until I knew I'd won it — why should she waste time? (Don't count your chickens until they're hatched.) I went upstairs, got the book, and brought it downstairs to show Jill. It was quite a delight. And then I called my mom. She was very happy. She actually was crying but she said they were tears of joy; she insisted on that. She said it was all wonderful.

I had to get to work before my lunch appointment with the dean. I wanted to do as much as I could before noon, but the phone kept ringing: different people from public relations, a call from Japan an hour later confirming the award, and so on. Then I decided to go to the office and work there for a while. Finally I went to my lunch with Dean Hennessy.

---

* Phyllis Winkler (1933–2007) was DEK's secretary from 1970 to 1998.

John was waiting for me, with a nametag on his chest. He led me to the hall, and the next thing I heard was people applauding! I thought he had sent around an email message to people about the prize and organized a little informal celebration.

Well, it turned out that the dean had known about it all the time. He gave a little speech and then I said a few words. And then — all of a sudden, at the end of my talk — I noticed that my pastor was in the audience; and then there's my wife, there's my son! Suddenly I realized this was a party that had been arranged for a long time before, and people had come long distances. Among those present were some of my former students. It seemed they had all sort of come out of the woodwork. This was certainly the biggest surprise of my life.

Jill, of course, had arranged this. She had known about it all along; she also had told my mom. So when I called Wisconsin, mom had to keep it secret that she already knew. At this luncheon, a portable phone was brought to our table and it kept ringing. I got calls from my mom, also from my sister, and from my daughter Jenny who was in Boston at the time, and others. It was really incredible.

And what a happy occasion — except I don't know whether to trust Jill any more, because she was so good at deception. I mean, she had learned about it on Monday, which was our wedding anniversary; and we went through a big celebration of our 35th anniversary, and she didn't give anything away. When I woke up Friday morning I said to Jill, "By around noon, we'll know whether I won the Kyoto Prize or not." She said "Oh, I forgot all about that." We arranged that I would call her at Recording for the Blind, where she works. I asked her if that would interrupt anything, and she said no. I wrote down the phone number in case I needed to call her. But then Phyllis's call came through, and that was before Jill left for work. So when I went to meet with the dean I figured Jill was off at this other place; you can imagine my surprise at seeing her there along with everybody else.

She was so good at this subterfuge. When Phyllis called earlier that week and asked to speak to Jill — rather unusual, since when she calls my home she always talks to me — I was a little surprised. Later when I asked what Phyllis wanted, Jill had a really good explanation already prepared. She said, "Oh, one of the people who we'd met on our vacation needed some family history information, and he had only Phyllis's address so they had to reach me through her." A pretty good lie! [laughs]

It's really nice to win a prize that has a lot of money in it, not for the money but because people know that the prize wasn't awarded at random. A prize has credibility if it's got a hefty dollar amount (or a yen amount, in this case) behind it. Also, in America, every news item has to have a number; for example, if there's ever a disaster, we have to know how many billions of dollars the damage is going to cost, or how many people died. There has to be a number associated with every event; at least that seems to be the thing the newspapers are going after, to put in the headlines. This prize has a big number in it, so it's oriented to American culture in that way.

Shortly after the news, Jill and I decided to give the money all to charity. This was a pretty easy decision to make, because we were happy before we had the prize, and we didn't see how that money could change things for us. Nothing was holding us back as far as being happy or having a good life before the prize. We think we know a lot of organizations that will be able to use the money really well. Now we're trying to work things out so that the money goes directly from the foundation in Japan to charity instead of through us.

DK: You'd mentioned once that you wanted to make your home office more efficient. Why not use some of the prize money for that purpose?

DEK: Well, that's true; but we're just using money from our savings for that. We'll continue what we were doing. And we'll also use some of our savings to pay for the travel of my mother and my kids to Japan. So the prize will be a net loss in that sense [laughs]; but no, no, what counts is the happiness.

DK: Does your mother know about your decision to give the prize money to charity?

DEK: No, but she'll find out soon. For example, there's an endowment fund in my dad's name at the high school where he taught, and we'd like to add to it. There's also an inner-city church in Milwaukee where my mother's on the board of directors; that church runs the school where I got started, up to grade eight. It's a very nice school, attended by almost all black kids now, and we want to help that school. And, you know, we'd also like to help Stanford in some modest way. Nothing like Bill Gates giving a donation; but these kinds of charitable gifts are appreciated, I think, even when comparatively small. Also, we would like to help with improvements of the pipe organ at our church.

DK: What can you tell me about your family?

DEK: My parents had two children: first me, then my sister. My mother was the oldest of a large family, with eight siblings, and my father was the youngest of a family of four. So it's skewed, you know; my uncles and aunts on one side are much older than my father, but on my mother's side her siblings are younger. In one branch of the family, I'm the oldest cousin among 35 cousins. On the other branch, my sister and I are the youngest. Most of my mother's side lives in the Cleveland area.

Though we live far away from our relatives, we're close and the relationship among us is really warm. When I was growing up, during summer vacations and later when I went to college, my cousins and I used to get together every Sunday after church and spend the day together. We'd come from different churches to the house of one of the uncles or aunts — and from noon until about nine o'clock we did things together, playing horseshoes or whatever. The family had the most well-organized system for 30–40 people to eat together that I've ever seen in my life. Everybody knew their role as to how to set the tables, bring in the food, wash and dry the dishes at the end, and clean up, and mostly we'd play cards in the evening. We had two meals and then played pinochle. It was all very pleasant and I never was aware of any problems or strains or anything among all these people.

But I also knew that I couldn't live that way all the time, because that would be giving up one seventh of my life. I felt I had a mission to the world, where a lot of people are counting on me to do things that they can enjoy. I love my extended family, but taking one seventh of my life away was too much; so I knew that I'd be living somewhere farther away, and visiting them only once or twice a year.

They don't meet every week any more, of course; many more generations are involved now, although still all in the Cleveland area. Some of them live on an island in Lake Erie, and others live far off in the other suburbs, maybe up to 100 miles apart; it's not like they were all within a few blocks of each other as before. Now there may be five or six big gatherings a year.

DK: I recently went to a family wedding and was thinking about similar things. The grandfather of the bride died last year, so suddenly there were no more patriarchs. What's the situation in your mother's clan?

DEK: I'm not sure if there is a patriarch in that group or not, considering all the marriages. The main patriarch I guess would be my Uncle Paul, and the matriarch would be my mother. They're the survivors of the family, and my Aunt Esther would be another person in that generation. She's the one who gets gifts for wedding anniversaries. She would be the fourth oldest, I guess. But of the nine original children, those three are still around. And my mother is the oldest and still very healthy, I'm happy to say. In fact she's the only one not retired.

I was just reading that Stan Ulam once said there were two phases of his life: In the first phase, he was the youngest of the people he was with, and in the second phase, he was the oldest. There was no middle. I'm not sure if that's true, but it is a neat way to look at the situation, always being at one extreme or the other.

DK: Perhaps you don't remember it but over the years you've been very generous to me. When you were developing TEX and METAFONT you gave me a guest account on SAIL [the Computer Science Department timeshare computer with its own unique operating system] and invited me to join your discussion groups. This generosity showed itself in a far more substantial and massive way when you made both programs available to the public for free. And when you said you had a mission to the world, I interpreted the remark to mean that you were given a gift by God for a purpose and that you had to share it with other people.

DEK: Well, you're embarrassing me by being too generous yourself! When I spoke of a "mission" I wasn't thinking of a heavy obligation or anything scary like that. It's just that I do feel some sort of a calling, a natural sense about what's the right thing to do for a person in my shoes. I might be generous in some ways, but I'm selfish in other, more local and less visible ways. I let other people do the all-important stuff that doesn't make headlines.

Of course, I do daily chores like washing dishes, but I mean my father was completely different: He did volunteer work for about thirty organizations all the time, and he was indispensable to all kinds of groups. He was always insisting on doing something for which he would get no credit at all, except from the one or two people who would directly benefit from each of his efforts; in some sense, he lived by doing personal favors. Well, I tend to do things where there will be a hundred people who will benefit from my actions. But somebody's got to do these other things, which I don't do. Fortunately there are networks of volunteers everywhere you look; if everybody was only going to work on stuff that has a large impact, then the world would collapse.

So I'm selfish by not volunteering in my own neighborhood. But when I see that I have some unique abilities that could have a world impact, well, then, that's what I'm going for; I have a limited amount of time, so this way I can do more good. Or to put it differently, I tend to pass up chances to do things that don't require any uniqueness, any skills that large numbers of people could master. I found that there was something I could do that was fairly unusual and also had a payoff for others at long distance, and so that became my role.

Of course I can't say that the path I've chosen is the only way to go, or that I feel in some way superior because of this, because I know that computer science is just one of the things that makes the world go round. It's what I happen to be good at. You have to realize there are two sides of the coin: The world would be a terrible place if everybody was like me. I mean, you couldn't possibly read all the books, for example, if everybody wrote as many books as I do; how many trillion books would there be? There has to be a balance.

Computer scientists like to talk about binary search. Well, I think of life as a binary search: You try things, and you find out about yourself as to what you can do successfully and what you can't. I knew a long time ago I'd never be an Olympic athlete. [laughs] And the more you learn about your talents — the more you become adjusted to what you can do successfully — the better your life is, it seems to me.

The Stanford Development Office called me yesterday and asked if I would fly up to Seattle with President Casper and visit Bill Gates, trying to convince him to donate some more money to Stanford. And I thought about it overnight, and today I'm going to tell them, "Well, I have absolutely no political skills or persuasive skills; what good would I be to Stanford in such a situation, you know?" Instead, I'm going to suggest a better plan. They can tell Bill that I think it's very worthwhile to put his money into this venture, and I'll prove it in the following way: For every ten million dollars he gives to Stanford, I'll give one day of free consulting time to Microsoft. I'll do my best as a consultant. This way I can do something where my expertise is, and it also proves that I am in favor of the project that they want to raise money for, in case he thinks it's important to have my opinion.

OK, it might sound silly to say that I'm going to offer one day of consulting for ten million dollars; but it still is much less silly than saying that I'm going to spend a whole day of arm twisting, which just wastes everybody's time since I'm no good at it. With my alternative proposal, Gates can still get all the benefits of philanthropy to Stanford and also have value-added for Microsoft. I could come up and get some good messages across to his programmers, maybe about the beauty of programming, and how to get a lot of satisfaction about making programs efficient for the machine as well as elegant in their style. I could help them promote such a philosophy up there, if I went; and I could learn from the people there too, from the questions they ask and the things they do. Conversely, I don't want to take any time away from writing *The Art of Computer Programming* just to do a sales job. That's not my schtick at all.

Speaking of Bill Gates, I know that he and his company are contro-versial. I've met him a few times and seen what he does, and talked to his associates who work at Microsoft, but I haven't really read much of their code. I think a lot of it is mixed up, the way almost every large organization's code is; you expect it to be mixed up. It's very hard to have that many people working together and doing anything elegant.

I do have the impression that he is the most competent billionaire in the world, thus far. And he does a lot of things that are very forward-looking, like this Corbis company, where he gets some of the best people in the world to digitize art work and so on. Other people were talking about it, but he did it.

With any large organization, the more you learn about it, the more you know its warts and so on. I'm not sure — I haven't ever really been there — I don't understand the spirit of Microsoft the way I once did in places where I was a consultant. (Years ago, when I did such work, I found that if I went to five different companies, I would find five differ-ent cultures.) And I can't say what Gates is really like on the basis of some magazine articles that I've read. I've seen magazine articles about myself saying things about me that I don't believe, so what can you say?

I mean, when you experience something at first hand and then you read about it in the paper, the newspaper account almost never reflects your own experience, it always seems very distorted in almost every case. So I have to say that, on basis of the second-hand information that I've heard, I would be charitable to Microsoft. The worst technical work of theirs that I've ever looked at in some detail was their original design for — what's it called? — smart ligatures or smart fonts or something like that, whatever. The first design was pretty awful, you could tell they'd never tried to implement it. But they eventually got the bugs out; now it's working, and they fought it through in spite of the mess. The latest version seems to be doing a decent job for very difficult Arabic scripts and so on. But when you saw the first specs they were impossible.

DK: Let me go back and ask you to say more about doing something outside of your expertise. You used the example of washing dishes. I know that you volunteer your time to do menial or practical work for your church. My question is: Do you find that that kind of activity — working with your hands — in some ways helps you with your principal vocation?

DEK: Well, you're absolutely right. I can't do technical stuff all the time. I've found that I can write only a certain number of pages a day before running out of steam. When I reach this maximum number, I have no more ideas that day. So certainly within a 24-hour period, not all of it is going to be equally creative. Working in the garden, pulling weeds and so on, is a good respite. I recently got together with some friends at Second Harvest, repackaging food from one place to another. This kind of activity, using my hands, provides variety and doesn't really take away from the things I can do for the world. But something I would never do for my church is serve on the council, or anything like that. I mean, I do committee work so badly compared to anybody else, I would never volunteer to do it. If nominated I would refuse, saying that I just gotta do my books. I hope that answers your question.

DK: Yes, it does. At times church council meetings can get pretty petty.

DEK: Makes my stomach churn. [laughs] We don't have any of that in the church I belong to now. But in some other churches, it was ... every meeting was a downer, even though you loved the people there, there were people who just loved to argue.

Interesting: Yesterday I went to the funeral of a man from our former church — we went back there — and the new pastor is a real neat, frank kind of guy. And he said, "You know, the first time I met Lew" — the pastor had come maybe a year ago — "A week after I arrived, Lew came in to talk to me and said, 'You know, Pastor, I'm going to be very loyal to you, but I want you to understand the way I am.' He says, 'When we get to a meeting, I'm going to challenge everything you say, and make you prove that you really want it.' So now I know that's how he's operated, see? He told me that he would be the Devil's advocate or whatever, never rubber-stamping anything and letting matters go through until they're thoroughly discussed before taking a vote. Then he said, 'And once we've passed the motion, I'll be on your side and stick to it.'" Well, after hearing this anecdote yesterday morning, I got to thinking: If I had known that the people at the church meetings were playing this kind of game, I wouldn't have felt so bad. [laughs]

DK: Sometimes church affairs go against Christian ideals.

DEK: Right. It's a paradox, but churches aren't for holy people, because there aren't any such people. Sinners are all over the place, and church is for them. But we muddle through, and try to learn from good examples. Certainly you're not going to find a place where there are only perfect people, or people that are always acting exactly as they should. That will never exist.

When I wrote the book *3:16* I was most surprised to find out — I sent the manuscript to a lot of people for reading, and they started telling me about their experiences — I was surprised to learn about the depth of hatred many of them had for what they felt were really bad deals that they or their parents had gotten from some church or other, and that these petty squabbles had sort of turned them off to the whole idea of religion. I grew up quite oblivious to such things, in my family, so I had no idea how many people were, you know, really carrying a tremendous grudge against the church. They weren't indifferent, which would have been worse; but it's tragic that they carried those scars.

DK: Going back to Kyoto and the distribution of the prize to different charities, have you decided to which ones you'll give and have you made your decision public?

DEK: No, no. Jill and I, we just decided this morning to distribute the prize. But we have an appointment with our lawyer next week, to find out about how to work this out. She's out of town, so we have to wait ten days before we really know how to proceed.

I'm writing a letter to the foundation in Kyoto to let them know that we're going to give the prize money to charity and ask them if there is a way to deposit it directly into the charity's bank account, so that we don't even touch the money. That should be a simpler way to distribute the prize. It makes us happier than if we had to do it ourselves. Perhaps this way we can avoid the rivalries and jealousies and so on that might arise. You know the saying, "Don't ever say you know someone until you've split an inheritance with them." Money might kind of spoil everything, so why should receiving a prize have any negative effects on our lives, right? Forget the money part.

DK: It's admirable, and also consistent with everything else you have done.

DEK: You're exaggerating. It's a matter of ... Let me put it this way. When I developed TEX and realized that it could be profitable, I didn't need any of the potential profits. I already had plenty. If writing software was the only way I'd had to make a living, naturally that would have been my living. But TEX was a spin-off of something else, so I didn't need to capitalize on it.

There are people who are very good at managing fortunes, and they can be philanthropists and so on; they can enjoy maximizing their nest egg and really doing more good that way. Jill and I learned that that's definitely not us. We had some investments in condominiums that we thought would be a good deal. Originally we had stock, we had this and that, and then we decided to diversify, to invest in real estate. So we bought these condominiums, we painted them, and got some tenants, and ...; well, it was the worst decision of our lives! It turned out that every time we had to deal with the condos, that activity took us away from what we really like to do. I'd have to sit down and write landlord-like letters; the toilets would suddenly stop working; we'd get phone calls from the police saying that wild parties were going on; and all sorts of things, you know. We were making a profit but oh, it was a terrible nuisance.

Then we found out that if we just donated the condominiums, lock, stock and barrel, to Stanford's management agency — the people who manage Stanford's endowment — those folks are very good at it. They know everything about condos, how to get new tenants and deal with them as they move in and out, and so on. We had four college kids in one unit, and a young family in the other (but that guy lost his job), so the management required lots of time and skill. After we turned them over, our life improved dramatically: Not only did Stanford appreciate this gift, because their staff was good at that kind of work, but they also took the time to figure out all the tax forms we needed for it. Thus Jill and I didn't have to pay any income tax for the next three years, after making that donation. It was so much nicer for us to be out of it than in it.

But there are other people who are really good at managing a fortune. You can think of David [Woodley] Packard, for example, as the epitome of this sort of thing. He's done an enormous amount of good that wouldn't have happened if he'd given everything away that he received, because he has that talent. Jill and I know we definitely don't have that talent. As I said before, when we find out what we can do well, we concentrate on those things; we don't worry about building up areas that we aren't really good at. That's somebody else's life.

DK: To put a little variety in today's interview let me ask you about a French mathematician we were talking about the other day, Philippe . . .

DEK: Philippe Flajolet. Yes, you were asking about whether or not there were certain national trends: Are people from some country perhaps much better at certain kinds of theoretical work than others? And you asked about the French in particular. I was saying that I knew a Frenchman who I could say was "impressionistic," in the manner of famous painters. But I was not thinking of Philippe, but rather Maurice Nivat. Philippe is much younger.

I first met Maurice in the 60s. He went on to become the founding editor of *Theoretical Computer Science*, an excellent journal that has now published more than a hundred volumes. Today he's one of the leading professors at the University of Paris, and he's also on lots of other editorial boards. With respect to "political power," as far as publications in French computer science and mathematics are concerned, he's one of the tops. But when I first met him, he was a junior student, hadn't gotten his doctorate yet. I had read his thesis; Frenchmen do two levels of theses, and I read his first thesis, which was about context-free languages. After I wrote him a letter with some questions about his work, he said, "You know, in France nobody reads your thesis, they just know who signed it; it's all a matter of prestige and not content." But I had written and expressed appreciation for his theories, so we got to be friendly. He came to America for a visit and we went camping in the Anza-Borrego desert, down there by San Diego, shortly before I left Caltech.

He's the one I could describe as an impressionist mathematician. He would write something down and say, "Don, do you know this formula?" Well, I'd look at the formula, and both sides of the equation were wrong. Still, indeed, I did know the formula! I knew that on one side he meant to switch j and k around, and that on the other side, he meant to square the one term, or something like that. And so he had the right impression of the thing; he had mathematics in his head the way Monet or Renoir would have the scene.

DK: Someone else would have said, "This is wrong," and just moved on.

DEK: Well, that's interesting. I never thought of it that way before. But I guess you're right. By knowing my limitations, by understanding that I have a distorted lens by which I look at the world, I can understand that other people also have their own ways of thinking; so I try to compensate by seeing the world through other people's eyes.

For example, I know from personal experience that a lot of difficulty goes into designing a font. A lot of my colleagues can't see any of that; they think font design is kind of a trivial thing to do, so why should anybody ever pay for it? But I believe that the ability to create a good font is extremely rare. And in general, I know that there are many varieties of expertise. Unfortunately, a lot of people view everybody else through their own filter.

Perhaps computer scientists understand this better than other people do, because computer science deals with representations. The real world has to be codified and represented inside a machine. We know how to model different kinds of expertise; so we can understand what it means to adapt, since we have to adapt things to computers. I suppose that might account for my attitude, at least in part.

I do know that people will evaluate ideas by projecting them onto their own scale of merit, based on what they themselves are good at.

They have a right to do this; in fact, it's very important in their own work to operate in that way. But if you apply such reasoning to conclude that somebody else doesn't deserve a salary, or isn't contributing anything of value to the world, that's a terrible error.

Computer science is a little bit more open-minded in that way, it seems to me. The models that we have may well match the world better than the models that a physicist might make; some physicists see everything only in terms of differential equations, say. It seems to me that computer science models are able to build in non-uniformity, the way the world is; they're a little more true to life.

DK: When you say you're selfish, I interpret that to mean you're less generous with your time. But sometimes I find it amazing how you will take time to explain something trivial, in cases where one would expect you to say, "Please do this by yourself, and let me advise you about something else."

DEK: Watch out: With this Kyoto Prize, my head keeps swelling. The more you talk to me, the worse it gets! You should put some kind of ego meter on these tapes, so that you can figure out whether or not I've completely lost any humility.

DK: I can give examples.

DEK: There's really just a simple pattern. I try to do a good job at whatever I'm doing, because it's more fun to do a good job than not. And when there's a choice between different things to spend time on, I try to look for things that will maximize the benefit without making me burn out.

For example, when I was working on the TEX project during the early 80s, hardly anybody saw me when I was sweeping the floor, mopping up the messes and carrying buckets of waste from the darkroom, cleaning the machines, and doing other such stuff. I did those things because I wouldn't have dared to ask graduate students to do menial tasks that were beneath them. I know that every large project has some things that are much less fun than others; so I can get through the tedium, the sweeping or whatever else needs to be done. I just do it and get it over with, instead of wasting time figuring out how not to do it.

I learned that from my parents. My mother is amazing to watch because she doesn't do anything efficiently, really: She puts about three times as much energy as necessary into everything she does. But she never spends any time wondering what to do next or how to optimize anything; she just keeps working. Her strategy, slightly simplified, is,

"See something that needs to be done and do it." All day long. And at the end of the day, she's accomplished a huge amount.

Putting this another way, I think that the limiting thing — the thing that determines a person's success in life — is not so much what they do best, but what they do worst. I mean, if you rate every aspect of what someone does, considering everything that goes into a task, a high minimum is much more important than a high maximum. The T_EX project was successful in large part because I quietly did things like mop the floor. The secret of any success that I've had, similarly, is that in all the projects I've worked on, the weakest link in my chain of abilities was still reasonably strong.

Chapter 8

Conversations, 1996: Printing

[Recorded 15 July 1996.]

DK: How did you get interested in typography?

DEK: Well, I had some ink in my blood from the beginning. My father had a mimeograph machine at home when I was young.

Do you recall what a mimeograph was? It was a comparatively inexpensive printing apparatus, based on a kind of oily black ink that never dries. The ink would ooze through thin spots in flexible stencils, which could be prepared by typewriter and/or stylus, and it was pressed onto absorbent paper, eventually sinking into the paper so that it wouldn't smear too badly. In the days before xerography, black mimeograph and purple "ditto" or "spirit master" printing were the near-universal alternatives to expensive typesetting equipment.

Dad's mimeograph didn't belong to us; it belonged to an architect, who let us use it in our house if my dad would help him print up specifications. So my dad would type the specifications for buildings, and he could also use the machine for various charitable projects. For example, he made programs and newsletters for churches and schools in the Milwaukee area. He would also reproduce music that way: If one of his friends composed a piece, dad had special equipment and templates with which to make stencils, from which the music could be printed. Choral music was the hardest thing he had to do, because it was necessary to match words to the notes; dad would have to line the words up very carefully on his typewriter.

I watched him do this and found it pretty interesting. Soon I learned how to type a mimeograph stencil by myself; eventually, in fact, I wound up printing a weekly newspaper for our high school. Once per week, during my senior year, I'd stay up all night editing and making the stencils for *The Knight's Page*, which was mimeographed on two sheets of

legal-size paper, printed on both sides.* My summer job in 1956, just before going off to college, was actually to run the Hasler Printing Company in downtown Milwaukee, a small firm that produced mimeographed newsletters and brochures, etc. Clients would come in and tell me or Mr. Hasler what they wanted; I'd type up the stencils and draw in any necessary illustrations. Then I'd run the machine, putting slip sheets in between the pages to keep the ink from bleeding from one sheet to the next. Finally, if necessary, I'd use a big "guillotine" knife to cut the results to size. I didn't have to do any binding. Mr. Hasler would leave about 9 o'clock in the morning and tell me, "OK, let's do these jobs"; then I would be on my own for the rest of the day, and I'd finish them.

I did that for about two to three months during the summer in Milwaukee. Of course this was just amateur printing, not really high quality; you can't do very much with mimeograph. But my dad kept developing his part-time business. He got an offset press from the A. B. Dick Company, a fairly good-sized offset press in our basement; and he would compose copy with a Varityper machine. That setup was much better than mimeograph, but still inferior to "real" letterpress printing. Again this work was mostly for churches and schools in the Milwaukee

---

* The second issue even included some music (see the illustration above). Another example of mimeograph output is the basketball score sheet reproduced in Chapter 23 of *Selected Papers on Fun and Games*.

area, but he actually did all kinds of jobs. I once went through his old files and found three or four thousand folders, including films from which the offset printing plates were made. In one case, for example, he had printed about 4,000 envelopes for some bank in Indianapolis.

My next experience with printing came when I'd written *The Art of Computer Programming*. I began in 1967 to proofread hundreds and hundreds of galley proofs, destined now for the high end of quality printing. The first editions of Volumes 1, 2, and 3 were done on a Monotype machine, as used in the finest technical books. The second edition of Volume 1 (1973) was also produced with Monotype. I met the talented people who were composing the type on that complex machine.

Suddenly, when looking at the first galleys for the second edition of Volume 2 in 1976, I was shocked to see a serious degradation of quality. The new proofs looked terrible, so I asked, "What's going on here? Why are you using a different font in the subscripts than you do on the main line? This doesn't look right. It doesn't come close to matching what we had before." And they said, "Well, Monotype machines are getting too expensive. You have to go to phototypesetting. Nobody knows how to run the Monotype machines any more. The guys are dying off and our equipment is becoming replaced by these other machines."

The new phototypesetting machines did well at the big money-making jobs, like the printing of magazines and newspapers. But nobody cared about making them work well for mathematics. I had an emergency meeting with the typographers at Addison–Wesley to discuss what to do. I said, "Look, I chose to publish with you primarily because of the quality of your typesetting and layout." Indeed, Addison–Wesley was unique among technical publishers, I think, because of their in-house composition. They had a man named Hans Wolf who employed his own compositors and ran his own Monotype machines. Other publishers like McGraw–Hill would farm their work out to different places, to independent suppliers, but Addison–Wesley had their own composition department — right in the building next to the editorial offices. Unfortunately Hans was now retiring, and they could no longer continue the tradition.

After I had argued rather passionately, Hans agreed that he would try to figure out how to use photo-optical typesetting equipment to match the appearance that he'd been able to achieve with the hot-lead Monotype methods. But he said that nobody had made fonts for mathematics symbols (the so-called "math sorts"). Nobody had adapted the classic Monotype math sorts to the new machines; even worse, the text fonts that had been used for books like mine, "Monotype Modern 8A," had never been adapted either. They were unavailable, and Hans said there were legal questions, copyright issues, about whether such font conversions could be done. But he'd heard of a place in Poland that would make photosetter fonts if you sent them proofs of the characters that you want.

Well, they tried that, and went through several iterations. But oh man, was it ugly! It was horrible. Some of the letters were much darker than others. Some of them were slightly tipped. They weren't spaced well. After getting the new proofs I felt sick.

In fact, I was just thinking about those proofs this morning, because I've got to prepare the talk that I'll be giving in Kyoto. The proofs are now in the Stanford Archives; I'm going to blow one of them up and make a slide to use in my presentation.* The people in Kyoto have asked to see indications of the struggles that I've gone through, so that the audience will understand that it wasn't a smooth road. The bad galley proof will therefore fit in perfectly: I'll be able to compare the awful typography that triggered my typographic research with the elegant typography in the Japanese translation of the same book.† One of my points will be that, if I had lived in Japan, there would have been no need for me ever to have gone into typography, since I wouldn't have had this problem. Paradoxically, though, the Japanese have now adopted my system enthusiastically; not for the increase in quality, but because it allows everybody to have access to this kind of quality.

Back to my story. I had to reject those ugly proofs, and I was faced with a dilemma. I didn't want to write books if they were going to look so lousy. One of the joys ... A book has to be something that I'm proud of visually, æsthetically, as well as having good technical content. The prospect of an ugly second edition was making me feel dejected. I didn't know what I was going to do.

Meanwhile, life went on. I did some playing around with the Xerox Graphics Printer at the AI Lab; you remember that old thing, the XGP. Its resolution was variable, 140 dots per inch at the edge of the page and 240 dpi in the middle of the page; it didn't produce a square grid. If you printed the Stanford seal, it would look like an oval instead of a circle, squashed horizontally on the left-hand side of your letter but squashed vertically in the middle. So we had two versions of the Stanford seal, depending upon where you wanted it to appear on the page.

---

* See Slide 10 in Chapter 1 of *Digital Typography*. That slide shows an excerpt from Addison–Wesley's final attempt to rectify the photo-optical letterforms (March 1977); previous attempts had been considerably worse.

† See Slide 24 in Chapter 1 of *Digital Typography*.

Despite the poor quality, we found it interesting to play with this pixel-oriented device. People would say, "Isn't this neat, we can make different styles of letters." Lots of fancy fonts for the XGP were created by members of the Lab.

In fact, our computers were hooked up to TV channels, so that we could watch old movies. Somebody developed software so that, if you got to the title of a film and saw a font that you liked, you could freeze that frame, crop out the letters, and enter them into a font. One guy watched a TV serial and captured its subtitles, week after week, until finally getting the letter 'X' that he needed to complete the alphabet.

People really appreciated the Xerox Graphics Printer because of the variety it allowed. The quality looks atrocious to our eyes now, but it was much, much better than we could get from a line printer, which was the traditional way of getting computer output. The fact is, on a day that the XGP was not in operation, the parking lot would only be half full! People would just not come to work if they couldn't use the XGP; it was that important to their work.

I typeset our family's Christmas newsletter with the XGP at the end of 1976. Earlier that year I had also used the XGP to print errata lists to *The Art of Computer Programming**, a task that required math fonts, superscripts, subscripts, and so forth. But I never had the slightest notion that XGP-style printing could ever be considered as a substitute for real printing in a real book. It was just a curiosity.

One day in February of 1977, however, I happened to see some galley proofs that were done on a high-resolution laser printer. No, not a laser printer — it was a machine made by Information International, Incorporated (III, Triple-I), and I guess it used some kind of a CRT beam instead of a laser. But it definitely was based on a completely pixel-oriented, digital process.

I was on a committee to reevaluate our reading lists for the grad student comprehensive exam. Pat Winston had written a book called *Artificial Intelligence*, and we were trying to decide whether to put it on the reading list for our students. One of Pat's students had reportedly taken magnetic tapes containing the page-image information from MIT down to Los Angeles, to get the book printed on this machine down there at III, and they sent us a copy of the galley proofs. This company, III, had been commissioned by the *Los Angeles Times* in the late 60s to develop a machine for typesetting the newspaper. (I think the company had been founded by Ed Fredkin from MIT, hence Winston

---

* See paper R33 in Chapter 20.

knew about their equipment.) The same company had also developed a similar machine to make microfilm copy, in which the resolution was incredibly sharp.

Anyway, I didn't know the details. All I knew was that the galley proofs of Winston's book looked amazingly good — just like real type! There was absolutely no difference in quality between the proofs I was looking at and the best metal type I'd ever seen. The XGP quality that I was familiar with was much worse than the difference between margarine and butter, you know; so I assumed that even if you could improve the XGP by beefing it up to a higher resolution, it would still give you only a poor imitation of real printing, like when the sound of an electronic organ is compared to the sound of real pipes. I thought pixels just couldn't cut it. But here, before my eyes, was a example of the highest quality ... and I knew that everything I saw on that page was produced by 0s and 1s. It was not done by any mysterious metal process or by any mysterious photographic process or by any other process that was hidden from me or scary. It was digital yet beautiful.

So, the next morning I woke up and I knew that my life was going to change. I thought, "Whoa!" I'd been faced with this terrific problem about how to make my books look right, but now I was faced with tangible proof that a solution to that problem was all within my power. All I had to do was to find out a way to put 0s and 1s on a grid, with 1s representing ink — and, you know, I'm kind of a conceited guy, I think I can do 0s and 1s as well as anybody in the world. Not only that: Because I was good at 0s and 1s, and because 0s and 1s now were clearly destined to be the wave of the future for printing, it was my *responsibility* to think about how to get those 0s and 1s there. Other people needed to use digital typography too. As a computer scientist, I *had* to work on typography to solve this problem, because it wasn't just holding *me* back — it was holding lots of people back.

Therefore I said to Jill, "You know, honey, I'm supposed to write *The Art of Computer Programming*, but I just can't go on doing that until after spending a year to work on printing." The time was right, and I felt a special call to do such work because of my years of experience with different aspects of printing. Indeed, I had a unique mathematical and algorithmic background, because some of my students in a problem seminar had recently figured out ways to break text between lines so that paragraphs would look better.

Furthermore, my sabbatical year was scheduled to start in the fall of 1977. Jill and I had planned to spend it in Santiago, Chile; we had tentatively arranged for me to visit one of the universities there. Once

I realized that I should really spend my sabbatical year working on typography, however, I had to change all of those plans, because a lot of special lab equipment would be needed.

I had also visited Xerox Palo Alto Research Center (PARC) the previous year, where I'd seen a bunch of guys working in one of the rooms as I walked by. They had a big capital 'B' on one of their monitors, and they were fitting lines to the edges of it; I remembered seeing how they were playing around with this big letter. I hadn't really gone in to watch; but now I thought "OK . . . , that's the way I'll do my letters. I'll go over to Xerox and use their program. I'll take the letters that appear in *The Art of Computer Programming*, and I'll fit lines around the edges; then I'll have mathematical definitions of all the characters that are needed in the book. That will solve the problem."

So I went over to talk to the folks at Xerox PARC and asked, "What if I spent my sabbatical here, could I use this equipment that you have?" Unfortunately there was a hitch. They said, "Yes, fine, but we would have to have the ownership of anything you do." Oops — I didn't want any of this stuff to be controlled by proprietary rights. I figured that I just needed a mathematical description of letters; I didn't want anybody to own those formulas.

Therefore I decided to work at Stanford's AI Lab. Our equipment wasn't anywhere near as good as the machines at Xerox, but at least we did have equipment. Like TV cameras. Also, the following week I flew down to Triple-I with Les Earnest to discuss getting one of their snazzy machines. How much would it cost?

Oops again: It turned out that their high-resolution typesetter was way too expensive for us. An alternative was to rent time on such a machine. The internal coding that they used was secret, but they would give us permission to write our own software that would produce fonts in their format. Still, the cost was probably more than the Lab could afford, and there was no research support for such things.

All of this took place in February, within a week of my seeing those proofs of Winston's book. It was immediately clear to me that I'd be working hard on this project for awhile; but I didn't think it was going to take very long. I thought a year would be plenty. Surely I could finish arranging those 0s and 1s in say 15 months, with three months of summer preceding a sabbatical year.

My big thing that summer that was a trip to the far East. Jill and the kids and I were scheduled to spend a month in China, about one year after Mao had died. I continued to work on *The Art of Computer Programming* through the middle of April, by which time I'd finished writing one of the opening sections of Volume 4. Then I put that book on hold, and started thinking about a language to express typesetting commands. (My diary entry for 14 April says that I was "thinking about hy-phen-a-tion versus co-or-di-na-tion and hy-phen-at-ed.")

Meanwhile, I had more discussions with Addison–Wesley, and we wrote letters back and forth. I told them that I'd solve the problem myself; they should abandon this Polish fantasy, which was never going to converge. They were anxious to help as much as they could, so they sent me the original printing plates that had been used to photograph the original edition of my book.

I told you that my book had originally been composed and printed with Monotype machines, but that wasn't the whole truth. In the late 60s, a book like mine would be created in several stages. Most of the copy would be typeset as individual slugs of Monotype letters; but a lot of hand work was also necessary because of the mathematical formulas. A technician would drop the big mathematical symbols in by hand, then tighten up the results. After I had corrected galley proofs, the technician would arrange the metal type into pages, and I'd get page proofs to check. Finally everything would be tightened up one more time by hand, and they would print *one copy* on stiff paper — using very heavy paper stock, almost like light cardboard.

That one master page would be photographed, using a very large camera; and the photograph was converted to a plate for *offset* printing. The metal type was melted down to be reused, but the photographic negatives were kept on file in case more copies would be needed. (Lead is expensive to keep around, and it also wears out after about 5,000 copies have been printed. It was better to make just one copy from the lead type, then do everything else by offset.)

Addison–Wesley had also retained a few of the original master pages that had been photographed after being printed from lead type. They sent me a bunch of those, enough to encompass all of the alphabets that I needed to digitize. (Last year, while cleaning out their warehouse, they sent me another shipment of those "historic" original pages.)

Addison–Wesley had also hired a commercial typesetting firm, Universities Press (Belfast) Ltd., to key in all of the copy for the second edition of Volume 2. (At that time Universities Press was handling a substantial number of the world's mathematical journals.) The result didn't look good — it was the source of those unacceptable galleys I mentioned earlier — but at least we did now have all the words and formulas recorded on paper tape, expressed in a typesetting language called Cora. Phototypesetting machines got their input from such paper tapes.

Thus I began in mid-April 1977 with a few dozen perfectly printed pages of the first edition of Volume 1, plus an approximation to the second edition of Volume 2 in this paper tape form. We figured that the tapes would save me much of the labor of keying in a 700-page book.

DK: Didn't you have any more information about the original fonts?

DEK: No, Addison–Wesley couldn't supply that. Several years later, Richard Southall found the definitive letterforms at St. Bride's type library in London. He found original proofs used by the Monotype Corporation in 1907, or whenever they first made the 8A font, photographed at a rather large size. So we eventually knew the gospel truth about what the letters were supposed to look like. But in 1977, all I could work with were the prints that had been used to do Volume 1 in 1968; that's all Addison–Wesley had.

I wasn't thinking of designing typefaces yet; that idea had never even occurred to me. At first I was just thinking of copying the typefaces that would be needed.

DK: How did your project get to be called 'TEX'?

DEK: I didn't actually have a project or a name for it, although the name 'TEX' came to me rather early on. By the end of April I was thinking of designing a language for typesetting that would be called TEX. That name changed to 'TEX' quite awhile later. But I did have a name, yes; the minute TEX was named, I started to get ideas about it.

The main problem, as I saw it then, was to put 0s and 1s on the page, so I had to know how much space to leave between things. I wasn't thinking yet of how I was going to make the character shapes. For the shapes I was thinking, "OK, they can be handled with something like the program that I saw at Xerox PARC. I'll come to that soon." First of all, I had to have a language to describe where to place those shapes.

One day I went up to the AI Lab and drafted an initial design for TEX, staying up all night until 5:00 a.m. before finishing it, and I still have a copy of that memo. I'm going to print it for the first time in the digital typography book, you know, the next volume in your CSLI series.* It was my specification of a language that could describe *The Art of Computer Programming* as it was to be typeset. The TEX language was only going to be for Phyllis and me to use at that time, although I did already try to make it extensible for other projects.

To make this design, which included a detailed test case, I went through Volume 2 and typed in almost all of page 1. Then on page 2,

---

* See Chapters 24 and 25 of *Digital Typography*.

I typed only the things that were different from page 1, and so on, until I had gone through the whole book and had examples of all the different kinds of typesetting that needed to be done in different parts of Volume 2, producing a five-page document.

By the way, that sample document still survives. David Fuchs and I wrote a paper where we used it as the example of our method for optimizing the communication between a typesetter and a computer.* We worked out a nice theory by which we could keep the Alphatype machine going fast even though it only had a very limited memory for characters. We had to keep sending it the shape information for new characters while it was typesetting, and it could remember only about 50 characters at once. Hundreds of different characters were needed, so we had to keep swapping new information into its memory; we had to do that in a clever way so that another shape could be described while the machine was moving the film a little bit. We worked this out and illustrated our method with the five sample pages in my original design of TEX, because those pages showed a lot of variety.

DK: When did you start to tackle the problem of character shapes?

DEK: After mocking up the TEX language, I turned to the font question. The problem was to define patterns of 0s and 1s for each letter of the alphabet in each of the needed styles.

Jill helped me at this point: She took 35 mm slides of the master pages that I'd gotten from Addison–Wesley, by holding her camera as close as she could to take each shot, maybe three feet away from the original copy. To enlarge those images, we used our home projector, by setting it up in the longest corridor in our house and projecting the slides onto a wall that was about 25 feet away. I stood there at the wall with a piece of paper, sketching the outlines of the letters. That was our homegrown technology for magnifying the original font samples; very crude, because the letters weren't at all sharp after being projected, but I didn't realize as yet that the fine details would be all that important.

I figured that I could probably live without extremely precise measurements. After all, I had spent many years looking at letters. Once I had shapes that were approximately right, surely I could simply take a look at sample pages; my eyes would tell me what's wrong, and I could twiddle the patterns until I got them right. That was my overall game plan at the time.

Well, as I was standing there with a piece of paper and drawing the letters as they appeared fuzzily on the wall, I began to lose confidence,

---

* Paper P105 = Chapter 14 in *Selected Papers on Design of Algorithms*.

until an obvious idea dawned on me. Namely, I realized that these letters had been designed by a person, a human being who'd had some idea in his head. Right? My job wasn't really to copy the letters that were there; instead, I should find out what was going on in the designer's mind when he drew the letters. There was some intelligence behind the design. There was a scheme to it.

Indeed, after I started looking at some of the letters, I could predict what the next one would be. I mean, I noticed that the letter 'i' was five units wide. The lowercase 'h' was ten units wide, and so was the lowercase 'n'. The letter 'm' was fifteen units wide. And hey, a pattern became clear: The 'm' has three vertical strokes to it. The 'n' has two. The 'i' has one. There was an underlying principle, a rhythm, with one little stem coming every five units. In other words, I realized — which is now obvious of course — that the design wasn't random. The guy had planned his alphabet according to a logical system.

Thus it dawned on me that what I should do is not just blindly copy the letterforms. I should find a way to express the intent of the designer. Instead of just having a bunch of formulas for the outlines, one for each component of each letter, I should have a way to say definitively what constraints those formulas are intended to obey.

Just about this time, in mid-May, Jill and I went on a tour with Stanford's Library Associates, up in the gold country. We went to Sacramento and visited a typography museum where I could see lots of classic examples of typefaces. Then we went out into the hills and saw people's printing presses, where they made books by hand in their retirement homes. We saw what book lovers of the Stanford community were appreciating and collecting as some of the very finest local printing on private presses. Right after that tour I read the works of Goudy and Zapf, and everything else I could find on the subject of type design.

Stanford has a great collection of materials on printing called the Gunst Collection, which was donated by the family of one of those book lovers. I studied books that explained the history of type design and gave many examples of how it was done, how the designers would mark up their own proofs. I was very conscious of not wanting to make the mistake that a typical engineer often makes when he tries to solve a problem all by himself, forgetting to incorporate the things that people have learned over hundreds of years. No, I wanted to learn as much as I could from the wisdom of the past. I got the idea that Fred Goudy, if he were alive, would never have come near a computer. But Hermann Zapf was the other way; his books sounded like he wanted to adapt properly to changes, to continue making progress.

These books taught me that 10-point, 9-point, 8-point, and 7-point letters were not simply scaled versions of a single design; each size was subtly different, when you looked at real typography of good quality. I needed a systematic way to represent the variations. Furthermore I would have to do more than just make letters in different sizes: I needed to make bold letters, I needed to make typewriter style, and so on. So I began to ask if it would be possible to have a unified idea that could adapt to different stylistic conventions. Could I accommodate both bold and normal weight in the same design, if I just changed certain numbers in the specification?

Pursuing this quest, I started to compare the different alphabets more closely, trying to see how they changed in different circumstances. In most cases the changes were very smooth as the strokes got thicker or taller or wider.

However, the lowercase 'a' was an example where the changes were not smooth, in the Monotype fonts of my book: The bottom right corner of a boldface lowercase 'a' has only a normal serif ('**a**'); but the non-bold one has a curly little hook in that place. If I tried to attach a bold curly hook to a bold 'a', the strokes came too close to each other, making sort of an ugly blot instead of a hook. That's why the designers rounded off their 'a' with just an ordinary serif in the bold version.

On the other hand, that little hook was the only significant difference between bold 'a' and normal 'a'. None of the other letters had such a little hook; I'd never actually noticed the funny hooks that were sitting there under my nose, on each 'a' but nowhere else. So I thought, "Hey, I don't need this. I'll just make all of my lowercase 'a's without a curly hook." I figured that the hook was, you know, left over from some archaic alphabet — like an appendix supposedly has no use in a human body, as a relic from evolution somehow. To verify my hypothesis I looked around and found a couple of fonts that, indeed, had hookless 'a's.

So I began to plan for a unified design in which all the shapes would change gradually as the overall specifications of an alphabet were varied. I started with my measurements from projecting onto the wall, and I went from that to graph paper, and from that to a computer program, thereby starting to obtain machine-drawn letters in June.

Before long the computer had produced somewhat decent shapes for every letter except the 's'. I've often told the story about how I couldn't get my 's' to look like an 's'; how I was unable to sleep for two nights until I finally figured out some mathematics to describe an 's' in a way that would be satisfactory in both bold and Roman styles. It was very tricky to specify how it should curve first to the left then to the right.

Eventually I wrote a paper about the letter 's', explaining the solution that got me over that hump.*

Of course I had greatly underestimated the difficulty of type design, and I had to reconsider everything later. I soon found, for example, that I *did* want to have hooks on the 'a's, after all; so then I had to decide when to make the transition, as the font became bolder. But if I hadn't been so naïve in my early thoughts about making the shapes, I never would have come up with the ideas that are presently embodied in METAFONT.

The next step in my plan was to tune up the initial shapes by making measurements that were much more accurate than I was able to obtain with projected slides. I took the Addison–Wesley master pages to the AI Lab and aimed a TV camera at them. I mentioned earlier that people could look at old movies and freeze the screen; well, I could use the lab's TV camera, and freeze that view. I thought this process would be simple, as it apparently had been when I'd watched the experiments at Xerox PARC.

But lots of problems arose because there was significant distortion in the camera. Our TV camera wasn't at all accurate for such measurements, and it was *completely* unsuitable when I tried to capture the character shapes. If I adjusted the lights in the room by just a little bit, the characters would double in thickness! I couldn't make any decent measurements whatsoever; any images you could freeze on one day would be quite inconsistent with what you'd get the next day. I began to realize why the people in Poland had not been successful at converting fonts from one medium to another.

Even though absolute measurements were out of the question with the unreliable AI Lab equipment, I still could make *relative* measurements. I could figure out, for instance, how far down the subscripts had been dropped by the compositors who had originally prepared the given example pages. I could certainly measure how much space there was between lines, and how much space there was between words, and so on.

At this time I measured not only my own books, but also several other works that I chose as standards of good typography. I took a journal called *Acta Mathematica* that was printed in Stockholm at the turn of the century. At that time, *Acta Mathematica* had the best budget in the world for mathematical typesetting; it was the pet project of a leading mathematician, Mittag-Leffler, whose wife was rich, and he made sure that this journal would be produced with the best quality that

---

* See Chapter 13 of *Digital Typography*.

money could buy at the time. Therefore I studied it carefully and analyzed how they printed the formulas. (Two years ago, incidentally, *Acta Mathematica* decided to convert its operations to TEX, thus coming full circle and making me very happy.) Another standard of excellence that I measured was a Dutch mathematical journal from 1950, *Indagationes Mathematicæ*, because its printers also did an especially nice job.

I also found books in Stanford's library about the typesetting of mathematics. These books had conflicting information about how the spacing should be done; I compared what they said with what the professionals were doing. I could also look at the paper tapes from Belfast, because all the spacing of mathematics had been specified painstakingly by their compositor in the Cora language. For instance, he would skip to the right four units before an equal sign and four units after an equal sign. (Actually, TEX now uses five units, not four, because the Addison–Wesley pages from 1968 used five.) By combining the recommendations of three library books with several examples of really good stuff, which represented the true best practice, I was able to put together a picture of how a decent job of mathematical typesetting could be done.

DK: And you were scheduled to visit China.

DEK: Right. By now it was July, and we had this trip to China coming up, so I had to put the whole font thing on hold. But I had an alphabet that I thought would probably be a reasonable starting point.

Summer had begun, and I started some students working on the implementation of TEX, from the specification that I'd drawn up. I figured that the specs were pretty complete, so the programming would be fairly trivial — just a routine student job for two guys to do during the summer. The students that I picked on were Mike Plass and Frank Liang, whom you know.

Jill and I went off to China; so Mike and Frank had no way to talk to me or to ask me questions if there were any problems in the specs. And I learned later that the specs were actually *loaded* with problems. That is, when I got back and my sabbatical really began, I started writing the final program for TEX, and every five minutes I'd come up with a question that hadn't been answered in those specifications.

If I had been in my students' shoes, doing the programming for my professor, I would have had to schedule an appointment with him every time a question came up, and then I'd have to spend maybe twenty minutes explaining the problem. Then he would say, "Oh, yeah, do it this way"; and I'd go back to work for another five minutes and come up with another question, schedule another appointment, and so on. I now think that it's impossible to build a first-generation system efficiently when the designer and implementer are different people. A designer/specifier never sees the whole picture. People can't really perceive the issues clearly until they are faced with writing a computer program.

Mike and Frank must therefore have been faced with enormous problems while I was gone in China. But they came up with programs that implemented a mini-TEX. And they actually printed a page, by applying their system to a test file that got all the way through from the beginning to the end, with a couple of test letters and a horizontal rule on it or something like that. It was kind of a triumph, really, that they finished as much as they did — although my first reaction was surprise that the whole project wasn't already complete. Afterwards, by looking at their implementation, I got helpful ideas for the overall structure of the final program that I would write later.

In the fall, when my sabbatical year officially began, I visited various manufacturers in hopes of finding a digital typesetting machine that Stanford could afford to buy. The III machine, which was called Videocomp, was too expensive, as I said; so I looked at other machines that were being sold by Compugraphic, Autologic, etc. Finally we decided either to get Monotype Corporation's new Lasercomp, or to purchase an Alphatype machine, which was smaller and cheaper and slower but had higher resolution. With Addison–Wesley's help, we finally installed an Alphatype, which arrived in the spring of 1979. (So much for my hopes of wrapping up this whole project during my sabbatical year.)

In order to get ready for that event, I needed to have all kinds of things in place, each of which needed something else. Like, I needed the typesetting system in order to test the characters, but I needed the characters in order to test the typesetting.

First I wrote the basic parts of TEX, the routines for typesetting ordinary text exclusive of mathematics; that took a month. I couldn't test the programs yet, having no fonts to work with; but that didn't really bother me, because I was using the principles of structured programming and had a fair amount of confidence that the code wasn't too far from being correct.

Then I did fonts. I made a Roman alphabet, italic alphabet, some math symbols, lots of special characters for mathematics, and punctuation. (At first one thinks only of 26 letters, times two for uppercase and lowercase; but the number of different shapes needed keeps growing and growing, the more you look, and eventually you end up with about 500 altogether.) And each of them was designed with parameters so that you could make them bolder or less bold, or in typewriter style or whatever.

Notice that if I could finish five characters a day, the whole task would take 100 days. The letter 's' alone required nearly a week, but on other days I could maybe get through a dozen different characters. Of course I had to do all the Greek letters, etc.; so I wasn't totally ready with the test fonts until March of the following year [1978].

I still had no good measuring tools. But it was possible to print my trial letters on the XGP at huge size — like each letter would be about two inches high — and then I could Xerox the output to make a bunch of copies. After cutting the resulting letters with a scissors, I could do typesetting by hand, pasting up some proofsheets and putting them on the wall for viewing. I could also use a reducing Xerox to take those samples down to smaller and smaller sizes, in order to see if they began to look like regular type.

Yes, that was the "high technology" available to me when I initially designed the first fonts. I had to rush, because I wanted to show this work to the mathematical community when I gave the "Gibbs lecture" at a national meeting in January 1978.* After giving that lecture I took a month off from font hacking, to write the math-mode parts of TEX, before finalizing the mathematics fonts and finally getting ready to do some actual testing.

Anyway, I was sitting up there in the AI Lab during most of my sabbatical, writing these programs, and I was kind of enjoying it because McCarthy's lab was a nice place to work. One of the best things about it was that everybody could see what everybody else was doing. Unless you specifically said, "hide my screen," others could type a couple of keystrokes and see what was on your monitor. I knew, for example, that Hans Moravec had four monitors on his desk, and he always had one of them tuned to what I was doing. He liked to watch me, because my screen was usually showing letters that were being designed in various styles. Conversely, I knew that Hans was enjoying my font experiments, and that knowledge made me happy as I was doing it.

John McCarthy had helped design the display system that we used. You might recall that this DataDisc had 32 channels, one of which was the "Take me, I'm yours" channel for logins. After logging in you could work with your own screen, or display the TV picture (which was another channel), or you could display up to four channels simultaneously. Gray levels were possible so that you could get 16 shades of gray.

There was an intercom too, so that you could broadcast a message like "Does anybody know how to work around this bug?" You could

---

* See Chapter 1 of *Digital Typography*.

even type on somebody else's screen: You could give them a hint as to what to do. Yeah, it was a fun place to work.

And I sat in the office right next to John McCarthy all that year. He very kindly gave me a desk there, and visitors would come through all the time because ... there were about 35-40 researchers up at the Lab, so people would drop in at all hours. And they would stop by my office and see what I was doing. So the word got out that I was working on this typesetting thing, and pretty soon it became clear that I wasn't going to be the only user. Other people wanted to do typesetting too. In fact, within a month after I had TEX running, Guy Steele had ported it so that it ran on the MIT computer.

Of course you know that my sabbatical year ended long before I could declare that my typography project had been successful. TEX went through a long evolution as it gained hundreds and then thousands and then hundreds of thousands of users. The entire font generation system was redone in 1979, making it interpretive rather than compiled inline. And the hardest job of all was to get the letterforms to look right. My early alphabets looked funny, but I didn't know why. I had to learn all kinds of lessons about fonts, and the Computer Modern letters didn't begin to please my eyes until five more years had gone by. Five years of tuning and more tuning.

I felt ashamed that such an apparently straightforward task should have taken me so long to accomplish. But then Matthew Carter cheered me up. He said, "Well, five years is about the normal time frame for a font designer's apprenticeship." The reason, I guess, is that people's eyes play tricks on them, and many years are needed for a designer to train his eyes to see the important and subtle nuances that must go into a successful font.

Throughout that period, I wanted to keep in touch with the world of letter artists and I wanted to incorporate their knowledge. Fortunately, the American Mathematical Society (AMS) got interested in my work, and a guy from Rochester who knew Hermann Zapf was a friend of one of the leaders of the AMS. In those days Zapf came to Rochester every summer to teach a one- or two-week class on type design. This mathematician in Rochester had met him and thought that Zapf would actually be delighted to meet me. I never would have dared to approach this famous German artist on my own, but with an introduction like that I could do so. Hermann came out to spend two weeks with me in February of 1980 — almost three years after I had made my first trials — and we hit it off really well. Through him, I gained credibility with other artists. I was eventually able to work with all of the leading type designers in those days, with the exception of Adrian Frutiger who was ill. Thus I had fantastic tutors during my years as an apprentice. In particular, they showed me why the lowercase 'a' needed that little hook (namely for balance), and they showed me how to put it back on. In fact, I learned that the real problem with my original lowercase 'a' was not with the hook at the lower right, but rather with the upper stroke in the bowl at the lower *left*.

Chapter 9

Conversations, 1996: Life

[Recorded 25 July 1996.]

DK: Let's begin today by continuing the conversation that we started while driving to the restaurant this noon.

DEK: You were saying that you'd been worried about issues that faced your son as he was growing up, and I was saying, "Right: That's a sign of being a good parent." I mean, if you didn't worry, and if you didn't go through some spells and crises, then you'd be missing a part of life. Even though such things aren't pleasant when you're doing them, they are the defining experiences — things to be glad about in retrospect because they happened. Otherwise you might be guilty of not feeling guilty!

On the other hand I've noticed in myself that there were times when my body was telling me to be unhappy, yet I sometimes couldn't readily figure out a reason for any unhappiness. I knew that I was feeling "down," but sometimes I had to go back several months to recall anything that anybody had said to me that might still be making me feel bad. One day, when I realized how hard it was to find any reason for my current unhappiness, I thought, "Wait a minute. I bet this unhappiness is really something chemical, not actually caused by circumstances." I began to speculate that my body was programmed to be unhappy a certain percentage of the time, and that hormones or something were the real reason behind moments of mild depression.

If so, we can get a better understanding of why "power corrupts." When people have more power and they get richer, and they find themselves rich but still unhappy, they think, "Hmmm, I'll be happy if I only get rid of all the sources of my unhappiness." But the action of removing annoyances sometimes involves abusing their power. I could go on and on in this vein, I guess, because you find that in the countries where there is a great difference between rich and poor, the rich people have their problems, too. They haven't any motivation to change the way they're living, exploiting others, because as far as they can see, their own life isn't that happy. But if they would only realize that their unhappy spells are part of the way that they're made, and basically normal, they wouldn't make the mistake of blaming somebody else and trying to get even for imagined misdeeds.

This morning's paper had an article about psychologists finding evidence for what they called a person's "set point"; it's the psychologists' way of measuring the level of happiness. Some people are normally glum, some people are normally happy, and so on. Their new data came mostly from studying identical twins, who had quite different circumstances in life but the same genes. In their terms, such twins generally have the same set point. This study seems to confirm what I've been suspecting all the time lately.

In fact I've concluded that it's really a good thing for people not to be 100% happy. I've started to live in accordance with a philosophy that can be summed up in the phrase "Point eight is enough," meaning "0.8 is enough."

You might remember the TV show from the 70s called "Eight is Enough," about a family with eight children. That's the source of my new motto. I don't know that 0.8 is the right number, but I do believe that when I'm not feeling 100% happy, I shouldn't feel guilty or angry, or think that anything unusual is occurring. I shouldn't set 100% as the norm, without which there must be something wrong. Instead, I might just as well wait a little while, and I'll feel better. I won't make any important decisions about my life at a time when I'm feeling less than normally good.

In a sense I tend now to suspect that it was necessary to leave the Garden of Eden. Imagine a world where people are in a state of euphoria all the time — being high on heroin, say. They'd have no incentive to do anything. What would get done? What would happen? The whole world would soon collapse. It seems like intelligent design when everybody's set point is somewhere less than 100%.

DK: The journey is more important than the goal, more important than getting to the finish line.

DEK: Yeah, that's the key. Enjoy the path, don't think of the bottom line too much! Of course, we're all entitled to a certain amount of happiness. Don't let me stress the negative thing. I'm not saying that unhappiness should increase beyond a healthy level. But I think a little bit is healthy.

Today I've been preparing my Kyoto commemoration speech, and I began by reading the speeches of other laureates in the past. One of them was starting to speculate about the future, and he had a very good essay about comparing life to riding on a ship. He was able to bring out that analogy in really great ways; then he concluded: "There is no way to know the future. There never has been and probably never will be. Although we continue to make progress, I can't say that the future is going to be one in which life will be easy for everybody." Of course when I read that, I wanted to write in the margin, "I *hope* that life will not be easy for everybody," for exactly the reasons that I've been telling you. A certain amount of struggle defines our life, and so on.

Every time I have a choice to make between something that is going to make someone's life easier or harder, I will always choose the one that makes it easier, in spite of what I just said. And I'm certainly not in favor of wars, in order to define more people's lives! But there are plenty of ways to have a healthy struggle against difficulties without hurting another person, without abusing another person.

I know that the "0.8 is enough" attitude was helpful when I was advising graduate students. A PhD advisor also has to be a counselor, although we have no professional training in such matters. My discussions with students were private, of course; suffice it to say that I had 28 students and there were 28 different cases. And at times there were a lot of tears. Once I remember, for example, that there was no way to discuss what we were talking about in my office, so we had to go walking around the campus. Eventually I became convinced that it was good for the student to go through a personal struggle at the time, although it was very serious for him. Several of my students had to get over important crises in their lives, and they all are brilliant people. As I say, I encountered 28 different situations.

I don't plan to dwell on any of this in my Kyoto speech, but I do have a paragraph or two where I start to talk about my early life. When I was a baby, it was not fashionable for parents to introduce their kids to anything that they would learn later in school. The whole social picture was quite different from today; the concept of "preschool" was basically unheard-of. So my parents were really frowned upon by their friends for reading stories to me when I was three years old. There were children's books around, but you weren't supposed to have them until you were in first grade, or kindergarten anyway. The reason was that people said, "If you do that, the student is going to be bored when he gets to school."

I think I talked to you about that maybe once before, where I think this idea of being bored is cockeyed. When someone says to somebody else that they are bored, I think it's a shocking, almost shameful admission, or at least it ought to be regarded as such. My view is that it's not the world's responsibility to entertain me, it's my responsibility to see what is interesting about the world. I mean, I can admit that some college professors give boring lectures. But I still think that, no matter how bad the professor is, the student is at fault if the student doesn't find something interesting.

In general, I myself tend to make the mistake in the other way, to err in the other direction: I am *too much* interested in stuff. But I really think that if there were more social pressure, saying that boredom is the fault of the bor*ee*, instead of the bor*er*, then a lot of people would have a much fuller life. If you go through life with the expectation that external sources are going to be amusing you all the time, you're going to miss a tremendous amount.

The key is to learn as soon as possible how to find interest from within yourself, how to ask interesting questions about what you are experiencing. For example, if I have to wait on a street corner for a bus to come by, I will count how many Volkswagens are passing, or if there are more cars going north than south, or whatever. There will always be something to do that is interesting, it seems to me.

I probably carry this attitude to an extreme, doing it too much, because I tend to be very interested in Chapter 1 of every book that I read. So much so, that I hardly have time to look at the last chapter. For example, when I studied calculus in college, the first chapter talked about the absolute value function, before getting into meatier things like differentiation. I first saw the absolute value function at that time; it's something that people usually skim past in a second so that they can go on to the hard stuff, but I was fascinated by it. I spent weeks thinking about different constructions involving the absolute value function. In general I always go very slowly through the Chapter 1 of whatever I'm doing, what I'm studying, thus I get a good knowledge of fundamentals; but I don't very often solve a problem on the frontier. I tend rather to hone my basic skills, because I find that to be interesting in itself.

Maybe that's why I got into typography — designing letters: Not only did I see the interesting words in Chapter 1, I also saw the interesting letters that they were made of! I keep looking at lower level stuff. I'm not a high-level, broad-brush type of person.

I can see the great gift that generalists have; but the difference between them and people like me might even connect up with our previous discussion of nationalist mathematics or whatever. Henri Poincaré was one of the great mathematicians of all time, but in fact I can't understand a thing he wrote. He just lived in a completely different universe. Well, I did find one day that he wrote a book on number theory, and there were some parts of it that I could actually understand. It came as a tremendous surprise. Anyway, that's the way I am.

The technique of asking questions is something that I don't know how to teach, but I've tried to encourage it in my classes. I say, "Now, here is a situation, ask an interesting question about it." I'm sure there must be some way to write a book about how to find interesting things in our everyday circumstances, but it remains for somebody else to do.

DK: Can you tell me a little more about your childhood?

DEK: The first thing in growing up, as I said, was that my parents read to me when I was young. But I don't ever remember being bored in school. Furthermore, my parents never promoted me to an advanced grade. I was born in January; in Milwaukee at that time, I would have gone to school a year earlier if I had been born in December. So I was generally the oldest in my class all the way through. My parents had a chance to move me to another class, but they very wisely did not. And this absolutely did not mean that I sat there bored, because there was always something to do.

In fact I think I was a behavior problem when I was in eighth grade. I probably sat in the back and made wisecracks with my friends, which was not good. But at least I wasn't bored, OK?

And I always wanted to be a teacher. When I was in first grade, I wanted to be a first grade teacher when I grew up. When I was in second grade, I wanted to be a second grade teacher, and so on, until I got to college; and then I wanted to be a professor. I was good at certain things, but of course, I also was bad at other things.

Among the things I was not good at were sports and penmanship. Sports were basically a disaster; for instance, I never could throw a baseball. I threw like a girl, and I still do. I'll probably never learn to throw a baseball. But that wasn't a big problem. Some big kids did beat me up, probably in first and second grade, but I got over that.

The only time I remember ever being really upset was when I got mad at my third grade teacher for some reason. I don't remember what the reason was, I just remember that I was upset. At the end of every class we all would walk by her desk and say something like, "Good-bye." But, that day I said, "Good-*bye!*" and she said, "Donald, please stay after class and write 100 times, 'I must not ...'", whatever.

All in all, my school days were pleasant. The teachers made sure that there were always extra projects to work on. For example, in music, maybe the class would try some three-part singing and I would be the only one on one of the parts. As far as I know, I didn't have enemies in the classroom, we all got along fine. We had a kind of a club. We would go to each other's houses. I started a newsletter for my classmates when I was in sixth grade. I did this with a ditto machine, actually. You remember the purple stuff?

DK: Like the machine your father had?

DEK: Nope, he had a mimeograph. This was a ditto machine, yeah, the smelly stuff! I had learned how to use it up at camp.

I went to summer camp for six or seven weeks every year, from the time I was seven years old to when I was 14 or 15, in the countryside near Wautoma, Wisconsin. One of the things I liked especially well at camp was the nature, the flowers. (Weeds, really, but they were nice-looking weeds.) I learned the Latin names of all the weeds, but when I'd come back the next summer I had forgotten them, so I had to learn them again. Finally, when I was maybe 11 or 12, I made a book for the campers where I drew pictures of each of the common plants around our camp, and gave the Latin names. This was a little handbook that was distributed to the campers for several years. I did it with ditto masters — in fact, we had the fancy version, with two colors. You could use both red and purple, so I could draw those flowers in two colors. And I used a typewriter to type the names, using a "hunt and peck" method.

Anyway by sixth grade I knew the ditto process, and I must have gotten encouragement from the teachers to make a little newsletter that would tell, you know, what was going on in the school. (It also featured some really corny jokes that I undoubtedly found in books.) The point is that there always were plenty of things to do that would keep me amused, even though I wasn't advanced into the next grade level.

My dad also had a wire recorder — these were the machines that came out before tape recorders — which captured speech on magnetic wire. My friends and I would write scripts for make-believe radio programs; I reproduced them on ditto and gave copies to the other kids, so that they each could read their parts into the recording machine. Yes, lots of extracurricular things were available to keep me busy.

In high school (Lutheran High in Milwaukee), I played piano to accompany the chorus. We had a very good choir. I think the best-sounding voices of all are probably high school kids when their voices are blending and singing choral music; so I enjoyed the opportunity to play the piano accompaniment for some of their numbers. And I worked on the school paper and the yearbook.

Similar activities continued in college, at Case in Cleveland. Case had set up a system to measure how many extracurricular activities you had. If you were in a certain student organization, you might get one point or two points; if you were in the band, maybe four points; and there were points for varsity letters, and so on. If you worked on the newspaper or if you joined a fraternity, you could earn a specified number of honor points. The rule then was that if you had more than 50 honor points at the end of your senior year, you received the honor key, the Case honor key. Well, I had accumulated more than 80 honor points when I was a junior! The scoring system corresponded perfectly with the kinds of things that I wanted to do anyway.

DK: Isn't it true that your father was a schoolteacher?

DEK: Yes, but he always was careful not to have me in his class. He was the second- and third-grade teacher when I was in first grade. Then he moved to being fifth- and sixth-grade teacher, when I went to second grade. In fact, the school had just gotten bigger, so they hired two new teachers for the second and third grade classes. I did have fifth and sixth grade together in the same classroom; but not with my father, who had by now begun to teach in high school.

When I was in sixth grade, I had already heard what the sixth graders were learning, because it had been taught the previous year. So that would be the year for me to get bored, if any year was. And that was the year when I started working on this little newspaper.

By the time I got to high school, dad became an administrator. So, he always stayed a step ahead of me. He didn't want to have me in class, and he never ... he always ...

Well actually, I think the only problem that I can remember about my showing strange talents was that dad maybe seemed to feel that he hadn't been successful enough himself. In other words, I suppose, you know, like when I got a PhD, he wished he had a PhD too. He clearly was the kind of person who always was helping everybody around him: Whenever he could see a chance to pitch in and help, he would do it. He devoted his life to those selfless activities. But perhaps, in the back of his mind, he also thought that if I had succeeded in some way, shouldn't he have done it too?

The funny thing was that, during all these years, I always was faced with challenges; there always were things that other people did better than me, so I never felt like I was on top of any heap. I worked hard because I thought I was a bit behind the 8-ball. The vice-principal of our high school called me in one day for a brief talk before I went to college, and he said, "Don, you've been successful here, but you're going to be a failure in college. It's just going to be too hard for you." I don't know why he was telling me this, but he said that I should get ready for failure; that was his advice to me.

In my high school, the administrators kept percentages instead of a grade point average, so you got a numerical score on your report card. I don't remember exactly, but an 'A' grade meant 92 or better, and 'B' also corresponded to a certain interval of numbers, and we actually got a numerical score instead of a letter grade. And my overall average in high school came out to be somewhere between 97 and 98, which was an all-time record for the school. So I knew that I was doing OK, and I participated in lots of extracurricular activities, and so on; but I also knew about other things that other people were doing a lot better than I was, so I never stopped working.

Actually, I was pretty much of a machine at that time, a test-taking machine. I didn't have feelings so much, I just did things. I could pass my exams. I could obey instructions. I could find an interest in what I was doing, but I never really emoted. I started to mature rather late, when I joined a fraternity and went through Hell Week.

My horizons broadened a bit during my first sabbatical year, at age 30, when for the first time I started reading great literature that I hadn't been assigned for homework. For once I began to read books that I chose myself, instead of books that a teacher had told me to read. I went through the Harvard shelf of fiction. I learned that I loved Tolstoy but hated Dostoevsky. I enjoyed Dickens, you know, *David Copperfield*, *Oliver Twist*, ... all the classics, *Jane Eyre*, the greatest things. But I started reading them only when I was fairly old, when I was becoming more of a human being. Yes, I think I was pretty much a machine, during my student years.

DK: What about other activities outside of school?

DEK: I loved music. And I dated girls and stuff. (I had huge crushes on several girls at school and at summer camp; but they didn't like me much in return.)

Maybe I suppressed feelings because it was a guy thing. But since I was enjoying what I was doing, well, I really didn't have any time for long-term reflection. Nor did I have any crises that would make me stop and think. So I think I postponed that part of my life until later.

I was oblivious to enemies or political maneuvering all the way through. I could have focused on that, but I never did. I was involved in other matters.

I took piano lessons, beginning when I was seven years old. But I was doing a lot of other stuff, and didn't have time to practice my piano lesson every day. As a result, I got pretty good at sight-reading, so that I could fake it.

Probably the least happy time while I was growing up was Christmas each year, in a sense — I mean, not Christmas Day, but the preparation for Christmas — because all the activities that I was in would come to a climax at Christmas time. The choir would give special performances, and every other activity also went into high gear. If you were involved in five activities, you'd feel temporarily as if you were in more like ten, come December.

I always felt that I had to prove myself. Is that an inferiority complex? I constantly thought that I should be doing better. And when I got to college, I was the first person from my high school who had ever gone to Case, so I didn't know how to calibrate myself with respect to people from all over the country. It was the first time I was inside of a world-class institution. I'd been in a small, loving church community, but now I was in a big place. And Case's dean warned us, right off the bat. Just before classes started, he said, "Look to your left, look to your right, one of you three are not going to be here next year." I was scared stiff that I wouldn't make it. I had enough confidence to keep me happy, but I did feel a constant need to prove that I could cut the mustard.

DK: Did your mother and father put pressure on you to emulate them? I'm wondering to what extent parents should attempt to direct their children.

DEK: Because you are so democratic. Yes, that's an important concern. Several of my PhD students have suffered from a parental heavy hand.

I always wanted to obey my parents, but I never felt worried about not being exactly like them. I think my kids, well, you know, they have a lot in common with Jill and me, but we never put any pressure on them to be much like us. I know that my daughter wouldn't dare take a computer class at Brown University, for fear that they'd expect her to ace it. And my son is a terrific math teacher, but he doesn't like computers. So, you know, they aren't exactly the same, but they have a lot of similar characteristics. Contrariwise, my son is a world-class athlete; I don't know where on earth he got that talent!

Speaking for myself, when growing up I never felt much of a sense of rebellion. I guess maybe I was just blessed with some really neat parents. We did have disagreements, of course.

DK: You grew up during the depression years.

DEK: Oh, yeah, there were financial hardships galore. My dad hardly got a living wage. Working for the Lutheran school system was really a mission, not a career, in that sense. The church didn't have much money to pay its teachers. I don't remember the exact numbers, but essentially, the principal of the school told him that they would be cutting his salary from $12.00 a month to $10.00 a month, so that he would learn how to be thrifty. He had to find part-time jobs to supplement his salary.

Dad wanted a piano, so he started teaching piano lessons. With the money he could get from teaching piano outside of his school duties, he could pay interest on the money that he had borrowed to purchase the piano. (By the way, I still have that piano.)

Furthermore, my mother started working as soon as my sister went to school. She managed to be a full-time mother and a full-time secretary, and kept being promoted so that she's been in the real estate business now for 50 years — still hasn't retired, at age 83! I can't help but mention that she was the first woman ever to have been a member of the Building Owners and Managers Association in the United States. The organization was all men until she got involved, in the late 1950s, as a national officer. (That's when she met Khrushchev: During his visit to their convention in Iowa, she shook hands with Khrushchev!)

Yes, mom worked. And that was unusual for an American woman at that time; the prevailing opinion was that working women were abdicating their family responsibilities. So she probably felt guilty about that and worked extra hard cooking all of our meals and everything besides. Anyway, her work gave us enough income so that we could afford to buy a car when I was 11 years old. Up until that time we used bicycles for transportation. Finally mom and dad were able to purchase an old Chevy, so that we could drive to my grandparents' houses for the first time instead of taking the train.

Then, as I mentioned before, dad started a part-time printing business in his basement, a hobby that developed into another source of income. Later on, in the 60s, he became treasurer of the high school, and the high school was having trouble meeting its payroll; so he stopped writing checks for himself. He just started working for free, in order to help balance their school budget. I don't think he told anybody what he was doing.

Certainly my parents were never rich; they worked hard to get out of the depression years. They continually volunteered to do stuff where only a few people at a time could see the good that they were doing. Yet little by little they gained many, many lifetime friends.

Before I forget it, let me mention another thing, because I plan to bring it up in the Kyoto talk. My parents told an interesting story that supposedly happened when I was five years old. During the summer of

1943, I'd been going to a children's reading hour at the library, which was in downtown Milwaukee. It was about a 30-minute streetcar ride from our house to the middle of the city. In those days Milwaukee was a very safe city, drug-free; so my parents let me, a five-year-old, ride the streetcar by myself to the library one day. (I don't remember this occasion, but they certainly do.) They say that I went there into the children's book section and I got fascinated by it and started reading, oblivious to time. Apparently, when the lights went out, I took some books over by the window where I could continue to read, and nobody saw me. So I didn't come home, and naturally they were worried because they had let me go downtown all by myself. "Where is Donny?" So they phoned the library. Somebody on the night staff answered the phone and said, "I haven't seen anybody, but I'll take a look"; and he found me there, sitting in the stacks reading books. I guess that incident was sort of predictive for my later life.

DK: Were you an only child, or did you have siblings?

DEK: My sister Paula was born when I was $3^1/_2$, so there were two of us. She was three years behind me in school, so she was a freshman when I was a senior. Alas, unbeknownst to me, she always felt inferior to her brother. That was a side effect of my academic success. When she graduated from high school she was first in her class, but she still didn't feel like number one. She kept thinking that our parents were expecting her to do exactly the same as a normal child like me would do.

We see each other fairly often — most recently, last month. She went to the University of Wisconsin, and then to the University of Minnesota for graduate school, and specialized in what I suppose they used to call Home Economics. In graduate school she met the man who she soon married, a Canadian who is a specialist in weed control. He comes from a farming background, and he has won a lot of awards now for his research on agronomy, on weeds. He just retired this year, and they moved just last week. They have some property in an area of British Columbia near ski resorts, and they're building their dream home now. For many years they've lived in Beaverlodge, a small city 300 miles north of Edmonton; just east of the Rockies and a little south of the ALCAN highway. It's very cold up there: It gets up to 40° below zero in the winter; I mean, that's the *high* temperature. It'll be 50 below, and then it'll warm up and be only 40 below. However, no matter where you are on earth, you have the same total number of hours of sunshine during an entire year. The difference is that the distribution is more skewed, the farther north you get. The folks in Beaverlodge get fewer but longer periods of sunshine; so Paula's husband studied what crops would grow well in that kind of climate. Paula is also a music teacher with many students, mostly flute, but also other instruments. She has four children. Thus my parents have six grandchildren altogether.

DK: Did you grow up entirely insulated from politics?

DEK: I think you're probably thinking about the Progressive Party, which was born in Wisconsin, or maybe about Upton Sinclair, who spent time in Chicago. But no, topics like that were not on my radar screen when I was young.

The mayor of Milwaukee was Frank Zeidler, who wasn't a member of any party. He just was a Milwaukeean. And he was so good that he was reelected about five or six times. I mean, he was just totally committed to the city, and totally apolitical. That was the atmosphere where I grew up. We didn't really know much about politics.

Marty Schreiber, one of my not-quite-classmates, a guy one year behind me, went into politics and became Lieutenant Governor of Wisconsin; then the governor died and Marty was governor for awhile. His father had been an alderman for the city of Milwaukee.

But I never knew the political life very much; as I said, I was kind of a machine. I lived in a happy enough world. I didn't worry about any other parts of the total picture.

DK: When I mentioned the word politics, I was thinking of personal politics, cases where you have to iron out problems between people, clashes between groups.

DEK: Ah, I guess I don't even understand the *meaning* of that word! Actually I've always shunned controversy. Fortunately the computer science department at Stanford has been amazingly free of such disputes. George Forsythe set the tone for that, minimizing conflicts. Disagreements naturally arise, but when there's a real problem we all work together.

I know that I'm no good at resolving disputes. But I'm glad that there are people who have political skills. The world would be terrible without peacemakers.

Similarly, I'm glad that there are people who do price-comparison shopping, so that I don't have to take time to do it myself. I concentrate on things that I can do well; and I say thank goodness for the people who have a talent for the other things that I don't do well. I don't like to take anything on that I'm not good at, unless *nobody* is good at it.

Chapter 10

Conversations, 1996: Printing (Continued)

[Recorded 25 July 1996.]

DK: Let's change the topic back to something we've already discussed. After thinking over what you told me last week, I crave more details about the early days — about Monotype machines, and about the Linotype machines that you didn't mention.

DEK: Both Linotype and Monotype were invented in the 1880s, and both companies have eventually switched from hot lead to digital typesetting in recent years, so it's easy to get them confused. But the original Linotype and Monotype machines were quite different from each other.

A Linotype machine made one "line o' type" at a time, by passing a whole bunch of matrix molds to a casting machine, after which the whole line would be cast in molten lead. Then that line would be fixed, unchangeable; to correct any character you had to remake the whole line. By contrast, the Monotype machine cast individual letters, as needed, and individual pieces of type could be pulled out and/or inserted later.

A Monotype machine acted in two phases. First the operator would punch a paper tape using a huge pneumatic keyboard. (In fact, I counted the number of keys this morning, because I'm mentioning that in my Kyoto talk, and it turned out that there were 284, not counting shift keys.) The keyboard layout incorporated four regular typewriter keyboards within it, among many other special keys; and air ran through them so that it had a special touch. When you pressed a key, it would punch a row of holes on a wide paper tape: 31 channels actually, about so wide [spreading his fingers], looking like a player piano roll.

Then the operator would take that paper tape over to the casting machine, which would spit out one little piece of individual, loose metal type for each row of holes on the tape, and arrange those pieces into neat little lines of movable type. This feature was extremely important for math typesetting, because a second person could go through and do all the hard stuff by hand. He would put in all the big $\sum$ and $\int$ signs, all the big parentheses, and various special symbols. When I'd get my galleys, they would always say that Eric had run the keyboard, while the hand work was done by Joe. I once met Eric; I've never met Joe. Those guys both had a lot of complicated work to do.

Hans Wolf's group at Addison–Wesley had rigged up their Monotype in a special way, more sophisticated than what was being done in other places. A famous book by Chaundy, Barrett, and Batey was published by Oxford University Press in the mid-50s. It was one of the main books that I consulted when developing TEX, and it explained how to typeset mathematics with a Monotype machine, but their method required more hand work than Addison–Wesley's method did. Hans Wolf figured out how to typeset half a line, while Oxford always worked with full lines.

I mean, if lines with a 12-point base were being set at Oxford, every line coming out of the casting machine would consist of pieces of type that were 12 points high. But Addison–Wesley was able to make pieces of type that were just 6 points high, although the bottom half of a letter would stick out below that 6-point base. That bottom half would normally be supported by putting a 6-point blank underneath, but subscripts and superscripts could also be handled easily when necessary. Addison–Wesley worked the lines in two passes, one for ordinary letters and superscripts, and the next pass for the blanks and/or subscripts. That would be the other half line.

To achieve this, Eric had to know the width of every letter, and had to count so that he could insert the right number of blank spaces to make the subscripts appear where they belonged. So it was a two-pass operation, while the Oxford system I think needed much more hand work. I'm not absolutely sure about the details, but I've described what I believe they showed me when I visited Addison–Wesley in the 60s.

And Eric could do this at a tremendous speed. He was the fastest typist I've ever seen, including Phyllis, and he told me that his speed was due to the wondrous touch of the pneumatic keyboard.

Eric spent day after day typesetting math books, and on the day that I came to meet him he was actually working on a fourth-grade book about arithmetic. It was a primer with great big type, and with carefully aligned arrays of numbers showing how to divide, say, 316 by 2. When I saw what he was doing, I realized to my surprise that the typesetting of fourth-grade math texts is considerably more complex than what's generally needed in *The Art of Computer Programming*, because all kinds of tricky alignments have to be handled. I had thought that my books were just about as hard as a typesetter would ever face, but elementary texts turn out to be even harder.

So I started talking to him, and Eric had the strongest Cockney accent that I've ever encountered. He had obviously grown up in South London, and he almost certainly had never had any training in calculus, but he was responsible for typesetting much of the most advanced stuff in mathematics. Later I felt sorry for him, because I suppose he lost his job when Monotype machines were phased out five or six years later.

Monotype was invented in the United States by a Mr. Lanston, but he didn't have enough financial backing to make it in quantity. He met a rich lady on a boat trip to England, and sold her on the idea, after which he built a big Monotype factory in Redhill, England, near the present-day Gatwick airport. The British company spawned an American subsidiary, Lanston Monotype, which also became strong and quite popular in the 20s.

Monotype was generally used for high-end printing: for books, not for newspapers. Newspapers didn't need the fancy stuff. I have no idea how many thousands of Monotype machines were made, but at one time they were ubiquitous. Yet when I visited Redhill in 1977, I think I was told that they had sold 14 machines to Pakistan in that year, and they expected that shipment to be the end of the line.

There still were Monotype machines, you know, in the MacKenzie–Harris type foundry that we visited on the METAFONT class outing in 1984. Probably they still have one or two. That foundry has now been bought out by Andrew Hoyem, who runs Arion Press and prints fine books for collectors. We were told in 1984 that these machines were the last Monotypes to remain in San Francisco.

DK: I recall how our college newspaper was typeset with a Linotype.

DEK: Yeah, I knew Linotype too, from when I worked on Case's student paper. Once I had to go to the downtown office where the paper was printed, because we had to make a last minute correction. I was the copy editor of our paper, and one article had mentioned the Christmas party at which my fraternity had served hot buttered rum. Somebody pointed out at the last minute that it was actually illegal to serve hard liquor at a fraternity party; so I took a quick trip downtown and changed the phrase to "hot buttered popcorn." Only one line needed to be changed.

I guess I saw Linotype for the first time when I was in high school. I never had a chance to operate such a machine myself, although I had often encountered them. I knew, for instance, that the top row of the keyboard said ETAOINSHRDLU, representing the twelve most common letters in English: 'E' is the most common, then comes 'T', then 'A', and so on. The machine ran faster because of this arrangement, because the matrices for common letters didn't have to travel as far to the caster. A year or so ago I noticed that the Oxford English Dictionary has some really choice quotations under the heading 'etaoin shrdlu', taken from places where people had forgotten to remove erroneous lines of type.

A man named Mergenthaler invented the Linotype at almost the same time as Lanston invented the Monotype. Before then, typesetting was difficult and slow, because people had to put precast pieces of type into a composing stick, by hand. But after 1890 or so, Monotype became the method of choice for typesetting books, while Linotype was the winner for newspapers. By 1900 almost every small town in America had their own newspaper, composed by a local person who had purchased a Linotype. It was easy to have news every day about who visited whom, so Jill and I know a lot about the daily lives of our grandparents.

The situation with mathematics was different. There, hand methods prevailed until the 1930s, until somebody figured out a good way to do it with Monotype.

I should mention that Joe, the guy who did final adjustments by hand after Eric had keyboarded most of a math book's copy, was also responsible for making up the pages later. He would insert the spacing needed for displayed formulas, and he'd decide where to break from one page to the next.

I tried this morning to estimate how many people worldwide once had the skills that Eric and Joe had acquired. First I guessed that the total number of math pages made up each day is at most 2400, say. Then if a single operator could produce ten finished pages per day, there would be 240 people altogether who knew how to do it. Twenty dozen. That seems a high estimate; maybe the true number was 100. Anyway they probably all learned their trade from somebody else. But now almost nobody can do it. I was however glad to notice that the Hungarian translation of *The Art of Computer Programming*, three beautiful volumes published in 1987, was all done with the traditional Monotype methods pioneered during the 1930s.

DK: I recall that photo-typesetting machines were invented during the 50s, but hot-lead machines evidently continued to survive until the 70s.

DEK: Yes; these machines were expensive, and people bought them with the idea that they would amortize the cost over a period of about 20 years.

DK: But most of the switch to cold type happened already in the 1960s.

DEK: Of course the amount of printing that was for mathematics was just a tiny, tiny fraction of the total. So people had little reason to keep a Monotype when everything else could suddenly be done on another kind of machine that's a lot cheaper.

Unfortunately, the new machines were indeed cheaper, not only in their cost but in the quality of their output. The output looked cheap, too, and especially with mathematics it was awful.

I think the best way to study what happened during the 1960s is to look at *The Penrose Annual*, an amazing publication that came out every spring and showcased all the current best practice. The first examples of phototypesetting that were published in 1959–1960 were gorgeous. I mean, they actually looked just as good as the metal type. But then a lot of cheap imitations of the original machine came along, where the manufacturers forgot about spacing. The cheap clones were designed by people who cared only about speed, about how many ems they could process per minute; they started to rank machines by measuring the wrong thing. Soon the printed quality went into a downhill spiral. Almost every book that you see, printed in the late 60s with phototypesetting machines, was an æsthetic disaster. By opening a random page, you can almost smell the year of printing. "Oh, yeah, this was 1966."

DK: By now, I guess, TEX has become the method of choice for typesetting mathematics.

DEK: Well, TEX is leading the pack with respect to quality, but not for ease of use.

I got a wonderful surprise in the mail yesterday, from academic researchers who are *not* concerned with mathematics. It's called `EDMAC`, and it's a package that has been developed during recent years for people in humanities who are doing scholarly editions, critical editions of books. With these macros, they've found that TEX provides a nice way to deal with complex systems of footnotes, while mixing many languages and alphabets; there are tools that facilitate, say, a Sanskrit commentary on a Greek text, or whatever. `EDMAC` has resulted in the publication of many fine books that just wouldn't have existed otherwise. So that made me really happy.

There's a cautionary tale, though. The authors say in their preface that they couldn't get any credit for this pioneering work within the normal academic traditions. They're doing absolutely leading-edge research for the future benefit of all humanities scholars, but `EDMAC` doesn't show up on their publication record!

And I've heard of other cases where people did really great, trendsetting scholarship, for instance with multi-media presentations of classic works, and didn't get tenure.

Everybody makes mistakes, of course, but this backward-looking obtuseness has got to change pretty soon. Let's hope that academics will soon realize where the real scholarship is. I think people like the authors of EDMAC are doing heroic work, combining wonderful scholarship with a sense of what the future is going to ask of people in their field.

Chapter 11

Conversations, 1996: Travel

[Recorded 1 August 1996.]

DK: While getting ready to eat lunch, we were talking about traveling, and your earliest adventures abroad. Let's continue with that.

DEK: Ah yes, Jill and I were young, and all by ourselves for the first time. We had gotten married at the end of June, 1961, shortly after Jill's graduation from college; I had just finished my first year of graduate school. Our "nest egg" for this honeymoon trip was the princely sum of $5,500, which I had earned during the previous summer by writing an ALGOL compiler for the Burroughs 205 computer. We had read the guidebook entitled *Europe on Five Dollars a Day.* We had arranged through the auto club to pick up a new car in Germany. The honeymoon began in Toledo and Detroit, followed by a short flight to Montréal. (That flight, incidentally, was Jill's first airplane ride.)

After Montréal we stayed on the earth's surface. We sailed to and from Europe via the Greek Line: two six-day trips, setting our watches forward or backward by one hour each day. (Ocean liners were interesting, but not quite as romantic as they may sound, because of *mal de mer*!) The first ship departed from Montréal and dropped us off in Cobh, Ireland.

In Ireland we were impressed by the fact that the trains ran like clockwork. And we loved the greenery that had led to the name "Emerald Isle." We had no time for detailed exploration, but we saw the main sights of Dublin before having to catch a "boat train" to England via Holyhead in Wales.

The main thing I remember about arriving in Dublin is about water: All the guide books we'd read were unanimous in warning, "Don't drink tap water in Europe; be sure to buy bottles of fresh, pure water." So we went to a store and asked for a bottle, and were met with blank stares. All the water in Dublin was crystal clear, and nobody had ever asked for such a thing before!

By the time we boarded the boat train, we had spent all of our Irish pound notes, but we still had 12 pence in change; British and Irish coins were interchangeable at that time. Our plan was to cash a traveler's check in England, since we carried all of our money in the form of American Express Travelers Cheques. The stage was now set for the episode that still stands out most strongly in my mind about those days.

We got off the eastbound train in a small city called Crewe, which we learned later is a famous (or infamous) junction point; we were scheduled to board a night train, a sleeper, from Crewe to Glasgow later that evening. It was a Saturday afternoon. We saw no place to cash a traveler's check in the station. But we looked to the right and saw a bus terminal, with buses to the city that cost only $1\frac{1}{2}$ pence each. "OK," we figured, "it will cost thruppence (3 pence) to get to the city, where we can get some British pounds and something to eat." (We hadn't had any food since breakfast, many hours earlier.) "Then with thruppence to return, we'll still have 6 pence left in the worst case."

The people in Crewe's shops were very friendly, and quite interested in seeing our traveler's check — a completely new experience for them; but of course they didn't want to give us any money for this quaint little piece of paper. So we went to another bus stop, and asked the attendant if this was the place to get a bus back to the train station. He replied by saying a lot of words in a thick Midlands accent, a dialect that I'd never heard anything like before; I thought his answer was basically a yes.

We got on the bus, but found that it seemed to always be taking the wrong turns. "Oh well," we thought, "it's just a loop, and we're going to see the other half of the loop." No; pretty soon we were out in the country. So I went to talk to the driver, who stopped the bus on the highway and told us to get out and go back the other way. (At least, I think that's what he said.)

We still had sixpence left. But when another bus came by, heading back to Crewe, its driver told us that the fare would be $1\frac{1}{2}$ shillings! Way more than we could pay.

By this time hunger pangs had begun to get to me, and I had no idea what to do. I sort of collapsed in the aisle, and started to cry. Fortunately a kindly lady in one of the front seats took pity on us; she paid our fare and, I think, gave us another sixpence. In return, we thanked her profusely, and told our story about how we were on our honeymoon and en route from Dublin to Glasgow, etc. We also showed her a traveler's check, which she thought was a delightful novelty.

It wasn't a traumatic experience, although I was in tears; I never was threatened or anything like that. (You hear all these horror stories of tourists getting robbed. Nothing like that has ever happened to me.) Everybody that we met was, in fact, extremely helpful and kind.

Back at Crewe station, I looked this time to the left, and now saw the lights of a hotel! (It was beginning to get dark.) We went to the hotel's restaurant and showed our traveler's check to the young waitress. She, too, had never seen one before; but her response was, "OK, how much do you want for it?" So we had a delicious and relaxing meal, on our first evening in England. (I also recall watching an episode of Perry Mason on the telly, while waiting for the sleeper train to arrive. And another factoid comes to mind, too: We got bit by a bedbug on the train that night.)

We went to church in Glasgow, but had time for little else in Scotland because this trip had been pretty tightly scheduled. Soon we were in London, seeing all the usual sights (Buckingham Palace, the Tower, etc.).

Then we took a boat across the channel and went to Cologne (Köln) to pick up our Volkswagen camper, a mini-bus with a camping unit built in. I believe my $5,500 included the cost of that car, something like $2,000. (Remember that this was 1961.)

It was about four o'clock when we got the papers for the car. So we had an hour to buy food, plates, and a camping stove. We found it interesting to begin communicating in a foreign language by gestures, by pointing at things. We never developed much of a vocabulary, but in every country we went to, we learned how to say the numbers; we also learned how to say "thank you" and "that's all." Those words were enough for shopping.

On that first night with our new car we went to a campground near the Rhine River in Cologne. People who live in Cologne tell me that they know where that campground is, still there today. That's where Jill cooked her first meal for me, in our married life, because we'd begun this trip right after our wedding. She remembers that aspect of it especially well: How she had to get the camping stove going, although all the instructions were in German. After an hour or two, with none of the skills that could ever be taught in school, she was able to make some tomato soup for me, with meatballs in it. Of course, it was very delicious — maybe the best meal we ever had, I don't know. Anyway, that was the inaugural eating experience of our married life.

We were camping and living pretty cheaply. It was very nice. Our accommodations cost two or three dollars a night, but gasoline was much more expensive than we thought and we also had to pay for various admissions. We didn't have any hot water but we learned to really like the cold showers. At first we found it a little bit different to bathe in cold water instead of having at least some warmth, but after awhile the cold showers were invigorating — except one morning in Switzerland, where it was really too cold. Glacier water! (According to the laws of physics, water can't get below the freezing temperature, but it seemed to us that the water in Zermatt was colder than that.) Otherwise, we enjoyed the cold showers and camping life in general. We drove from Germany up into the Netherlands, and camped around Amsterdam and Rotterdam. We traveled slowly through Belgium, went to Paris and then along the Loire Valley into the chateau country. Then we came through into Switzerland: Geneva and around the Matterhorn area, crossing over to Italy through a tunnel.

In Paris, however, we had already run out of money. We tried to figure out how to get more money from America by using some of our bank accounts at home. We were told that that was impossible, with just a passport for identification and without any security; but we found a branch of the Bank of America in Paris. The guy who worked at that bank was a graduate of MIT, and I could convince him that I was a legitimate credit risk, since I had come from a similar college in America. So he gave us another few hundred dollars' worth of traveler's checks. We still were three, four weeks from the time our boat was due to sail.

In Italy we went first to Florence (Firenze), camping on a hill overlooking the city. We had purchased some delicious honey, which unfortunately spilled in the car and was a sticky mess; but the local ants cleaned it up. We went to Lago di Garda, where I went swimming. I still think that was the nicest swim I've ever had. We went to Venice, Bologna, Rome, Pompeii; then our boat took off from Napoli and came back through the Mediterranean, to New York City via a stop in Lisbon, with our VW camper aboard. Our six-week journey had given us a general orientation to western Europe.

All the other trips we took were to attend conferences. Well, wait, I did spend a week in England during May of 1965, consulting with IBM about a computer language that later became known as PL/I. Otherwise I don't think Jill or I revisited Europe before 1967, but 1967 was a big year. I'll tell you more about it later, but we flew to Europe twice in 1967. In both cases our kids stayed home with their grandparents. We had baby Jenny, less than a year old, and also John, who was a little less than two years old.

I had befriended a couple of European computer scientists, like the mathematician Maurice Nivat I mentioned the other day. As I told you, he really was happy that I was giving him feedback, because nobody in France was reading his work.

I learned some French by reading two or three PhD theses at that time. I mean, I learned to *read* some French; I can't very well understand anything that people *say*. But I became able to read it pretty well, if it was technical, if it was mathematical, although never having any education in French. With a dictionary, and knowing that the material had to make sense, I could figure out enough of the language to read a thesis. Furthermore, the experience of a week in Paris, just seeing the advertisements on billboards and in the Metro, gave me a pretty good basis to work from. I still know very little of the vocabulary or structure, but being there was incredibly effective compared to just reading a book. Nowadays, when I look at captions in a museum or something, I pretty much know what they say, even if no math is involved; but that's as far as I've gotten in that language.

Maurice was our host in Paris in 1967. I visited Institute Blaise Pascal, then met with his friends in the Left Bank. That was when Jill and I first went to parties in people's homes and had liqueurs to drink — we'd never tasted liqueurs before. (At that time I was 29 years old, Jill 27.) I made several *faux pas*, like the night when I ordered soup and assumed that I was supposed to consume the whole large bowlful that was brought to the table. We also experienced a "general strike," on the day that we visited Marco Schützenberger and his wife at their apartment. Then Nivat drove us to Grenoble for another meeting, where I discussed my ideas about attribute grammars with Louis Bolliet.

From Grenoble we flew to Holland, where I spent a day at an international working group meeting, helping to develop the language ALGOL 68. Then we proceeded to our main destination, Norway, where there was a week-long conference about simulation. I had developed a computer language called SOL, "Simulation-Oriented Language," which was kind of interesting. It improved on other languages like SIMSCRIPT that had been developed for simulating discrete systems. If you have some model of a process, you want to describe it to the computer so that the computer can simulate it and tell you how the model behaves. Maybe you're modeling a highway system or some other kind of trans-portation, say; that was called discrete event simulation. Because of SOL I got invited to this conference in Norway.

We fell in love with Norway. It seemed to us that Norway was just the right size, and that things were working: You know, people had good values, a good balance of ideas, a good lifestyle, so we really enjoyed our time at that conference. We were captivated by Norway, so it's not surprising that we decided to spend an entire year there in 1972–1973 and to return rather often ever since.

We became friends with many people during our first week in Oslo, especially with professor Ole-Johan Dahl. During the conference he introduced me to his favorite kind of piano playing, "four-hands piano." He's a wonderful pianist, and he brought his copies of piano-duet music to the conference center, saying "Does anybody here like to sight-read?" I hadn't done it for years, but we sat down and played Mozart and Brahms pieces that I had never heard before. They were beautiful and it was a completely different style of music than I had ever experienced — chamber music style. Even though my father was a piano teacher in the American midwest, I'd been exposed only to pop-culture styles of music, sort of like "Mozart's Top Ten Hits." I knew nothing of the attitude towards chamber music that you find in Palo Alto now, or that you find all throughout Europe. It was a revelation to me, to learn about chamber music and real classical music, instead of classical music that had been regurgitated and warmed over and modernized and edited over and over again into different forms. This was the real thing.

After the conference we were invited to go still further north to the University of Trondheim, up near the Arctic Circle. That university was planning a new curriculum, and they wanted my ideas about it. I don't know why they wanted my ideas, because I don't think they knew I was writing *The Art of Computer Programming*, but anyway I was pleased to help in whatever way I could. They had also invited another computer scientist to advise them: Peter Naur. Peter and I had written letters back and forth about ALGOL, because he was a big shot in the programming languages community, but I had never met him in person. We met in the historic little town of Røros, suggested by our hosts, then went to Trondheim. During our discussions with the curriculum planners, it developed that a marvelous serendipity had brought us together. Peter and I were probably the two people in the world at that time who had been writing books about the entire field of computer science, as it existed then. And the amazing thing was that the two of us had been working quite independently of each other, yet we had come up with almost identical tables of contents for our books.

DK: Tell me more about 1967.

DEK: Yes, that was the most active year of my life, an incredibly busy year. For one thing, I was interviewing for a position at Stanford. My offer to Stanford came in February of '68; in '67 I was interviewing at Stanford, Cornell, Harvard, Berkeley. And I also had come across some brand-new research discoveries, which I had no free time to investigate. There were two main ideas, quite unrelated, one that's now called the

Knuth–Bendix algorithm, and another one called attribute grammars. I was able to publish only one or two papers to launch each of those subjects; afterwards they each led to careers for numerous other people who have developed the ideas considerably further. Both of those ideas came to me during 1967, and I didn't have enough time to pursue them, although I did write up the original papers.

During February I had been an ACM National Lecturer, scheduled to give 17 lectures on 10 campuses during a period of two weeks. The trip started out to be fun, but it soon became a real drag to repeat myself; so I was glad to be able to cancel one leg of the itinerary because of an unseasonable snowstorm in the southeast. I did, however, have memorable discussions about attribute grammars while visiting frozen Cornell and sunny Stanford on that trip.

I spent a week in April at a conference in Chapel Hill, North Carolina, meeting many mathematicians. In May, I lectured in Madison, Wisconsin, en route to France and Norway. During all this period my "spare time," when not teaching classes, was totally consumed by reading galley proofs and page proofs of Volume 1 and by writing the second half of Volume 2. (And, of course, by helping Jill with two toddlers.) I also was called on again to be organist at my church in June.

The strains caught up with me in July, when I was suddenly laid up with a bleeding ulcer.* It was a big turning point in my life; I drastically cut back on the number of hours that I had been working, and among other things I resigned from my editorial positions in ACM publications. The doctor gave me strict instructions to work only five hours per day for the next month.

That month was in fact another month of travel in Europe. I lectured for a week at a summer school in Denmark, introducing new material on methods of top-down parsing. Then we visited Klaus and Nani Wirth for several days in Switzerland; I stopped briefly to consult with IBM in Stuttgart; and we spent a week at a conference in Oxford. That's where I presented the so-called Knuth–Bendix algorithm (having written the paper at odd moments during the trip). Once again, Jill and I weren't tourists any longer; we were meeting people, making friends. One of the key benefits of travel for me during the 60s was to put faces to names and to see how people operate in different parts of the world.

---

* Further details appear in Chapter 19 of *Selected Papers on Computer Languages*. At the time of the ulcer attack I was working on the answer to exercise 4.5.2–20 of *Seminumerical Algorithms*, an event that I've commemorated by listing it under "Brute force" in the index to that book.

DK: With the publication of Volume 1 in 1968, I expect that you began to get many more chances to visit other countries, without having to foot the bill by yourself.

DEK: Yes; but just before coming to Stanford, I worked in Princeton on cryptanalysis, and one result was that I wasn't supposed to travel abroad. My employers said that if I traveled, I might get kidnapped or something, because I knew things that needed security clearance. I was therefore supposed to get government approval before I took any trips. So I stopped accepting most invitations to travel.

The first exception occurred in 1970, when I got permission to go to Nice to the International Congress of Mathematicians. I'd been invited to give a lecture there, and people said that such an invitation is a once in a lifetime experience. Jill wasn't with me on that trip.

At that congress I actually ran into unpleasantness for the first time. The organization turned out to be really sloppy: After the participants waited in line for two hours and got to the front of the line, we would get permission to go to another line. And finally there was a huge mixup about the housing. They didn't have nearly enough housing for the delegates, and I was an invited speaker so they should have made some reservations, but they had slipped up. Finally they gave me the name of a place out on the outskirts of town, and a few of us took the bus to go out there, after having waited many hours. We reached the place and found a concierge sitting at a table. About 20 people were already waiting in line when we got off the bus. We joined this line; but eventually, when only four or five of us were left, the man suddenly looked at his watch and said, "Time to go home." So he closed his books and there we were, with no place to stay. That was his attitude. I remember on that trip I also learned this gesture the French have of raising their shoulders. "There is nothing I can do," you know.

It was pretty late at night by then. One person in our party knew his way around a little bit, and we took a bus back into town and got an incredibly malodorous hotel room near the railroad station, with people screaming in the next room all night. It stunk to high heaven. It was really incredible, but not too expensive. Things got straightened out the next day. From Nice I had a chance to visit Cannes and Monte Carlo briefly. I was surprised to find rocky (not sandy) beaches.

While we're talking about trips, let me continue with the story of our big journey in 1971 to the IFIP Congress in Ljubljana, Slovenia — a large international conference of computer scientists. Again, I was an invited speaker, and had permission to travel even though Slovenia was on the other side of the Iron Curtain. Jill came with me this time.

Ljubljana is a really charming place. I'm so glad that Slovenia hasn't experienced the troubles that Bosnia has gone through. Slovenia was spared this and I'm happy because the people there were so wonderful to us at this conference, the young people especially. The older people looked sad, but the young people were enthusiastic and healthy and happy and had high spirits. They hadn't had much chance to see people from the outside world. They wore special uniforms — jump suits — and spoke many languages fluently. All the attendees were quite happy. Quite a contrast to my time on the Riviera in 1970!

The IFIP Congress was held every three years in those days. That was the first time I'd ever given a lecture to more than a thousand people at once, in a huge sort of arena. The acoustics were so bad I don't know if anybody understood my lecture, but there it was anyway. The organizers had even arranged for me to try out the pipe organ in the main cathedral. We also had one of the most delicious meals I've ever experienced, chunks of lamb roasted on large spits; and we went to the beautiful resort at Lake Bled.

The following week I was at another international congress in Bucharest. That one was on logic, methodology, and philosophy and it was organized by Pat Suppes. We went by train from Ljubljana through Belgrade and into Romania — not on the Orient Express, however; that one went further to the south. We had a sleeper cabin at night, making the journey rather a nice adventure.

I sort of gave diametrically opposed talks. At the first conference, in Ljubljana, my talk was about the beauties of computer science, more or less, but in the second conference I spoke on the dangers of computer science. I figured that then, no matter what side of an issue I wanted to take, I could always quote myself.

The main thing I learned during this trip to Eastern Europe was that communism was not at all uniform. Each country had a different sort of flavor, all very complicated and different. (Later we'd go to Poland, and to Russia, and to Uzbekistan, and China, all of which were different from Slovenia and from Romania and from each other.) As I said, the young people in Ljubljana had this glow to them while the older people did not. In Romania it seemed the opposite: The young people looked glum and the older people seemed happy. At least that was my impression.

I met a lot of people from other parts of Eastern Europe at that time because they could go to these places but they couldn't travel to the West. Thus I made some Polish friends and some Russian friends for the first time. But the most unforgettable thing about our trip to Romania was the amazing weekend excursion that our hosts had arranged for the two of us. My host was Dragoș Vaida, one of the leading professors of computer science in Bucharest. His wife, Constanța, was an architect. When she was a student, she had studied the architecture of the churches in the Bukovina area, in the northern part of Romania just near the Ukrainian border. Those churches have wonderful frescos, dating from the early 16th century. The walls, both inside and outside, are covered with icon-like images that tell a story. Those pictures made it possible for illiterate people to see their religion in front of them. The artwork was quite stylized and very beautiful.

Dragoș and Constanța drove us north to visit Constanța's friend George, who lived in a village near the monastery of Suceavița. We got to this little town where there was no electricity and no running water, and everyone lived in wooden houses that they had built themselves. No roads went into the village, so the car went on a little dirt track. Dozens of children met the car three miles out and sang us all the way in, with geese running along at our sides. I don't think the people were literate, but Jill disputes that. We were told that it was unusual for Romanian people to have more than a seventh-grade education, at that time, but I think even a seventh-grade education was unusual in small villages like the one we visited.

You've probably read that Ceaușescu decided to destroy thousands of those villages. Maybe there were 15,000 and he obliterated 8,000 of them with bulldozers, or something like that. I'm not sure what the numbers were, but I've seen such stories. He must have thought that his country was too backward and had to be modernized.

On the other hand Jill and I lived for a couple of days in one of these villages and it was an incredible experience because we felt part of history. This must be the way people lived hundreds of years ago. Except that George and his wife had a few things like colored pictures pasted on their wall, which had been torn from newspapers; their log cabin was now decorated with such mass-produced, fading artwork. Otherwise, the way they lived was by all kinds of handmade things and hand built things. They had clever ways of using sour milk and cheese and keeping them without refrigeration. They killed a chicken to serve us for dinner, in our honor, and they insisted that we sleep in their own bed. They were the happiest couple I've ever met in my life, laughing all the time. I've never encountered anyone who had more *joie de vivre* than these two people who lived in this extremely primitive village. And on Sunday everyone dressed up in native costumes and went to the church to dance in the fields all day long.

Recall that I had to get special permission from the U.S. Government to go to this Eastern European country, because I'd worked on secret projects. A man had come from Washington to Stanford to brief me on what to do if, say, I would meet a female spy! They gave me telephone numbers to call if I got into any trouble. I should give out no information except name, rank, and serial number — that sort of thing. In my wallet, I had these telephone numbers; but the whole idea of security or potential danger had completely gone out of my mind by this time, because I was enjoying myself very much.

Anyway, here we were in this little village and I got entranced by it. I decided that it would be nice to own one of the native costumes that the people were wearing, so I asked, "Does anybody have a spare one that I could use?" The answer was yes; they thought one of their neighbors had an extra outfit, which had belonged to a dead nephew and was still kept in some chest somewhere. So I went out with George and we walked through the woods a little ways to get to somebody else's house. We met the other family and they said, "Sure, we'll get it for you." The man asked me to sit down, and went into another room. Of course, everybody was speaking Romanian, and I had no idea what's going on. Jill wasn't with me at this point.

About five minutes later, back comes the man of the house from the back room, all dressed now in a military uniform. And all of sudden it hit me: "Oh my gosh. I'm separated from my wife; I'm in a remote place, I have no idea where it is; there is no telephone; I'm about to be kidnapped. This soldier is going to take me somewhere. How on earth am I going to phone the embassy, as I was told?" It was unbelievable, but there I was.

Well, it turned out that he was the postman, and he had just put on his uniform because he was about to go out on his route. A minute later they brought out the costume, and I bought it, and we went home and everything was fine.

But there was a definite undertone of fear in Bucharest. I was out walking one day, just sort of rambling at random and not looking very much where I was going, and a man in front of me with a machine gun said, "Get away." Apparently I was on a street where I wasn't supposed to be. Later on, just as we were about to leave our hotel, they separated Jill from me and gave us some kind of cockeyed story that she had stolen a comb out of the room. It was preposterous, but they held her up while I was gone and for awhile I didn't know where she was. We couldn't help noticing a deep-seated undercurrent of great fear, except in the little village.

When our plane finally lifted off, taking us west, we both felt as if a big burden had somehow disappeared from our shoulders. It's hard to describe, and we can't understand exactly why it was, but it was definitely a phenomenon.

I should also mention that, two days before going to the peasant village in Bukovina, we had experienced a completely different side of the culture. In fact I had actually spoken to and shaken hands with Premier Nicolae Ceauçescu.

DK: How on earth did that happen?

DEK: It's traditional at an international conference for the mayor or some other political dignitary to host a banquet at some point. In this particular case the banquet was held in the communist party headquarters, and Ceauçescu himself had decided to be the host.

It was basically impossible to find good food in any of Bucharest's ordinary restaurants. No matter where you went, you'd get a menu that had about 30 items on it; but whatever you asked for, they would say, "No sir, I'm sorry, but why don't you try the pickles?" You could get some kind of sausage and pickles at every place, just exactly the same — *except* at the communist party headquarters, where the food was really splendid. You should have seen those guests gorging themselves on it! The Russian men at this party commandeered an entire tray of *hors d'œuvres*. They hadn't been given very many rubles to spend, and they wanted to spend them on something else, so this night was their chance to have a good meal.

The guards at the door objected at first to Jill going in. Our invitation had not been clear as to whether or not wives were permitted, but she finally was allowed to enter. Moreover, she was wearing a backless dress, and Romanians are very conservative in their standards of clothing. Maybe the guards had thought that it was too shocking for a guest to have some skin showing. Romania is nothing like a Muslim country, but still they were much more conservative in this way, much more than in Slovenia for example.

When we got inside, we entered a big room where you could eat good finger food. Then, all of a sudden, there was a tremendous rush of people, and everybody was sort of trying to get up close to a man at the center. There were bright lights, and television cameras were recording every syllable that Ceauşescu spoke. He had the power and everybody tried to be associated with it somehow, maybe to absorb some of his energy or influence. Never have I seen such a focus of attention on one person. The funniest thing though, was a rather elderly lady who had gotten into the room somehow or other, not a member of the Congress; she began talking to him and complaining that some scientists refused to admit that she had invented perpetual motion. She claimed that her perpetual motion machine had solved an age-old problem, but she was being discriminated against by the scientists of the academy. In spite of all the security, a "crank" had gotten right to the center of activity.

Soon Dragoș introduced me to Ceaușescu and, you know, we shook hands and he said, "I hope you're enjoying our country." And I said, "Oh yes. This is my first visit, but I hope I can come again later." That was the extent of our conversation, but maybe I got onto Romanian TV.

At the time of this conference, Ceaușescu had just started a program to improve scientific research in Romania, and especially computer science. He was subsidizing the publications of many books; in fact, *The Art of Computer Programming* was destined to be published in the Romanian language already in 1974, before it had been translated and published in any other language. He appropriated funds to establish Romanian technical journals — not especially good ones, because of inexperience and a shortage of referees, but it was a start.

I saw more bookshops in Bucharest than probably in any other city I've ever been to. This was part of Ceaușescu's idea, that education was going to change the whole character of the country. It was a good idea, but not something that you can do instantly. There were many bookstores and zillions of books, but they just sort of had the form rather than the substance of science. They looked like science, they used the words of science, but they didn't really — well, Romania had half a dozen really world-class scientists and those guys were way too busy to spend a lot of time bringing others up to their level. It was surely a big problem. Anyway Ceaușescu wanted to promote science, including computer science, and that's probably why he visited this symposium in person. Certainly at that time I had never met anybody who was anywhere near that rank in any other country; I can't imagine the President of the United States at such a gathering. (Although I did get a chance to meet President Carter, in a roomful of scientists at the White House, when I received the National Medal of Science some years later.)

As I said, my talk in Romania was about the dangers of computer science, the dangers of theoretical computer science, and I meant it to be partly tongue-in-cheek. But I also had a serious purpose. I gave a dozen examples of how people had misunderstood what certain theorems really meant, and because of that misunderstanding we had a worse situation than before the theorem had been proved. People mistakenly thought that certain theoretical results would solve certain problems that didn't really match the theorems, and this had caused a step backwards instead of a step forward. I gave a dozen such examples, because this was a conference about methodology and philosophy of science. But after my lecture, professor Schützenberger said to me, "Don, this was a brilliant lecture, but maybe not given in the right country. Now is when they have their big chance to get funding; you're telling them it's more dangerous to have the theory than not to do so."

So that's the whole context of my meeting with Ceaușescu. You know, I think he had some good ideas about how to modernize his country. But in order to make such big changes you also have to preserve people's dignity, and worry about the way the generations are going to adjust, and everything; the way he was actually going about it turned out to be rather chaotic.

For example, we were told that he'd just changed the rules so that everybody in Romania was now going to get twelve years of education instead of seven, or whatever it had been. My hosts thought this was appalling; their attitude was, "What will the people do with this education?" "All these gypsies, what are they going to do, why should we teach them things they'll never use?" Maybe they were right — you have to bring along jobs as well as education — but still I think it was reasonable to think of having more education.

Now the Chinese have the same problem and they're doing it more sensibly. Although pandemonium still reigns there, they seem to be managing the changes better.

We passed by many other villages on our way to the primitive village. These places had electricity and, unfortunately, everybody had installed really ugly television antennas on their houses. They lived in mass produced, Soviet-designed condos, and outside of every house there was this huge cable leading up to a huge antenna on the roof. It was clear that nobody cared about visual pollution at all.

I suppose I'm reactionary, because I don't like telephone wires in our country either. It's my pet peeve. I'm so glad that I can live on the Stanford campus where we don't have to see them. Still, when I saw all those ugly TV antennas, I thought that the suburbs of Bucharest had shockingly sold their souls to technology in place of beauty.

Ceaușescu had this terrific problem of how to take a country rapidly through centuries of development. I have mixed feelings about it, but I suppose he was right; or was he? Even though the people I'd met were so happy, I could never live that way myself. I suppose everybody has got to become part of the modern world, but there must be a sensible way to do it.

DK: How're ya gonna keep them down on the farm, after they've seen Paree?

DEK: Right. I guess there's no good way to sustain a country of illiterate but happy people who are living without any of the modern things like telephones and plumbing and automobiles. If you accept that the old way must go, then it's still pretty rough to figure out how to change, while preserving self-respect, employment, and beauty in everyone's life.

I'm undoubtedly very naïve. I've had only a few days of experience in only one or two parts of the developing world. I've never been, say, to São Paulo or any place where the people reportedly now live in shantytowns because they think this is their chance for the future, because they believe that a miserable job is better than life in the jungle. But in Romania, where I had a chance to observe an authentic primitive lifestyle in action, I couldn't help but think it would be a shame to change the life I saw, the unspoiled people.

Their culture evolved over a long period of time, as a system that knew the other parts of the system and had adjusted to itself. When you change it drastically, you have to figure out how to change the other parts in order to keep everything in balance. People have to know every day what they're going to do, how they fit in, how they're tied to each other and to the past as well as the future. It's really a tricky thing to do, and probably impossible to do by central control, with somebody making all the decisions. I think it has to be a distributed control, it has to be a lot of people making mistakes and discovering their mistakes and putting it all together. Somehow the whole thing has to change together, and I don't see any way that anybody could mastermind that and be able to understand the ramifications of everything. Nor do I see how to accelerate such changes to fewer than one or two generations, if the change has to be made at all. But I do think that we have to accept the fact that the world is getting smaller; there's no longer a chance to live the way people lived a thousand years ago.

Groups like the Amish in America have created strong communities where they can live the kind of life they want. A lot of tensions exist between their world and the outside world. Their life has changed tremendously over the past hundred years. But it seems that they have found a viable way to live in an oldfashioned style in the new environment. Certainly there are many different criteria for success, not only one criterion; centralized control tends to emphasize only one criterion.

Chapter 12

Conversations, 1996:
Why Computer Science?

[Recorded 9 August 1996.]

DK: How did you decide to become a computer scientist?

DEK: I started as a math student. There was no such thing as computer science at the time.

Well, no, let's rewind: I really started as a physics student. I liked my chemistry and physics teacher [Edward Stoll] in high school the best, and when I applied to colleges there were two main finalists. I had narrowed the choices down to two places where I might go to college.

One was Valparaiso University, where I would major in music. During my senior year in high school I had done quite a bit with music, composing a little, mostly arranging things, plagiarizing things, learning how other composers did it. Anyway I prepared various pieces for our band in high school (none of them ever performed), and I played piano for the choir.

The other choice was Case Institute of Technology, where I'd be a physics major instead. Case in Cleveland was recommended by my mother's family, who all lived in Cleveland. The consensus was that Case was an extremely selective college, with very high standards, so it would be tough to succeed at Case.

I think I chose Case because I wanted more of a challenge; it also sounded like the place I would learn the most. On my visit to Valparaiso the students I met seemed to emphasize having fun and getting through, without working real hard.

The main fork in the road was the question about whether to major in music or in physics. I took physics, which in retrospect was actually the easier of the two branches. I learned later that careers in music are extremely tough, involving enormous competition and hard work, also requiring lots of talent. When I eventually got to Stanford as a full

107

professor, I could enjoy the best of both worlds. I could enjoy music, both as an amateur performer and in the audience; and I could sit on the PhD oral exam committees of music students, as the outsider that Stanford traditionally has on such exams, admiring and learning from the people who had chosen music as a career.

In other words, I thought at the time that I was taking the harder road, but it was really the easier road because of the mixture of abilities and non-abilities that I have, and because society as a whole doesn't give musicians as much credit as they give to scientists.

DK: Did your parents encourage you to select a particular major?

DEK: I don't remember that they expressed a preference. My dad was a good musician. He always played the organ on Sunday in church, and he was director of the choir. Many of my cousins on his side of the family have had their own bands and things like that, they're quite musical. Conversely, on my mother's side of the family there wasn't a piano to be found. My mother likes to sing, but it's not a thing in her family to play an instrument.

The key factor in my decision, I think, was the high standards at Case. They had sent me some terrific materials. I found their brochures and letters in our files a few years ago, and was impressed by the really excellent way they did their recruiting. They made it fairly clear that we were going to have to work hard and love it.

As I said, my science teacher in high school had been my favorite. But we didn't have a very strong program in science, especially compared to the public schools; Lutheran schools were competent in science, but not outstanding. Our school was outstanding in things like English grammar; in fact, my seventh grade training in that subject was significantly better than that of most of my college classmates.

Anyway, I got to Case and I could pass the exams with 100%. I could do well in physics, gradewise, but deep down I knew that I didn't really understand it. I could read what was in the books and I could see what I needed to answer for the test questions, but I didn't have any idea how I could ever have discovered the material that was in those books.

I took graduate courses in physics as an undergraduate, some classes in quantum mechanics and things, and . . . well, the way I might describe it is that I could understand the material only "locally." I could follow the train of an argument, but I didn't have an overall feel for any of the stuff we were doing.

Furthermore, when we were studying the physics of color, I asked my teacher, "Where is brown in the spectrum?" and he couldn't tell me.

When I had questions that weren't in the book, I didn't have the right teachers to answer those questions, either.

During my sophomore year I took a class called Basic Mathematics. I'm not sure why I took it; maybe physics majors were encouraged to take it, or maybe I chose it as an elective because my favorite teacher in the freshman year had been my calculus teacher.

Let me go back a bit. I'd never learned calculus until college. Nowadays people often take two years of calculus in high school, but in those days it was very unusual to have any calculus at all, and I doubt if anybody at Case had had calculus in high school. During my freshman year I was part of what Case called the "honor section," an experimental program in which about 30 of us all took exactly the same classes, supposedly taught by Case's best teachers: the best physics teacher, the best math teacher, the best chemistry teacher, the best English teacher. Each of us in the honor section had the same daily schedule during our freshman year.

The teachers were all nice people, and very smart. But my chemistry teacher seemed to know only chemistry, while my physics teacher seemed to know both physics and chemistry. And then there was my math teacher, Paul Guenther, who topped them both: He seemed to know math, physics, *and* chemistry. Furthermore it was impossible to impress him. So I worked very hard in the calculus class, and began to panic that I wasn't going to pass. (I told you the other day about how my high school vice-principal had warned me about flunking out of college.)

My training in high school had probably been weaker in math than in anything else. The teachers I'd had didn't understand anything that wasn't in the book; I had found a way to prove that $+1 = -1$, and they couldn't help me figure out what went wrong. They were good chess players, and one of them was a good athletic coach, but my mathematical education was stunted until I came to college.

Then at Case, as I said, I had a great math teacher but I was scared. We had a terrific textbook, Thomas's *Calculus*, which served as a model for the books that I would later write myself. (My son is now using a descendant of that textbook in his high school class.) It is probably the most famous calculus book ever written. Thomas was a professor at MIT, and he made friends with the men who founded Addison–Wesley publishing. Addison–Wesley really got its start with Thomas's *Calculus*, about 1950; it was a milestone in the history of high-quality math typesetting. Addison–Wesley also published my physics text, another big hit.

But I digress. At the back of Thomas's calculus book are what were called supplementary problems, maybe 500 or 600 of them. They were interesting problems; they weren't just drilling you by asking, "What's 2 plus 2?" They'd state a situation for which you might well want to know the answer.

As homework assignments in freshman calculus, we were asked to do a small number of the usual problems in the front part of the text. You know, we should do all the even-numbered problems, say. But I did *all* the problems, and I did all the *supplementary* problems too. I was scared, and I also wanted to learn this stuff, so I worked very hard.

And that's the best thing I ever did. I mean, being scared was wonderful. If I hadn't been scared, if I had been overconfident and hadn't felt somehow inferior, I never would have worked on those supplementary problems. For several weeks, at the beginning of my freshman year, I think I was working much harder than any of my classmates, as far as time spent on homework was concerned. I didn't have time to play ping pong or bridge very much, like the rest of the guys. But by the end of the year I could do all the problems *and* the supplementary problems faster than the rest of the class could do just the assigned problems ... because I had learned problem solving! I had learned how to attack that stuff. And so I've been sort of coasting ever since.

DK: Apparently your latent mathematical talents were not cultivated in high school or at home.

DEK: People say that if somebody shows a special talent they ought to be advanced above their age level, and my parents never did that. But when I was ready for it, I got it. I worked hard and I've been, you know, a happy man. I mean, I can't say that there was anything wrong in the way things came out after I got this slow start.

An extreme example of a similar situation occurs in biology where, you know, you have a newborn cat and you have a newborn child, and the cat stays way ahead of the child for a long time. But the child catches up and is able to outsmart the cat after awhile.

Back to my story. In spite of working hard for my freshman calculus teacher, I never was able to come up with anything that impressed him. Then in my sophomore year, I took the class called Basic Mathematics. Professor Louie Green was the teacher, and he was reputed to be the hardest prof in the whole college because, in either the previous year or two years before, he had failed an entire class. You know, he gave 'F' to everybody. He thought that the engineers in that particular class would never learn the material; he was kind of an uncompromising guy.

DK: He didn't believe in grading on a curve?

DEK: [laughs] He certainly didn't. He was famously eccentric.

He wrote his own textbook for this class, Basic Mathematics. It covered fundamental topics that ought to be known; he typed up his notes and handed them out to us. I don't remember why I took the class, but anyway, I took it and a lot of my friends from the previous year's honor section took it.

Early on he announced that he would tell us a problem, and if anybody found a solution to that problem they would automatically get an 'A' in his class. No matter what else they did, they could cut class or anything else, if they solved this problem that would be it. (So he was not only eccentric, he was kind of stupid; I mean, I would never make such an offer to my own students.)

The problem that he gave us is hard to describe in words, but I'll try. If you have a certain number of variables in a mathematical formula, in how many ways can you combine them, by grouping two adjacent things at a time? His problem turns out to be equivalent to what we now know is an important problem in computer science, namely to count binary trees. And there are many other equivalent formulations, extremely important in combinatorial mathematics; for example, in how many ways can you take a polygon and divide it into triangles?

He stated it as a problem that he didn't know how to solve. So, naturally, none of us tried to solve it either. We figured that if Louie Green gives up on such a problem, there is no hope, you're out of luck. Especially if he's also willing to reward you with an automatic 'A'.

Well, one Saturday morning I was supposed to take the bus with the football team. I was the tuba player in the marching band, and the game was out of town, so I'd planned to spend the whole day with the team. But I got up late or something, and missed the bus. So I was standing there, you know, kind of despondent, figuring "Nuts, the day's shot." I decided to take a look at Louie Green's impossible problem.

By that time I had an office in the computer center, because I had to work to supplement my scholarship during my freshman year. I'd been obliged to work part-time, and got a job in the computing center. My first assignment was to run an electronic sorting machine. I don't think Case had an electronic computer in 1956; computing was done by hand. But they did have card sorters, and I could run them and gather statistics from which I could draw graphs. Soon they got a computer, an IBM 650, and I could bend your ear for hours telling how I spent the whole summer between my freshman and sophomore year learning about computers and becoming addicted to programming.

Anyway, I was still a physics major, but I took the math class, and I had a Saturday to kill, and I had a desk in the computing center.

I went there and started looking at the problem and, lo and behold, I found a solution. I think the problem might even have been discussed explicitly in William Feller's famous book on probability theory, a book that my fellow students had told me was impossible to understand. Feller's *Introduction to Probability Theory and Its Applications* is now considered to be the best elementary exposition of the field ever written, but among us guys at that time it was considered to be hopelessly obscure. So I never really started at page 1 or gave that book a fair try. In fact, it wasn't until maybe five years after my PhD that I dared to read it, and discovered all of the good stuff inside.

It was easy to derive a recurrence relation for Green's problem, by which the answers could be calculated quickly in small cases. Two variables can be combined in one way, three variables in two ways, four variables in five ways, and so on. Therefore I had some data to start with.

Several math books were sitting on a shelf near my desk, and I opened them at random. Aha, there was a recurrence relation in Feller's book that looked very much like the one I was struggling with. Looking a bit further into this formidable text, I got an inkling of how to resolve such problem by using "power series," which I'd learned about in calculus during my freshman year. If you set up a power series that represents the sum of all ways to combine variables, the product of this power series with itself represents the sum of all ways to hook those combinations together, two by two.

In other words, I got a clue out of Feller's book without really being willing or able to read much of that book. I realized that the sum of all solutions, multiplied by itself, would give you almost the sum of all solutions again, because all solutions are either the simple one with a single variable or they are made from two other solutions.

It's really a simple idea, which all of today's students regard as obvious, because teachers now stress the importance of power series methods under the name "generating functions." It's also very much like what I would later encounter frequently in the study of context-free languages, and it ties together with lots and lots of mathematics.

By the way, I never had a chance to ask Green if he had actually known that there was a nice solution. I eventually learned that this classic problem had already been solved during the 18th century, independently in China and in Russia. Furthermore George Pólya had presented a really beautiful solution, using a version of power series that he called "picture-writing," in the *American Mathematical Monthly* for 1956 — a journal that Green certainly read, or should have. So it's quite possible that he was intentionally egging us on.

At any rate, I wrote up the solution and showed it to him the next Monday and he said, "OK, this is right. You've got your automatic 'A'." I cut class the rest of the year and took part in many extracurricular activities, and he came through and gave me the promised 'A' — actually two of them, because the class lasted for two semesters.

DK: What was the following year like?

DEK: Well, the next year I felt guilty that I had gotten an 'A' by cutting class, you know, after taking advantage of his foolish offer. So I agreed to be his grader for homework that year. I got to know the rest of the material in his course through that experience of grading papers.

DK: But were you still a physics major.

DEK: Let me tell you about my sophomore-year experiences in physics. All physics majors were required to take a lab course that covered topics like welding. That was my first college class in which I found that I just couldn't handle the material. I'm not good at all with my hands. During my freshman year, in my chemistry labs I would break the test tubes, and I'd be the last to finish all the experiments. I was just horrible in lab work. I almost poisoned myself a couple of times, and once I almost asphyxiated myself. I could tell you lots of horror stories about chem lab; I mean, like when I got this sulfur fire going and I thought, "OK, I'll blow it out." The fire didn't go out. So I took a deep breath, in order to blow it out good, and oh, man, I keeled over.

Physics lab was worse. In physics lab I was supposed to do welding, and one of the assignments was to take a metal plate and a bolt. By brazing we were supposed to attach the bolt to the plate. The test of whether or not we had a good joint was that we could put a threaded screw through the bolt, and it should break the plate before the weld would rupture. Well, when I tried to test mine, the joint came out so fast that the instructor said I was lucky that it didn't drop off on my way crossing the room over to the testing apparatus.

Welding was emphatically not my thing. First of all, in order to do welding, I had to take off my glasses, thus becoming basically blind, in order to wear the goggles. Then, all the welding had to be done on the table; but the table was built for people who were about five feet tall. Not only couldn't I see, but I had to work way down where I didn't have much control. I was supposed to be holding these dangerous rods with thousands of volts of electricity causing sparks to leap from one piece to the other; oh man. But physicists were required to do this.

On the other hand, in my math class I'd gotten an 'A' by solving a problem the teacher apparently didn't think could be solved. So I switched to mathematics as my major. I think there were only five math majors in my whole class, compared to maybe 40 physics majors. Math wasn't a known subject to major in.

Of course, computer science wasn't a known subject to major in either, because it didn't exist as an academic subject until ten or so years later.

Purdue and Michigan claim that they had pre-computer science programs, with Purdue in '62 probably coming the closest to what we now call computer science. But Stanford's CS department, founded in '65, was one of the very first. Anyway, I had to choose my undergraduate major much earlier, in '57 or '58. I was working part-time in computing, to make a living, but I was a math major at college because that was a known career path. I knew that I wanted to be a teacher, but had absolutely no idea that I would some day be teaching about computing.

I told you the other day that I'd participated in lots of extracurricular activities during those years. I was not only in the marching band, I was manager of quite a few sports; so I had five or six letters, varsity letters, although not for actually doing the sports. I was a good scorekeeper. In fact I might have been the best basketball scorekeeper the college had ever known, because I programmed a computer to help.

DK: What was this basketball computer system?

DEK: Well, I figured it wasn't fair that the people who were getting all the credit were the ones who scored the most points in the game. We can take another view of basketball, by saying that possession of the ball is worth something. Suppose, for example, that possession is somehow worth one point for the team who has the ball. Then if somebody makes a 2-point shot, his team gains two points on the scoreboard but loses possession, while the other team gains possession; so the net overall change is nil.

Continuing this example, suppose you come into a basketball stadium at a random point and the score is 47 to 45, but the team with 45 has the ball. Say team A has 47 points, team B has 45 points, but team B has possession. It wouldn't be unreasonable to regard the "true" score as being roughly 47 to 46, so that team A is effectively ahead by only one point. If now team B makes a basket, it's 47 to 47; but team A now has the ball, team A is still effectively one point up.

When, then, does the score really change? (I assume that there aren't any 3-point goals; such things weren't in the rules when I was at Case.) Well, change happens if one team misses a shot and the other team gets the rebound, or if somebody double-dribbles, or if somebody steals the ball, say. But under the traditional ways of keeping statistics, players weren't losing points for a double-dribble, they weren't losing anything for missing a shot, and they weren't gaining anything for getting a rebound, except maybe in some stats listed off to the side.

So I tried to make up a formula that would describe each player's true contribution to a game. I don't really believe my formula anymore, but I wrote one down.* It was based on the idea that, after the game was over, you could figure out that possession of the ball was really worth maybe 7/10 of a point, or something like that. If a player took a shot and missed, there was a certain chance that his team would get the rebound and a certain chance that the other team would get the rebound; thus you could figure out how much to penalize a player for missing a shot in that game. If a player made a shot, you could credit him with the true net gain for the team, based on loss of possession. Making a foul would cost something; stealing the ball would be worth something; all such things entered into my formula. What came out was a number representing roughly how many total points or fractions of points each player had really contributed, as a sum of all the gains and losses on particular plays. Sometimes, of course, a player's net contribution would be negative.

In order to take all these statistics, I had to develop a special way to record all kinds of microscopic details of what went on during the game. In fact, so many statistics were needed that I had to have a spotter who was calling things out to me continually; I'd be entering them furiously onto a special data sheet, pretty much with my head down. Then after the game I'd take all my statistics and punch them on cards, so that I could plug them into my formula.

The coach liked this. He thought it was good to have the players competing to be best in this ranking, not just best in total field goals or whatever. Our team did very well that year, and of course I'd like to take all the credit. But our athletes were really good, and the fact that Case had a good season was probably just a coincidence.

Anyway the public relations people at Case got wind of my system and told the Cleveland newspaper columnists. Then it got into *Newsweek* magazine, and it even appeared on Walter Cronkite's *Sunday Evening News*: a video of me taking my statistics, walking over to the computer, and getting the printouts. This activity earned me a varsity letter in basketball, because of scorekeeping.

---

* See Chapter 23 in *Selected Papers on Fun and Games*.

In high school I had been a five- or six-letter man, too, without having to do any real athletics. Nowadays you might say that I was a "virtual jock"!

DK: Tell me more about the television appearance.

DEK: Well, the whole episode lasted only about a minute. IBM had commissioned the preparation of a short "documentary film," giving themselves some publicity although they weren't sponsoring the show. An extra-large sign saying 'IBM' was attached to the machine when the computer appeared in one scene.

This experience led me to understand how movie stars must have a hard life. We had to retake the shots for this little film five or six times, even though in most cases I just had to walk from one place to another, or put punched cards into a hopper. How did Audrey Hepburn do it?

One nice result was that my aunt and uncle in Florida could see me on television. It was a rare time when I got into the "mass media."

DK: Your parents must have been very proud of you.

DEK: Well, the newspaper stories and the TV show gave me some credibility in the eyes of my relatives. Fortunately the stories weren't overly flattering, they were written in a humorous vein.

DK: Let's go back to that summer between your freshman and sophomore years, when you first encountered computers.

DEK: I worked full-time in the computer center during the summer, and part-time during the school year, in order to support myself. After my sophomore year, my teachers recommended me for a better scholarship, so it was no longer necessary for me to have extra money. Still, I kept up the computer job because, well, I could keep the money and also use it to go on dates with Jill.

Jill was at Western Reserve, the campus next door to Case. The two institutions hadn't merged yet. I met her when I was a sophomore and she was a freshman. I had been dating her roommate. I have a feeling I've already told you this story?

DK: No. Please do tell the story. It sounds intriguing and interesting.

DEK: OK. In my freshman year, I pledged a fraternity, then went through what they called "Hell Week" at the beginning of summer. Hell Week was ... well, it's called hazing now; it's illegal. You know, the active members had wooden paddles which they swung very freely at our rear ends, whether we did anything wrong or not, until we said "Yes, sir" exactly the right number of times. Basically, with hardly any sleep, we were forced to do all of the most disgusting cleaning jobs that have to be done once a year to keep the house in shape, jobs that were no fun whatsoever. And we would do this with "sergeants" watching every move we made, and using us for batting practice. There were lots of tears, etc. Yet in retrospect, I think ... on balance, it was a very worthwhile experience for me to go through. I matured tremendously during Hell Week.

DEK at the end of "Hell Week," 1957.

Anyway, by sophomore year I was ready for girls. So I was dating three girls. One was Catholic and one was Jewish and one was, I think, Lutheran. The Lutheran one was the most beautiful; she was from Estonia, and she was also a math major at Western Reserve. I found her tremendously appealing, but she didn't really like me at all. I don't know if she ever even accepted a date with me; maybe once, but that was enough for her. But I went out several times with Becky, the Jewish girl, and Betsy, the Catholic girl, and I liked them both. They both had very nice personalities, and both were pretty.

After awhile I started getting most serious about Betsy, the Catholic girl. And we went on double dates, my roommate and I: My roommate was dating Jill and I was dating Betsy. So we went out together, and I got to know Jill. After I started getting a bit serious, I started to think, hmmm, I wonder what Betsy really thinks about me? And is there going to be a problem because we have different religions?

So, I made an appointment with Jill, to have lunch, so that I could ask her some questions about my relationship with Betsy. I don't remember exactly what advice she gave me. But it was very good advice, and afterwards I started dating Jill.

(And then my roommate was mad at me for awhile, because he liked Jill pretty much. She didn't really care for him, and it took him a little while to get over that. Actually he started drinking; our fraternity had some stores of beer for the parties, and he knew where they were. A person who couldn't control himself could easily fall off the rails, and I felt pretty bad about his drinking problem. But he got through those years, and now he's a very successful professor at Ohio State, an excellent professional mathematician who has edited leading journals. I see him on the Worldwide Web these days, actively making educational innovations. Like me, he switched from physics to math while at Case.)

Anyway, that's how I got started with fraternities and with Jill. Jill was an art major. There was a joint program between Western Reserve University and the Cleveland Art Institute, which was a good deal.

Jill was a Methodist, and I started going to Bible class with her on Sunday mornings. I had been attending churches, but nothing else on Sundays; you know, I'd been brought up in Lutheran schools where we had religion Monday, Tuesday, Wednesday, Thursday, Friday, so we took time off on Sunday. But for her, every Sunday was a day for religion, including Bible classes. Naturally I wanted to spend more time with her, so I went along and found out that Bible classes were . . . that there was plenty more to learn after grade school and high school, religion-wise.

In fact, I suppose every young person more or less goes through a religious crisis at some time, when they start to decide what they really believe instead of what they are expected to believe. I too went through that experience. Several of my college professors were atheists, so I had to get used to that fact and come to a better understanding of God. When I visited home I had some discussions with my pastor in Milwaukee, which were very important to me, to help understand the tradeoffs and things. I read a whole bunch of books at that time, trying to sort out the views that I thought were too extreme on one side from the views that I thought were too extreme on the other side.

You know, everybody is extreme: You can't be neutral about religion. Or if you're neutral, you're really taking an extreme view of neutrality. Of course I kept learning and questioning. I think I was willing to accept whatever I was going to learn from my reading and other observations, and what I learned convinced me that I could basically remain religiously conservative and politically liberal.

DK: How did Betsy take this?

DEK: I don't think Betsy was real serious about our relationship. She got married a few years later and sadly died of cancer when she was in her thirties. Our relationship hadn't developed real strong, although I had been to her house and met her parents. They lived out near Akron, which is about an hour or so south of Cleveland, and I had gotten to know her family a little bit. Neither Betsy nor I were brokenhearted about splitting up. Platonic was the watchword, I guess. We liked each other's personality.

DK: And what about your relationship with computers?

DEK: OK, now back to computing. As I said, I worked full-time at the computer center, which was run by a wonderful man named Fred Way. He allowed students to contribute to the running of the center, trusting them to invent new software and to write manuals and to do basically whatever they thought was a good idea. Case was almost unique at the time, because Fred and his staff didn't farm any computer jobs out to professionals. Stanford, like most other places, did just the opposite; Stanford would hire people to write all of the software systems that were needed on campus. But at Case, Fred allowed us undergraduate students to do it, even though he knew that we were soon going to graduate and be gone. With his encouragement I wrote assemblers first and then I wrote compilers.

For the 650 machine my assembler "Case SOAP III" was definitely the world's best at the time. Then my friends and I wrote a compiler, "RUNCIBLE," which was a much more difficult task. I believe that it, too, was the best ever written for the IBM 650. Fred Way gave us youngsters the power to write world-class software, which was better than the competition we had from older folks at Michigan and Purdue and Carnegie Tech.

So I knew I had a talent for computer programming. On the other hand, the professional computer programming in those early days was actually quite pathetic, so that almost *anybody* would be able to do a better job in some sense. My original optimism about programming skills was largely based on comparing myself against a straw man. Fortunately, however, it turned out that I did actually have a bit more than a slight talent for my job.

During my senior year I was asked to be a consultant to Thomson–Ramo–Wooldridge Corporation (TRW). Some people at the Cleveland branch of TRW were planning to write a compiler. They had sent a proposal to Burroughs Corporation, to write an ALGOL compiler for the 205 machine, which was an early computer. They knew how to write proposals, and they'd heard that I knew how to write compilers; so they put me on board, with an agreement that I'd work for them, writing a compiler during the summer between my senior year at Case and my first year of graduate school. I began to prepare by learning the machine language of the Burroughs 205.

I believe their proposal to Burroughs asked for something like $50,000 for the compiler, an amount that was considered a bargain in those days for software. (With inflation, $50,000 in 1960 would come to something like $500,000 today.) I don't recall what my share of that money was supposed to be; probably something like $5,000. But that question is moot because Burroughs said no. TRW didn't get the contract from Burroughs.

This rejection occurred in May, by which time I had sort of put myself into a mode where I was planning to spend all summer writing that compiler. So I wrote to Burroughs myself, saying, "Look, I can write you such a compiler for only $5,000, but I won't have time to implement the full language; I'll have to leave out ALGOL procedures." They replied, "No, Don, you've got to give us the whole language or it's no deal." So I said, "OK, but it's going to cost you $5,500 dollars instead." That amount, while very low for software, was considered to be an astronomical summer salary. And they said okay.

So during the summer of 1960 I wrote an ALGOL compiler for Burroughs. (I didn't actually finish debugging it until the end of that year.) It's what paid for the honeymoon that Jill and I took the following year, which I told you about last week.

I applied to graduate school in three places: Caltech, Berkeley, and Stanford. (You can see that family vacations in California had made an impression on me, regarding where I wanted to go to study, because I didn't apply to any schools except in this state.)

I was admitted to all three places, with fellowship support; and I chose Caltech because my future advisor, Marshall Hall, had been recommended to me very highly by one of my professors at Case. Combinatorial mathematics seemed to be my *forté* in mathematics and Marshall Hall was probably the best person to direct me in that, certainly the best in California. So I chose to study with him at Caltech.

DK: Your receiving a master's degree at the same time you got your bachelor's must have helped you get in to the schools where you wanted to go. Can you tell us the circumstances how you came to have those two degrees simultaneously?

DEK: At Case I had started to take graduate courses. I think I told you, for example, that I took a graduate course in quantum mechanics. I took several other graduate courses, too, and the reason wasn't as laudable as it might sound — quite the opposite, in fact. The truth is that I'd made a strange discovery: Case's graduate courses were easier than its undergraduate courses, because Case had a rather weak cutoff for grad student admission, while being very picky when admitting undergrads. Thus, the teachers of graduate classes had to operate at sort of a remedial level. In those classes I didn't have much competition, so it would be pretty easy to ace them and have more time for extracurricular activities, like the things I was doing in our fraternity and on student publications.

The faculty didn't understand my strategy, so they thought it was pretty amazing for an undergraduate to be doing all this graduate work. Unbeknownst to me, some faculty member circulated a petition that they should do something that they'd never done before, namely to award a master's degree at the same time as my bachelor's degree was given. And it was a big surprise. The whole faculty actually voted to make this exception to the normal rules, and they gave me a standing ovation at the commencement ceremony. Case's president, T. Keith Glennan, took off his hat! Fortunately nobody recalled the class that I'd taken in welding.

DK: Then you spent the summer writing a compiler single-handedly.

DEK: I soon learned that the project would be much harder than I'd thought, because I also had to write a runtime library — a complete set of subroutines for floating-point trigonometry, logarithms, and stuff like that. Furthermore I had to do everything with a very primitive setup, because Burroughs didn't even have an assembly program for its 205 computer. There wasn't any software for writing software, so my first task was to write an assembler with which I could produce the other programs. I called my first assembler EASY, which was short for "elegant assembly system" (it was very short). Then I made another one, MEASY, the "most elegant assembly system yet." I wrote it only for my own use, but it was a big help.

Burroughs wanted me to make four or eight versions of my compiler, depending on different configurations of hardware that its customers had. For example, customers who couldn't afford a card reader would use paper tape instead. Paper tape was pretty awful: It was much slower than punched cards, and it was an incredibly awkward process because the tape would go spewing out all over the floor. I read in *Annals of the History of Computing* a few days ago that somebody had gotten my compiler from Burroughs and needed a whole day to get it into the machine because of the paper tape.* His paper tape reader evidently

---

* See *Annals of the History of Computing* **9** (1987), 81.

would get off track or something, and he'd have to start all over again. Paper tape was a bad thing, but it was the only way to get software into the 205 if you had the cheapest version of that machine.

I remember sitting one day at Burroughs in Pasadena during the fall of 1960, trying to debug my compiler on their own 205 system, when different parts of the machine kept breaking down. I had to work around each failure by patching various things by hand. It was almost like working directly with raw 0s and 1s, so I felt really master of the machine that day.

DK: Was your compiler widely used?

DEK: No, at least not in America, because Burroughs was actually phasing out the 205 computer in 1960. Their new machine, the 220, was just being delivered. Case had, in fact, received a 220 that summer, shortly before I left and drove cross country.

On the other hand, I did learn that my compiler saw fairly heavy use in South America, especially in Brazil. Many secondhand computers were shipped out of the country during those days, to places that couldn't afford the newer machines.

From a personal standpoint, the writing of that compiler improved my own life in three main ways. First, I made a lot of friends at Burroughs, which was a great place to work. (I continued as a consultant to them for eight years, all the while that I was at Caltech.) Second, I received enough money to get married and have a nice honeymoon. Third, word got out that I knew how to write a compiler, and that led directly to *The Art of Computer Programming*.

There was no book about the process of compiler writing, so one of Addison–Wesley's advisors [Richard Varga] suggested that they try to sign me up to write such a text. Their representative came out West and took me to lunch one day in January 1962, and shocked me by asking if I'd like to write a book for them.

Well, I think I told you that Addison–Wesley had published my favorite college textbooks, as well as some other math books that I had enjoyed reading. And you also know that I enjoyed the process of writing in general, because of my experiences with publications in high school and undergraduate school. So he didn't have to twist my arm before I decided that, yes, I'd love to write a book about compilers.

However, I didn't want to write *only* about compilers. On that first day I planned out a sequence of twelve chapters, where the early chapters would discuss basic techniques that apply to software in general, not just to compilers. The final chapter, Chapter 12, was going to apply the knowledge of the previous eleven chapters to the problem of translating an algebraic language into a machine language, and that would be the climactic conclusion of the book.

As you know, I had no idea what I was getting into when I made those promises in 1962. The "book" developed into a series of books, not yet finished. Here we are in 1996, and I'm still working on Chapter 7, having finished just six chapters so far. But the saga of *The Art of Computer Programming* is a topic for another day.

DK: You were a mathematics major at Caltech at that time, in your first year of grad school.

DEK: Right, and that's a crucial point, because I lived my life in two separate compartments. During most days, I studied combinatorial mathematics, a beautiful subject that I hoped to teach some day. The rest of the time, often in the evenings, I wrote computer programs and served as a consultant to the product planning group at Burroughs, making money to support myself. (I had declined graduate fellowships from the National Science Foundation and from the Woodrow Wilson Foundation, because those would have forbidden me to do any outside work.) My professional work was mathematics, and my informal work was computing. Those two worlds had essentially nothing in common.

In fact, I used two quite different styles of thinking: I had two different attitudes, one when I wore my mathematician's cloak and the other when I wore my programmer's hat. Inside the mathematics building, logic and formal proofs were my bread and butter. Inside the Burroughs plant, by contrast, I fiddled with programs until I couldn't make them fail, and I used my intuition, never imagining that mathematical reasoning might help in any formal way. Thus I saw absolutely no connection, really, between those two aspects of my life.

DK: As a lay person, I thought that mathematics was the heart of computer science.

DEK: Only very few people saw it that way in those days; certainly I didn't. And today people are tending to go back to the mistaken view that I originally had about math versus computing. Computer scientists have gone from a point where math was considered irrelevant to programming, say in 1960, to a point where math was recognized as the essential heart of our discipline, say in 1980, and now there are people who are once again questioning the value of mathematics in programming.

In the early 60s, only a handful of people, notably Bob Floyd, were connecting the concepts of proof with the concepts of writing programs. The rest of us never imagined that the correctness of a program could be proved rigorously. Such a strange, mind-blowing notion didn't occur to us at all.

Bob Floyd introduced me to his revolutionary ideas in the fall of 1962, when I met him for the first time. He showed me how math and programming could really mix, could coexist. Programmers sort of knew that their code was right or wrong somehow, but not in a logical way, only intuitively like a hunch. As I said, Bob and a few other people changed all that, and told us about the great importance of program verification. I certainly could not have written TEX and METAFONT and similar things if I had stuck to the philosophy that prevailed in 1960. Unfortunately a lot of our students are being told once again that proof has little or no importance in computer programming.

Before I met Bob, I did actually have some glimmerings of a possible connection between the two parts of my life, namely when I learned about the theory of languages. I was using that theory implicitly while writing compilers — because algebraic languages are, well, languages. That was one part of programming in which pure-math-type reasoning seemed to help.

I saw a copy of Chomsky's famous book *Syntactic Structures* about 1960 or so. I didn't have time to read it then, because I was a full-time student and had other commitments. But I took that book along with me on my honeymoon, assuming that there might be odd moments when I could think a bit about linguistic theory. And indeed, as I mentioned the other day, we went by boat back and forth across the Atlantic, and Jill was seasick, so I had some days with nothing to do but sit in the lounge and read Chomsky. That was the first time when I had ever noticed a possibly strong connection between mathematics and computing.

DK: My impression of math being central to computer science comes from talking to one of your students, John Hobby, whom you've described as one of your best students.

DEK: Hobby sort of *personifies* the idea that mathematics is the heart of programming. His father was a well-known mathematician. At the time John was here with us in the early 80s, those were the years we were spreading the word that mathematics and computer science are like two sides of the same coin.

On the other hand, paradoxically, math and CS are also quite different! Mathematical talent really covers three or four kinds of talents, at least, that are distinguishable from each other. There is a geometric kind of a talent, an algebraic kind of a talent, a logical-combinatorial kind of a talent, and a continuous-big-picture kind of a talent; I'm sorry that I can't think of better words just now. I mean, some mathematicians are really good at visualizing the fourth dimension, or at understanding how Fourier transforms make waves, or at dealing fluently with other things that are rather hard for me to understand. Some mathematicians are very good at far-out infinite structures, which are maybe not so important to computer science. So there are lots of kinds of talents; we can't just lump them all together into a single notion called "mathematical talent." Unfortunately we have only one adjective for all these different abilities. But if you don't have any of those talents, then you can't do computer programming.

The parts of mathematics that are more discrete as opposed to continuous, more concerned with case distinctions than with smooth transitions, are the parts that are most relevant to programming. Combinatorics and logic are examples of this discreteness; therefore computer scientists like me tend to talk more easily to people in combinatorics or logic than we do to people who study infinite-dimensional spaces, say.

I saw a neat quote just a few days ago, I don't recall where. Somebody said that when he was a student, he studied infinite-dimensional spaces; and after several years he realized that the most important infinite-dimensional spaces seemed to be those that were only countably infinite — which means the smallest kind of infinite, sort of the least infinite that you can be without being finite. Then still later, he found that the most important examples were really finite, as a special case of the infinite notions. A computer scientist usually uses infinity just as a simplifying tool for something that's large and finite, but doesn't think of it really as infinity. On the other hand a pure mathematician tends to think of infinity as part of his or her home territory. It's a different viewpoint.

So now I'm ready to summarize all this by returning to your original question: How did I decide to become a computer scientist?

While I was at Caltech I lived two lives, as I said. First, I "professed to be a mathematician," in the sense that I was a math professor teaching classes in pure mathematics. And I also had an active second life, outside mathematics, as a consultant to Burroughs and as programming languages editor for leading journals in that field. I was also writing a series of books, *The Art of Computer Programming*, accumulating many manuscript pages. That second aspect of my professional life soon acquired a name, "computer science."

Computer science and mathematics were beginning to have more aspects in common, yet they remained quite distinct. The unsolved problems of computer science excited me very much, and my talents for computer science exceeded my talents for mathematics. Therefore, when I had to choose between several opportunities to become a full professor, I selected Stanford University ... and henceforth "professed to be a computer scientist."

Chapter 13

Conversations, 1996:
Work Habits and Problem Solving

[Recorded 16 August 1996.]

DK: On our way here you were telling me about working on a problem that kept you up until 2:30 this morning. I'd like to talk about your work habits today.

DEK: Good idea. In fact, I try to study my own work habits in order to figure out how I might work better. I try to learn about different hangups that I have, and things that work more efficiently and less efficiently. But every once in awhile my scheduling apparatus breaks down and I do something totally irrational.

I'm inclined to think that this happens mostly after a period when I haven't been able to do anything creative, like solving a new problem. After such a nonproductive spell, I get onto a creativity jag and begin to do research — looking for a problem to solve, any problem. The first problem I find, I start working on it.

That's probably what happened last night after I went to the Stanford Theatre. I saw Audrey Hepburn and Gary Cooper in one of Billy Wilder's great movies, "Love in the Afternoon." I went because I've found out that I'm usually more efficient after I see a movie than if I just stay home and work constantly.

Just before it was time to go to bed, I decided to try one little idea that occurred to me while I was watching the movie. You know, sometimes your mind chews around on things. Well, $2^{1}/_{2}$ hours later I decided that the idea did not pan out and I needed to put it aside. By then it was way past my bedtime, I shouldn't have been up so late. So I didn't get much sleep last night.

Every once in awhile I feel this need. The first time I remember it happening was sometime in the 70s, when I stayed up all night solving about ten problems out of the *American Mathematical Monthly*. I just

127

started going through the published problems, as if I were a student taking exams again. Some kind of compulsion, maybe some kind of chemical was telling me to do this, some kind of a brain state that said, "Don, you've got to solve another problem, you have to do research of some sort."

Nowadays as I'm working on Volume 4, I know that I've got to spend almost all of my time writing up what other people have done. And I know that it's more important for me to finish that book than to solve another problem. Other people can do those other things as well as I. The creative part of my book-writing occurs in other ways, when I make up exercises, or organize the material, or find more elegant ways to present it. I've definitely resigned myself to never again work on an open problem that will take several days to solve, much less weeks.

Once upon a time, however, I gave myself the luxury of taking time off from *The Art of Computer Programming* to work on some really hard problems in mathematics, problems that required long and intense concentration, problems that seemed to have my name written on them. It was exciting to explore brand-new territory. Those days are over, but I still recall them with fondness.

I particularly remember the last two times that I embarked on major research topics; in each case I was sort of reliving my graduate-student days. While pursuing that work I knew that I wouldn't be able to do such a thing again, because, well, we have only one lifetime and I have plenty of other stuff to do. So I savored every minute of research on those problems and I couldn't put them down. Every discovery brought new questions, and I guess I didn't really mind the fact that "closure" was so difficult to obtain. One of those projects resulted in a 120-page monograph, and the other turned out to be even longer: An entire issue of a journal was devoted to it, a paper entitled "The birth of the giant component," in which my coauthors and I shed considerable new light on the process by which a random graph passes through a "big bang" moment.* We called it the Giant Paper because of its length: 125 pages.

I worked on the 120-page monograph while I was in Singapore waiting for my book *3:16* to be printed. I started thinking about the problem while on the airplane going over there, and began in earnest while waiting for the printing to start. I waited a whole week, sometimes in my hotel but mostly outside in public parks. I proved one of the main theorems while sitting under an exotic tree in Singapore's botanical gardens. Each day I'd walk and think; then every once in awhile I'd sit in the

---

* See *Selected Papers on Discrete Mathematics*, Chapter 41.

shade and write down another theorem on a big pad of paper that I had brought with me. The collection of theorems developed into a monograph that was eventually published by Springer in their *Lecture Notes in Computer Science*, under the title *Axioms and Hulls*.

I didn't include that monograph in the *Selected Papers* series because it's a book unto itself, with its own index. It's a work that belongs to huge area called computational geometry, which I have no time to keep up with although it is challenging and quite beautiful. Fortunately I found a way to explore a nice part of that mathematical territory in a logical way and to make an instructive story out of the quest.

I greatly enjoyed this last fling, this last chance to spend a largish chunk of time on a substantial, meaty work. Since those days, however, whenever I think of a problem that I can't solve quickly, I tell it to somebody else. I've had my share of the fun that comes with such breakthroughs; henceforth my fun will come from finding improved ways to describe the breakthroughs of other researchers.

DK: Can we go back briefly to the problem you were working on last night until 2:30 a.m.?

DEK: OK, excuse me for getting off on a tangent. The best way to understand how a person like me works is to zoom in on one particular more-or-less typical day, and to look at how I spent my time.

The problem that grabbed my attention last night is quite simple; it's a real-life problem that arose in a bridge club in Michigan, and it's still unsolved. There are twelve couples in this club, and they meet eight times per year. Every time they meet, they play three games. (Bridge players refer to "rubbers," but I'll call them games.) That means, eight meetings and three games each time, so everybody is playing 24 games of bridge during the year. They meet in a house with three rooms and two card tables in each room. The twelve couples are divided so that four couples go into each room and stay there throughout the night. One room might, for instance, have couples A, B, C, and D. Then they'll play three games: First A against B at one table, and C against D at the other; then A against C and B against D; finally A against D and B against C. The next time the twelve couples meet, they'll again divide up into three groups of four, but in a different way.

The club wants to figure out a system so that the 24 games are spread out evenly, with each couple playing each of the other couples about the same number of times. It's impossible to balance everything perfectly, because there are 11 other couples besides you and your partner, and 24/11 isn't a whole number. But maybe there's a schedule in which everybody plays twice with nine other couples and three times with two others; that works out fine because $2 \times 9 + 3 \times 2 = 24$.

Is there a way to do this? The authors of this article couldn't find a solution, although they described a way by which they got close.* Their problem might be a good one for me to discuss in Volume 4 of *The Art of Computer Programming*, but I decided it would be suitable only if a solution does exist; otherwise it wouldn't exceed the threshold necessary for getting into my book. (Obviously I have to be pretty hardnosed about what to include, because there are hundreds of thousands of pages of stuff that could be in there, yet I must boil the material down to just a few thousand pages.) On the other hand I didn't want to reject the problem out of hand. So I figured, OK, if this problem does have a solution, it probably has a nice solution, one that has some pattern to it.

So I started thinking about potential patterns. If a solution exists, every couple has two other couples that are their special rivals, namely the ones that they play against three times instead of twice. It's well known that if you have a system where every couple has exactly two special rivals, that system forms cycles or chains. (One of your special rivals has another special rival besides you, and that one has yet another, and so on until the cycle comes back to you again.) Therefore I began to look for a solution in which there would be four chains of three couples each. In such a system, if A and B are special rivals, and if B and C are special rivals, then also C and A will be special rivals.

I also looked for a solution that had some symmetry. Comparatively few of the possible schedules are symmetrical, so the search for solutions of that kind needs to examine many fewer cases. Furthermore when a symmetrical solution does the right thing for one couple, it does the right thing for all couples. So you sort of win twice when adding symmetry to the specifications; and a symmetric solution tends to be beautiful as well.

I thought I found nice patterns that would lead to a solution, and they looked good for awhile. But eventually they petered out. Maybe I made a mistake, working by hand. Anyway I had to go to bed.

Today I've decided to put the problem on hold. I know that it's an example of a so-called "covering" problem, with 66 columns and 5775 rows; I mean, there's a 5775×66 matrix of 0s and 1s, for which a solution to the problem is equivalent to choosing eight rows whose sum contains only 2s and 3s in each column. And I know that some day I'll

---

* See "Scheduling a bridge club" by Bruce S. Elenbogen and Bruce R. Maxim, *Mathematics Magazine* **65** (1992), 18–26.

be discussing covering problems in detail, when I get around to writing Section 7.2.2 of Volume 4.

The result then of about six hours of work, not counting the time I went to the movie, is that my files about covering now have a line that refers to the unsolved bridge club problem. I can't afford any more time to think about it today. When I get to that part of Section 7.2.2, I'll phone or write to the authors of this paper and ask them about the current status of the problem. If it has been proved impossible, I'll forget about it. If it has been proved possible, or if it's still unresolved at that time, I'll take another look. It might or might not turn out to be an instructive example of techniques for covering problems, or an excellent exercise, possibly even an exercise that's also a research problem.

DK: Do you find working on problems like the one you just described, which can be viewed as a game, helps your work?

DEK: Research always involves an element of play and fun. One of the reasons this question is appealing is that it arose in a real bridge club in Michigan. I could make up all sorts of covering problems, but most of them are uninteresting, but this one is fairly natural and easy to grasp. Mathematics is the science of patterns, and a schedule that solves this problem might exhibit a beautiful pattern.

A solution to this problem is not going to help computer science so much, although it might help a few bridge players in Michigan. But the method by which a problem is solved is usually much more important than the solution itself. The answer to a problem is usually not the bottom line, not the thing that I want my readers to learn. The bottom line is the path that led to the answer. Because the more you know about the path to a solution, the more ideas you'll have about how to tackle the next problem that arises.

It's very rare for a problem that comes up in practical work to exactly match a problem that appears in a textbook. Usually your problem is close to something in the book, but you need to tweak the book's solution in order to solve your own problem.

DK: In the movie you saw last night, what was it that triggered all this? Was it a particular scene?

DEK: No, no, the movie just freed my subconscious mind so that it could go to work. Last night my subconscious was also working on another problem, which I'm going to look at tonight, an entirely different problem that's related to number theory and cryptography. Tonight I'm hoping that my brain will be ready to think about another kind of mathematics. I think our brains store things far below the surface, and there's an ongoing process that keeps churning away underneath. The point of going to the movie was that it captured my conscious mind, so that my unconscious mind could be unfettered, not confused by too much stimulation. The advantage of the movie in this particular case was that it was totally *un*related to mathematics or computer science.

DK: Could it also be that a series of scenes in the movie collectively created an impression or triggered something in you that led to the approach you took on the problem?

DEK: Well, such things happen a lot in mystery novels, but I'm not sure if they ever happen in real life. You know, in an Agatha Christie story somebody might be crossing a bridge and the detective will see that and say, "Aha! The bridge! I understand everything now!" I rarely if ever have "Aha" moments like that, but I often find that my mind somewhat magically gets ready to solve a problem.

For example, let me go back to the 50s when I was a college student. I tried to solve lots of math problems, but for a long time I noticed that if I couldn't get anywhere after say five hours, then I never found a solution even after spending several more days on the problem.

But I distinctly remember the first time when I was actually able to solve something after having worked on it for ten hours. (I think it was the analysis of clock solitaire, but I'm not sure.) I had kept working for ten hours because at every point I wasn't quite stuck; I was almost stuck, but there was still something else to try, and then that led to something else, and so on for ten hours. Finally I did hit pay dirt. This was very reassuring, the fact that sustained work could lead to success; that really felt good, because up to that time my brain seemed to be limited in its reach to what I already could do easily.

I also remember two occasions in the 60s, when I had spent several weeks on research problems without solving them, so that I finally gave up and started working on something else. Then, a day or two later, I woke up and knew how to get the answer. My subconscious mind must not have given up on the problems after all. The first such case occurred when I worked on a technical question about parentheses.*

I've seen many graduate students working on their theses, over the years, and their research often follows a pattern that supports what I'm trying to explain. Suppose you want to solve a complicated problem whose solution is unknown; in essence you're an explorer entering into a new world. At first your brain is learning the territory, and you're

---

* See *Selected Papers on Computer Languages*, Chapter 13.

making tiny steps, baby steps in the world of the problem. But after you've immersed yourself in that problem for awhile then you can start to make giant steps, bigger steps, and you can see many things at once, so your brain is getting ready for a new kind of work. You begin to see both the forest and the trees.

When I start to investigate some topic, during the first days I fill up scratch paper like mad. I mean, I have a huge pile of paper at home, paper that's half-used, used on only one side; I've kept a lot of partially printed sheets instead of throwing them away, so that I can write on the back sides. And I'll use up 20 sheets or more per hour when I'm exploring a problem, especially at the beginning. For the first hour I'm trying all kinds of stuff and looking for patterns. Later, after internalizing those calculations or drawings or whatever they are, I don't have to write quite so much down, and I'm getting closer to a solution. The best test of when I'm about ready to solve a problem is whether or not I can think about it sensibly while swimming, without any paper or notes to help out. Because my mind is getting accustomed to the territory, and finally I can see what might possibly lead to the end. That's oversimplifying the truth a little bit, but the main idea is that, with all my students, I've noticed that they get into a mental state where they've become more familiar with a certain problem area than anybody else in the world.

When they reach this point I always tell them that now they have a responsibility to the rest of us. Namely, after they have solved their thesis problem and trained their brain for this problem area, they should look around for other, similar problems that require the same expertise. They should use their expertise now, while they have this unique ability, because they're going to lose it in a month. I emphasize that they shouldn't be satisfied with solving only one problem; they should also be thinking about other interesting problems that could be handled with the same methods.

DK: I wonder if role reversal — that is, assuming the perspective of another person, or someone from the opposite sex — might be helpful at getting to the solution of a problem.

DEK: It gives you a better way of understanding the world, and you can see balance. Acting something out helps you to see analogies and to understand problems, but I'm not sure that it helps mathematically.

Monty Python was real good at mixing roles. Some of the most biting sarcasm and humor came out of that group of actors when people with one accent or from one part of society would switch roles. And of course, *The Far Side* mixes animals and humans in this way, enlightening us by helping us to see things in a new perspective. But that's a different kind of problem solving. That's solving the problems of the world.

Well, maybe I've spoken too quickly. I can think of two ways in which role playing, if not role reversal, can be helpful for solving math-type problems. One is a story that I was told of how a mathematician heard a rumor that another mathematician had just solved a famous problem. And immediately, upon hearing that the problem was now solved, he said, "Oh, of course! He did it this way." In other words, you can sometimes solve a problem just by imagining that the problem is no longer unsolved.

Another aspect of role playing is considerably more important: We can often make advances by anthropomorphizing a problem, by saying that certain of its aspects are "bad guys" and others are "good guys," or that parts of a system are "talking to each other." This approach is helpful because our language has lots of words for human relationships, so we can bring more machinery to bear on what we're thinking about.

DK: There are some researchers who work hard on solving a problem but then completely lose interest in it once they have the solution, and are reluctant to put their discovery on paper.

DEK: Well, I have no sympathy with people who *never* write up an answer; it's selfish to keep beautiful discoveries a secret. But I can understand a reluctance to write something up when another problem has already grabbed your attention. I used to have three or four papers always in sort of a pipeline, waiting for their ideas to mature before I would finally prepare them for publication.

Frances Yao once described the situation very nicely. She said, you work very hard on a problem for a long time, and then you get this rush, this wonderful satisfaction when you've solved it. That lasts about an hour. And then you think of another problem, and you're consumed with curiosity about the answer to that new one. Again, your life isn't happy until you find the next answer.

The process of seeking solutions is certainly a big part of a researcher's life, but really it's in everybody's life. I don't want to get deep into philosophy, but the book of Ecclesiastes in the Bible says essentially this: "Life is hard and then you die. You can, however, enjoy the process of living; don't worry about the fact that you're going to die. Some bad people have a good life, and some good people have a bad life, and that doesn't seem fair; but don't worry about that either. Just think about ways of enjoying the journey." Again I'm oversimplifying, but that's the message I find in many parts of the Bible. For example, it turns up in Philippians 3:16, where the writer says that you don't race to get to the goal; the process of racing itself, of keeping the pace, is the real goal. When I go on vacation, I like to enjoy the drive.

In Christian churches I am least impressed by a sermon that talks about how marvelous heaven is going to be at the end. To me that's not the message of Christianity. The message is about how to live now, not that we should live in some particular way because there's going to be pie in the sky some day. The end means almost nothing to me. I am glad it's there, but I don't see it as much of a motivating force, if any. I mean, it's the journey that's important.

A very similar thing is true in mathematics and computer science. Theorems are there, but the important thing is the way that a theorem has been proved. Because we can use those methods to answer other questions that will arise tomorrow.

As I'm preparing Volume 4, I'm noticing that this way of thinking about problems might perhaps distinguish my book from a lot of the others. I've been reading all kinds of survey articles, and a survey article typically goes through a hundred or so papers in the literature and lists the theorems that they contain. It gives a catalog of facts, telling what problems have been solved, and who solved them in what year. But those bare facts are of comparatively little interest to me; I mostly want to know the techniques that were used. I want to classify papers by techniques and not by results. Those techniques, those methods, will solve many more problems than have already been solved.

The purpose of my book is to teach the techniques. I don't tell programmers how to use a subroutine, I tell them how to write new subroutines as needed. Of course I illustrate the techniques by applying them to the solution of real problems, thereby answering natural questions and satisfying our curiosity; but I try to emphasize the generality of the methods. Tens of thousands of problems have been solved, but fortunately there don't seem to be ten thousand different methods out there. I try to learn the basic ones and to see how they are akin to each other. That's where I get pleasure in reading and writing. It's something like singing a familiar song, or putting themes together in a new way. That's fun, that's beauty.

Richard Hamming famously said, "The purpose of computing is insight, not numbers." (Somebody else said, "The purpose of computing is not yet in sight"; I disagree, but it's a good joke.)

I can't possibly read all the literature, but I try to read everything that's relevant to what I write about. Therefore I subscribe to more than 30 journals, and I receive about eight of them in the mail each week.

I keep them in boxes for several months, while I'm in writing mode. But every once in awhile, like now, I spend a week or two catching up on journal-reading.

It turns out that I read everything at the same slow rate, whether I'm looking at light fiction or at highly technical papers. When I browse through a journal, the titles and abstracts of papers usually don't help me much, because they emphasize results rather than methods; therefore I generally go through page by page, looking at the illustrations, also looking for equations that are somehow familiar or for indications of useful techniques that are unfamiliar.

Usually a paper lies outside the scope of my books, because I've promised to write about only a rather small part of the entire field of computer science. In such cases there's nothing new for me to worry about, and I happily turn the pages, zipping to the end.

But when I do find a potentially relevant paper, I generally read it only partway, only until I know where it fits into the table of contents of *The Art of Computer Programming.* Then I make myself a note, to read it later when I'm writing up that section. Sometimes, however — as happened last night with that paper about scheduling games of bridge — I get hooked on some question and try to explore it before I'm ready to move on to reading any other papers.

Eventually when I do begin to write a section of my book, I go into "batch mode" and read all of the literature for which my files point to that section, as well as all of the papers that those papers cite. I save considerable time by reading several dozen papers on the same topic all in the same week, rather than reading them one by one as they come out and trying to keep infinitely many things in my head all at once.

When I finally do get into batch mode, I go very carefully through the first two or three papers, trying to work the concepts out in my own mind and to anticipate what the authors are going to say before turning each page. I usually fail to guess what the next page holds, but the fact that I've tried and failed makes me more ready to understand why the authors chose the paths that they did. Frequently I'll also write little computer programs at this point, so that the ideas solidify in my head. Then, once I've gone slowly through the first few papers that I've accumulated about some topic, I can usually breeze through the others at a comparatively high speed. It's like the process of starting with baby steps and progressing to giant steps that I described earlier.

DK: Were there times when you did your work without enjoying or appreciating the pleasure derived from the journey that you described?

DEK: Well, some parts of a job are always much less fun than others. But I've learned to grin and bear it, to bite the bullet and move on, to face the music, to take it in stride and make a virtue of necessity. (Excuse me for using so many clichés, but the number of different popular expressions tends to make my point.)

I schedule my activities in a somewhat peculiar way. Every day I look at the things that I'm ready to do, and choose the one that I like the least, the one that's least fun — the task that I would most like to procrastinate from doing, but for which I have no good reason for procrastination. This scheduling rule is paradoxical because you might think that I'm never enjoying my work at all; but precisely the opposite is the case, because I like to finish a project. It feels good to know that I've gotten through the hurdles.

DK: Did you always enjoy organizing things?

DEK: Ever since I was young, I guess I've always taken an opportunistic view of knowledge, in some sense. Instead of memorizing facts, I've sort of filed stuff in my head by remembering how I could use it later, as part of a system. Already I preferred methods to facts.

For example, I told you that I was quite interested in learning the names of flowers when I was in summer camp. Well, I was also interested in trees, and I made myself a little notebook by which I could identify the trees of central Wisconsin by looking only at their leaves. If the leaves were compound (I mean with leaflets, like sumac or a Kentucky coffee tree), my book said, "Turn to part B." Otherwise the leaves were simple, and part A divided simple leaves according to whether or not they had lobes, like an oak versus an elm, and/or whether the edges were smooth or toothed, like white oak versus red oak. Some trees, like cottonwoods and poplars, have flat stems, etc. So there were parts A.1, A.2, and so on. Or maybe the tree in question had needles instead of leaves; that was part C.

I learned later that biologists call this taxonomy. For me, at age ten or so, it was a method, a technique by which I could identify a tree quickly. (You have to remember that I went to camp only in summer, when the trees weren't bare.)

Dick Karp told me once that he'd noticed this opportunistic approach in my work, and he thought it was unusual. It's hard for me to recognize that my work is unusual, if it is, until I back off from it and look at it again years later.

When I wrote *The Art of Computer Programming* in the first place, I wasn't aware of doing anything out of the ordinary, in my approach to exposition. But later I began to understand what Dick may have been referring to.

For example, consider the way I introduced techniques of finite summation in my book, indicated by a big Greek letter Sigma ('$\sum$'). In Section 1.2.3 of Volume 1, I mentioned four basic rules by which formulas involving $\sum$ could be manipulated and transformed into other formulas. I thought that all mathematicians who used $\sum$ in their work were familiar with those transformation rules; and probably they were, in fact. But the funny thing was that no other book except mine seems to have stated the rules explicitly, and gone on to illustrate how to apply them in lots of examples.

Thus, instead of listing a bunch of correct formulas A, B, C, D, etc., I said, "Look, here's a handy way to get from A to B, and here's how to recognize when it will be helpful." I still don't understand why my approach was somewhat radical, for its time. But I guess it illustrates my basic attitude, my preference for methods over facts, for paths over destinations. It's the way I file things in my head.

Of course I can't actually remember all those methods, as I continue to work on new problems. That's why it's very important for me to include all the answers to the exercises in my books, because I often can't recall how I originally solved those problems. Now, when I'm in a hurry and have the problem on one page and the answer on another, with a quick turn I can figure out once again how to exercise the part of my brain that will tell me how to get from here to there.

This approach to knowledge was probably stated best by Richard Hamming. He observed that there are incredibly many facts, so many that we can't possibly remember fact after fact after fact; that would fill up space. The universe isn't large enough to record all the facts. So what we have to do is figure out ways to regenerate most of the facts from other facts. That's what mathematics is good at. By knowing a lot of techniques, you only have to remember a few things, because you can get from them to lots and lots of others.

In the extreme, Hamming said, let's consider all the facts of history, supposing that the human race will never die out. (Maybe that assumption is contrary to the laws of physics, against the supposed eventual heat-death of the universe; but for now let's assume that the earth and its inhabitants will keep going forever.) Well, there's a certain maximum total number of molecules on earth, some huge number, let's call it N. Whatever that number is, there will come a time when more than N people have ever lived. We'll have to forget some people, totally. Later on there will come a time when more than N centuries have elapsed, and we'll have to forget some centuries. Maybe we can keep around one molecule of information about the 20th century, and another about the 21st, but we won't be able to remember them all.

In summary, Hamming pointed out that as time goes on we *have* to learn methods to derive facts from other facts. We must learn to pack information so that we can regenerate a lot of it from smaller parts. And that's why I try to organize knowledge opportunistically in my head, packing it in by function rather than by fact.

DK: You seem to be saying that *The Art of Computer Programming* is different from other books in that it doesn't categorically tell the reader, "This is how you go about doing something." Rather, you tell the reader, "This is one of the ways of doing it."

DEK: No, that isn't quite it. If, for instance, I ever do learn of a nice schedule by which that bridge club in Michigan could play its games, I wouldn't just say "Here is a good schedule to use." I would explain one or preferably more techniques by which such a schedule could be discovered, and I'd try to evaluate which technique works best and when it should be tried.* I do get to the bottom line, but always I'm trying to stress the process of discovery.

My books have to take hundreds of pages of facts and boil them down to an essence. For me, the essence turns out to be the arsenal of techniques by which facts can be derived.

I don't claim that my books are easy to read, only that they could have been a lot harder. And they do seem to encapsulate a lot of relevant knowledge, for people who are somewhat like me in their way of thinking.

---

* In fact, when DK and DEK were having this conversation, Gordon Royle and Walter Wallis had already discovered that the Michigan bridge club problem can be solved in essentially only two ways. Furthermore, both of the solutions have a nice symmetry of order 3, without fixed points. The graph of "special rivals" turns out to consist of three 4-cycles in one case, and one 12-cycle in the other. (That's why DEK found nothing when looking for a case with four 3-cycles.) Since solutions were eventually found via several different methods, it's likely that this problem will indeed rise above the threshold needed for inclusion in *The Art of Computer Programming*. See Gordon F. Royle and W. D. Wallis, "Constructing bridge club designs," *Bulletin of the Institute of Combinatorics and its Applications* **11** (1994), 122–125; Donald L. Kreher, Gordon F. Royle, and W. D. Wallis, "A family of resolvable regular graph designs," *Discrete Mathematics* **156** (1996), 269–275; R. J. Simpson, "Scheduling a bridge club using a genetic algorithm," *Mathematics Magazine* **70** (1997), 281–286; Luis B. Morales, "Scheduling a bridge club by tabu search," *Mathematics Magazine* **70** (1997), 287–290.

DK: What about L^AT_EX? (I bring this up because it's based on your work.) L^AT_EX offers canned solutions, and that seems to go against what you are saying.

DEK: Well, I guess many users do treat L^AT_EX as sort of a black box with prefabricated formats, as a system that ensures consistency by limiting the typesetting tricks that can been used. It adds a layer of protection against doing things that are too original. But really, L^AT_EX is tremendously flexible.

Some books about L^AT_EX tell their readers how to produce books and papers with the popular canned formats. Other books, more advanced, explain how to create new L^AT_EX style files. The latter books are closer to *The Art of Computer Programming* than the former ones.

The Art of Computer Programming is more like Thomas's calculus book, which I mentioned last week. That book naturally includes the famous mathematical theorem that the area of a circle is πr^2, but it also explains where that formula came from, how it was derived. Therefore it taught me how to figure out the areas of shapes that are, say, parts of circles, maybe circles intersected with squares, or of shapes that are nearly-but-not-quite circles, things like that, including shapes that might become important although they've never been studied before.

DK: What you say makes me think that we can perhaps draw an analogy from literature. A literary critic and a writer often come from different disciplines, and their work seems to spring from different sources of talent. Perhaps you're working in both camps; in other words, you're writing computer programs as well as doing theoretical studies, akin to people doing work in literary theory.

DEK: I guess you're thinking about the process of writing. I enjoy exposition, but I can write best only for people who think like me. I'm not really the best writer for somebody who just wants to know the basic facts. Take *The T_EXbook*, for example. Some people think it is brilliant and just the right way to explain a system for typesetting, while others just hate it. They want another kind of "how to" book, one that just spells out and defines the features needed to support standard formats.

Perhaps a better literary analogy than *The T_EXbook* would be a novel, which tells a story but can also do much more. Some novels are just pot boilers. If you're going to write a romance novel you have got to have a certain exotic setting, maybe some kind of a castle; and you have got to have a hero, and a villain, and so on. Some readers are interested only in the story. They want to know who falls in love, who gets hurt, who does what to whom and where, but they don't care about the lessons they might learn about their own lives from the personalities or philosophies of the characters involved. Nor do they step back and think about the way the novelist has woven these things together.

For example, in the movie I saw last night, it was clear that Gary Cooper was going to find out that Maurice Chevalier was Audrey Hepburn's father. But the way that the author revealed this to him was particularly brilliant. That's what appealed to me, the fact that the author solved the problem of communicating this secret by putting John McGiver in a Turkish bath. You know, the whole story was both poignant and amusing at the same time, an uproarious comedy yet it brought tears to my eyes in parts. It's a complete farce, yet serious in a beautiful way. I not only liked the story but I greatly appreciated the process by which the story was told.

DK: There was a touching scene where Maurice Chevalier goes to Gary Cooper's apartment to turn in his report.

DEK: Yes, he finally says, this is my daughter. That was the wonderful climax where we experience his deepest feelings.

My main point is that we know the ingredients that go into this plot, the ten or so phases that govern it, but we also see them carried through with great finesse in every detail. I just can't get tired of admiring it, it's like a movie about how to make movies. It presents, by example, a sort of optimum solution to a problem of writing.

DK: Does Jill share your enthusiasm for this movie?

DEK: Yes, she loves the film; but she loves it, you know, because it depicts beautiful examples of French baroque architecture and because the art director decorated Gary Cooper's hotel suite with flair; she thinks that it's a tremendous visual treat. We love it on different levels.

DK: Do such literary aspects influence your own technical work?

DEK: In order to maintain a computer program or in order to do anything unusual with it, you need to know the story behind it and not just the final resolution of the story. So literate programming is intended to fill this gap. A program all by itself is just the outcome of a process, it doesn't show the process. So the most successful literate programs reveal the reasoning behind the program's code and the context of every part. That's what people will want to know when they look at the program next year and try to bend it into a slightly different direction.

Computer programming involves working on many levels at once. You're working down at the computer's level of zeros and ones, and simultaneously you're working up on the conceptual level. The more successful you are at having both of those levels in your mind at the same time and bridging them, then the more successful you are at computer programming. It's something like watching the plot unfold in a movie but also thinking about how the writer and actors and cameramen and director created that work of art.

So literate programming highlights both aspects. The computer understands exact instructions, and the human being understands intuitive motivations. Both are needed when you want to understand a computer program, or to maintain it or adapt it. Literate programming combines the formal aspects with the informal ones, with formalisms at the bottom level together with intuition and context on top.

DK: Most ordinary users of computers who do only minimal programming in the form of, say, writing a macro or a spreadsheet formula, don't bother documenting their work. A few months later when they need to do something similar they have to start from square one (unless they have an unfailing memory). [laughs]

DEK: Yes, that's exactly why I try to write in a "literate" way, so that a couple years later I can quickly put myself back into the picture and understand the reasons behind certain steps. You're right that setting up a spreadsheet is analogous to programming, because it's much more than checking options on a menu. In a large piece of software the problems you mention are multiplied considerably, so good documentation becomes even more critical.

But I myself am guilty of the sin you describe. Long ago, when I wrote the macros for plain TEX, I just wrote them down, without including much documentation at all. Now a guy in Poland has come out with a literate-programming version of plain TEX's macros. He presented it to me last summer, and it's very nice.* It's what I should have done a long time ago. He is teaching me literate programming.

---

*Włodek Bzyl, "Literate `plain` source is available!" *TUGboat* **16** (1995), 297–299.

Chapter 14

Conversations, 1996: Getting Started

[Recorded 23 August 1996.]

DK: Please give more details about things that we didn't have time to discuss two weeks ago, regarding your first experiences as a computer programmer and later as an author.

DEK: Before I even start to answer your new questions, I want to give a footnote to last week's conversation, because we were talking about getting inspiration from movies or from nature.

Last week I was thinking primarily about the mysterious process by which a person is inspired to discover how to solve a particular problem. But I realized afterward that I'm more often inspired in a different way: We can fruitfully be inspired by external influences to work on an entirely new problem, or to do something different. For example, you know the story of Newton sitting under an apple tree and then beginning to think about gravity.

This morning I got an inspiration from the real world as I was riding my bike to the swimming pool. Namely, I was thinking about European paper sizes, A4, A5, and so on, and I got an idea for a wonderful exercise to include in my book. It's a way to represent binary trees, related also to the layout of computer chips.* I'll add it to the book this afternoon.

Furthermore, inspiration often comes from other people, and the conventional wisdom is that we're inspired only when somebody else does especially good work. Paradoxically, however, every once in awhile I find that I'm inspired by reading a bad paper, one that I probably wouldn't have recommended for publication if I had been the editor.

In other words, when I'm reading journals this week I *don't* automatically ignore an article that was written by people who don't understand their subject properly. You might think that such bad work

---

* See exercise 2.3–22 in *The Art of Computer Programming*, Volume 1, third edition (1997).

143

inspires me because it gives me confidence that I'm not the worst in the world! [laughs] Well, that was probably true when I was just starting out. But now there's really a much better reason. Even though I see an article whose authors are barking up the wrong tree, I assume that they have made a serious attempt to do the right thing; hence other well-intentioned people will probably also tend to make the same mistake. By reading such papers, I can help to warn against such errors.

Conversely, if I confined myself to reading work by super-geniuses, then I could never write a book that is able to communicate to anybody but super-geniuses. I need to realize the common errors that people make, so that I can write a book that will help them.

Sometimes papers are bad from a scientific point of view, yet brilliant in other ways. For example, this morning I read a paper in which I thought the research was of no interest whatsoever; but it included a very beautiful technical illustration. So I made a note to myself, saying that when I get around to writing a certain part of Volume 4 I should try to think of a way to have an appealing image that's modeled after the style of the one I just saw.

If I do ever make such an illustration, I suppose I should also give credit publicly to the authors of the paper that inspired it. Unfortunately, however, I don't know how to do that without insulting them by having nothing good to say about the scientific content of their paper. Similarly, I can't politely give explicit credit to wrong-headed papers that have led me to write about what not to do, even though those papers have indirectly helped me to improve my books. Back-handed compliments are better left unsaid.

This issue actually ties in with what you want to talk about today, since my first encounter with a computer manual inspired me by being rather bad. When I saw the awkward example programs in the original programmer's guide to the IBM 650, I immediately knew how to do better. And, being just a college freshman at the time, my self-confidence as a potential programmer was boosted.

During the summer of 1957, between my freshman and sophomore years, I had no classes or other obligations during the daytime. So I spent almost every night of the first month sitting all by myself at the console of the computer, and I wrote three programs.

First I wrote a program to find the prime factors of a given number. For example, we know that $45 = 3 \times 3 \times 5$, so the prime factors of 45 are 3, 3, and 5. That was my very first computer program. At first it had about 80 instructions, but it didn't work at all. When I finally finished debugging it and speeding it up a bit, a week or two later, it had 140 instructions.* I was having a ball, staying up all night with this incredible machine.

My second program was much simpler. It changed a number from one notation to another, like from base 10 to 8 or from base 8 to base 10, something like that. I had already begun to use a symbolic assembly language called "SOAP," instead of machine language. I think the first version of SOAP came to us from IBM early that summer.

Those two successes gave me the courage to tackle something much harder: I decided to write a program that would play tic-tac-toe. Do you know the game I mean? In Britain it's called "naughts and crosses." I decided to implement tic-tac-toe in three different ways, using what I called Brain 1, Brain 2, and Brain 3 to choose the moves.

Brain 1 embodied an optimum strategy for playing the game. I had learned as a child how to guarantee a win or draw, and I simply programmed the strategy that I had been using for years.

Brain 2, on the other hand, was designed to learn from experience. It started out knowing nothing except the rules of the game, but as it played it gradually got better. If you would play against it, maybe it would win or maybe you would win; afterwards, it considered all the winning player's moves to be good and all the losing player's moves to be bad. It kept track of all possible tic-tac-toe positions in its memory; all positions initially were "neutral," but after playing a game the ratings of positions that arose were sometimes adjusted up or down. After about 70 or 80 games, Brain 2 could play a respectable game of tic-tac-toe against an expert like me.

Brain 3 was a variant by which the machine could play against itself. I could, for example, make Brain 1 play versus Brain 1, or against Brain 2, at high speed. The most interesting case was when Brain 2 played against itself, with neither side knowing any strategy in advance. It was like the blind leading the blind; at first both sides made their moves pretty much at random. If somebody happened to win, the other player would think, "Next time I won't do that." After about 350 games, these two blind learners converged on a very boring and very conservative strategy, under which nobody won or even came close. A good player could easily beat the strategy they had come up with, because they had investigated only very safe lines in which losses were virtually impossible.

Anyway, tic-tac-toe with Brain 3 was my first major program. I don't know how many lines of code were needed, but it filled the machine.

---

* See Chapter 13 in *Selected Papers on Computer Science*.

In July we received an amazing program from Carnegie Tech called IT, which was short for "Internal Translator." That was my first experience with a compiler, a program that could translate an algebraic formula automatically into a sequence of instructions in machine language to compute that formula.

I mean, I could take a formula like, say, $(x + y)/(z - 2)$ and punch it onto a card, and feed that card to the machine running IT; then the lights would flash for awhile and lo! The machine would punch maybe ten cards, on which there was a program that added x to y and divided the result by z minus 2. That blew my mind — I couldn't figure out how such a miracle was possible.

Near the end of that summer I got hold of the source program for the IT compiler, with all the instructions that had accomplished such a miracle. I joined most of my mother's family on a week-long vacation at a cottage on Lake Erie, and I spent most of that time reading the program, learning how IT was able to do this magical translation.

I learned that IT's basic method was excellent, but the programming style was terrible. So, again, my confidence increased after realizing that I could do a much better job, once I understood the algorithm.

Then, just at the end of the summer, I came across another program, which was done by a man at IBM named Stan Poley; it was a symbolic assembly program called SOAP II. And for the first time I had the enormous pleasure of reading a program that was brilliantly written. It was just like a symphony, like poetry . . . It was just gorgeous! Now, at last, I was receiving inspiration of the best kind, where I could learn from a master. I learned then that programs could be works of art, much more than just ways to get some jobs done.

DK: What is it that makes a person good at computer science?

DEK: I've been thinking about that question a fair amount, because I strongly believe that computer science is characterized by a particular, peculiar way of thinking, which some people have to a much greater degree than others. People like me have a certain way of understanding things, of structuring knowledge inside of our heads, that puts us somehow in harmony with computers, so we turn out to be especially good at programming.

Some fields are defined by a goal: a mission to pursue, like medicine. You know, a doctor's mission is to cure diseases, regardless of his or her skill set. But other fields are based on the abilities of its practitioners. People belong to specialties of the second kind because they happen to be unusually good at their line of work.

Computer science belongs to that second category. I've noticed that one out of every fifty people, more or less, has the peculiar way of thinking that makes them resonate with computers. Long ago, such people were scattered among many other disciplines, which didn't quite suit their abilities; but they discovered each other when computer science was established as a separate field.

I mean, I think it's likely that one out of every fifty people who built the pyramids, ages ago, would probably have been a great programmer if computers had existed in ancient Egypt. After reading the works of many scholars who lived in past centuries, I'm convinced that some of them were natural-born computer scientists. But they didn't have any way to make a career out of it at the time.

In fact, the existence of this "hidden" community of like-minded individuals explains why computer science rose so quickly: Within ten years of the establishment of Stanford's Computer Science Department, nearly every university in the world already had a flourishing department of computer science, under one name or another.

DK: Where did you get this number, one in fifty?

DEK: I think I first learned it from Fred Gruenberger, who wrote about it in the early 70s after observing it in the classes he was teaching. In 1979 I spent a day or two at the University of Illinois in Urbana-Champaign, and was talking to a friend about Gruenberger's observation. To check it out, I asked him how many graduate students were presently at UIUC. He thought it over, and said, "About 11,000." So then I asked, "How many of those grad students are majoring in Computer Science?" And he said, "220." I remember this because, you see, the ratio was perfect, exactly 50 to 1 at that time!

I'm not sure that an anthropologist who studies, say, Pygmy tribes would agree that about 2 adults in each village of 100 have the mindset of a computer scientist. That kind of experiment hasn't been done yet, although I wouldn't be surprised if it turned out to be true. The data I have comes from observing college students during the past twenty years.

People who have acquired this special way of thinking by the time they're adults might not necessarily be skilled at anything else. And of course a person like me might not even be able to devise a computer program that a majority of people will want to use, because I don't really understand users who are not like myself. I mentioned that I like to read articles by people who have a different mindset, so that I can understand their way of thinking a little bit and thereby make my books a little better; but still, the audience for *The Art of Computer*

Programming is limited to about 2% of the population, and I'm quite content with that. *Somebody* has to write books for the natural-born computer scientists of this world, therefore I've found my mission in life.

DK: Can this "peculiar way of thinking" be articulated or described in some reasonable way?

DEK: Yes, I want to go into that. What are the quirks that characterize a computer scientist like me? There are several aspects, and I'm not sure that I have discovered the real answers because it's hard to analyze one's self. But here's what I think.

First of all, computer scientists seem to have an uncanny ability to jump between levels of abstraction—to see things "in the small" while at the same time seeing them "in the large." Imagine, for instance, looking at nature: Starting at a sub-microscopic level, we have an atom, which belongs to a molecule, which belongs to a cell, which belongs to a bird, which belongs to a flock, which belongs to the earth, which belongs to the solar system, which belongs to the Milky Way galaxy, and so on to higher and higher levels. Lots of levels.

Computer programs also exist on multiple levels, with electrical pulses that correspond to zeros and ones at the bottom, and with the zeros and ones representing data at another level, and with data being manipulated by simple instructions that make tiny changes; those simple instructions implement more complex operations, which are part of a subroutine that is part of an algorithm that is part of a system that tries to achieve some goal. The programmer needs to zoom in and out between levels—to know, for instance, that by adding one to a certain number, we're getting closer to the goal.

The more fluent you are at jumping effortlessly from the low level to the high level and to levels in between, the better computer programmer you are, because a programmer has to be able to understand the small steps the machine is making as well as the overall algorithm and its subgoals at intermediate levels. That's peculiar talent number one.

The next thing is something that computer scientists might share with lawyers, namely an ability to deal with nonuniform rules. In other words, suppose we have a setup with four rules, all different: Case A, Case B, Case C, Case D. Mathematicians or physicists like to have only one rule. They like to have one or two differential equations that explain everything, some kind of unified field theory perhaps, a single unifying principle. But a computer scientist needs to write programs that consist of Step 1, Step 2, Step 3, and Step 4, where each step is different. A lot of mathematicians instinctively resent any theory that breaks down into many distinct cases. Case distinctions are mathematically unsatisfying, but a computer scientist has no problem with diversity. Programmers build data structures made from nodes of many different kinds.

This aspect of the computer science mentality is a weakness as well as a strength. It's a weakness because, when faced with a situation where a nice uniform principle exists, a person like me might not discover it; I won't be very unhappy with an awkward case analysis, so I won't bother to look any further. Thus I'll overlook a beautiful simple principle that another kind of scientist would pick up.

On the other hand, many important problems have no underlying unity, and there never will be an elegant way to attack them without delving into different cases. Mathematicians who excel only at uniform problems won't make headway on them. Thus an ability to be comfortable with nonuniform cases is another mark of a computer scientist.

The third aspect is somewhat related to the second: A computer scientist is happier dealing with "discrete" things like individual marks on paper, than with "continuous" quantities like measurements of temperature. We're digital rather than analog. We're more facile with exact integers than with approximate real numbers. I was able to tackle typography when it became a question about zeros and ones instead of about molten lead. Physicists deal with a similar distinction between particles and waves. A person like me is much better at dealing with alphabets than with soup. The new biology, which is DNA-oriented, is much more accessible to computer scientists than the older "wet lab" biology was.

And the fourth aspect, on my list of four, is an idiosyncratic way of looking at dynamic processes, at the way things change. A computer scientist often throws information away by saying something like, "Increase x by 1," or "Set x to $x + 1$." In other words, if x was 5, now x is 6. We don't remember anymore that x ever was 5; we just think of x as a single quantity, whose current value is 6.

Mathematicians never did that. In such circumstances they considered x to be not simply a number but a function of time, which was equal to 5 at one time and 6 at another. The computer-science notion, of state change with discarded information, seems so natural to me that I was astonished to read John von Neumann's early publications about programming and to see the awkward way in which he grappled with the notion of assigning new values to variables. Indeed, I still find it remarkable that such a natural notion was absent from essentially all published descriptions of mathematics in the pre-computer era.

I suppose a mathematician might ask me, "Why do you want to throw away the historical information about the previous value of x?"

The reason is that the assignment/replacement operation gives us a different kind of elegance, which is easier to explain to a computer. If we didn't have a way of throwing data away, we would fill up the computer too fast. Also our languages for describing algorithms would be cluttered up with unnecessary garbage.

So those are my four answers to your question. Within computer science there also are many other kinds of abilities that may be present to a greater or lesser extent, just as there are many flavors of mathematical talent. (You recall that we talked about different kinds of mathematicians a couple weeks ago.) But the four shared modes of thinking that I've just mentioned are the main ingredients that bond computer scientists together, in my view.

DK: Can we say that some of these characteristics you describe are driven by a strong desire on the part of the individual to put some order or structure in the world around us?

DEK: My comments have tried to distinguish computer scientists from mathematicians and natural scientists, but I didn't try to distinguish them from poets and painters.

You're right in implying that computer scientists embody some aspects of precision and organization, as opposed to a talent for understanding metaphysical or subjective concepts that can't be pinned down quantitatively.

One might say that a computer scientist tends to be a boundary-defining type of person ... although that is certainly not my own philosophy. I like gray areas. I definitely don't think everything is black or white—although Gene Golub did once tell me that he thought I had some extreme views! On the other hand I do like to have things wrapped up when they deserve to be.

The computer-science mentality is surely more complicated than what I've said. If I were more of a psychologist I could probably come up with several more key characteristics. I know, for example, that Jill and I are extremely different, but I'm not sure exactly why. Of course I say, "*Vive la différence.*" That is why I married her, I didn't want to marry a clone of myself.

DK: Tell me more about your undergraduate days, when you first began to write significant programs.

DEK: The administration at Case, in the person of a man named Fred Way, was quite enlightened, because people like me were allowed and even encouraged to write software although we were just sophomores. Several of us had discovered our natural affinity for programming, and we had converged on the computer center. I worked part-time during the school year and full-time during the summer, writing programs that would be used by other students and faculty.

By the time I was a senior I'd written "SuperSoap," which was certainly the best-ever assembly program for the extended version of the IBM 650 computer that Case had acquired by 1959. And with a half-dozen friends I'd also participated in the writing of RUNCIBLE, which was certainly the best-ever compiler for that machine.

The Association for Computing Machinery began to publish a magazine called *Communications of the ACM* in 1958, when I was a sophomore. A year or so later I happened to see a copy, in which some people described how they'd written part of a compiler. And I thought, "Hmmm, this method isn't anywhere as good as we've been doing in our lab." So I wrote up for this magazine a description of what we had accomplished with the RUNCIBLE compiler.

Well, that turned out to be the second paper on my list of publications, following what I had previously written for *MAD* magazine. And it became a source of embarrassment, because I didn't realize at the time that authors of publications get credit for the ideas they have described. To me, the purpose of a magazine article was to tell an interesting story, and I thought the task of a writer was to explain that story clearly. But my story discussed only the results; I neglected to mention any of the people I had worked with to create our compiler.

Nobody mentioned at the time that they were unhappy about my omission of their names. But two or three years later I began to realize that people were giving me credit for things that I hadn't invented. That was a huge surprise, because I'd never heard of "publish or perish." My experience had been only with popular magazines, which were published to tell about neat ideas but not to establish priority claims or anything like that. Some day when the RUNCIBLE paper is reprinted with my other works on programming languages, I'll finally be able to give credit to the people who truly deserved it.*

In later years I ran across a number of other young computer scientists who made the same mistake. They were blissfully unaware, when writing their first paper for publication, that people would be giving them credit for any ideas that they didn't ascribe to others. They tried to balance that gaffe by bending over backwards in subsequent papers, by giving more credit than necessary. Nowadays I believe there's an overemphasis on intellectual property rights, although I'm certainly in

---

* See Chapter 21's Postscript in *Selected Papers on Computer Languages*.

favor of giving credit where credit is due. And I do like to include the human element of research as an important part of any scientific story.

Anyway RUNCIBLE was a world-class piece of work at its time, considering that it was written for an extremely small computer. And it was written by a few of us undergraduates, having no credentials except for the trust placed in us by our wise supervisor, Fred Way.

I've already told you about the next summer, when I wrote a compiler for Burroughs, haven't I?

DK: Yes, but tell me more!

DEK: Before I could work on the compiler itself, I needed to write and debug the library of numerical subroutines that were needed for the runtime system. For example, an ALGOL programmer could ask for logarithms and sines and cosines and such things to be calculated, and those subroutines hadn't been written yet for the Burroughs 205. And I needed an assembler before I could write those subroutines.

The summer was slipping by, and I decided to write the compiler while driving cross country to California, where I was scheduled to begin graduate study in mathematics. My first step in those days was to use a technique that has long been outmoded, but it was all I knew at the time: I drew up flow charts for everything before beginning to write the program itself.

Do you remember the large-format paper that once was commonly used for computer output, those $11'' \times 17''$ sheets with sprocket holes for "tractor feeding"? I took 200 of those blank sheets and bound them together to make a notebook, in which I could write the compiler as I drove west. I gave myself about a month to make the trip, driving about 100 miles every day. After each short drive I'd get a motel room or stop at some national park or something, and I'd sit and write another 10 pages of flow charts in that notebook. By the time I got across the Rocky Mountains I was done with the flow charts and ready for the coding part. So I had all the code written and ready for debugging when I arrived, in mid-September, at Burroughs in Pasadena. Burroughs not only let me use their computers for debugging, they also hired me as a consultant to the product planning department.

I had been awarded fellowships by the National Science Foundation and by the Woodrow Wilson Foundation, but those fellowships had strings attached: "If you accept the NSF you can't accept the Woodrow Wilson, and if you accept the Woodrow Wilson you can't accept the NSF. If you accept either one you can't have a part-time job. The point of a fellowship is to allow you to be a full-time student." In particular,

I couldn't have a fellowship and also be working at Burroughs as a consultant. And Burroughs offered to pay five dollars an hour, which amounted to pretty good wages in 1960. I could go to Burroughs at any hour I wanted to, and earn five dollars. I could even sit in the park and write some kind of report, then charge my time to Burroughs. At forty hours per week I could make $10,000 per year, which was about the same as an assistant professor's salary; so a consulting job was much more lucrative than a fellowship, which paid only $2,000 or $3,000. (Wages and prices were substantially different in those days, pre-inflation.)

So I declined my fellowships in 1960 and I had this job, which made it possible for Jill and me to buy a house soon after we were married in 1961. Owning a house turned out to be really good for our life. We never had to rent. Renters essentially pay money down the drain, it just goes away; but home owners have equity. (I was beginning to learn that money is funny. Later on, for instance, when I bought a grand piano, I realized that the piano still retained its value; I could have sold it and gotten my money back, thereby having a wonderful piano for free. On the other hand food isn't free; food gets consumed.) Anyway, because of my consulting job, Jill and I never had to take out loans for anything except the house. And we paid off the mortgage rather early, so we weren't paying double for the house by paying interest. Even though I was a student, those decisions put us several years ahead of the curve, considering that everybody else who lived on our block was at least 20 years older than we were. Most of the young people at that time never thought of buying a house. I'm glad that my kids are now following the same policy; my son has a house.

That consulting job wasn't the same as being a regular employee, because it didn't include medical insurance or any such side benefits. But I could choose my own hours, and I found that I could really do valuable things for Burroughs. Because I was a consultant, because I had gotten onto an inside track and written a compiler for them, they decided that I had something worthwhile to say even though I was young and didn't have any kind of advanced degree.

After finishing the 205 compiler, my first assignment for Burroughs was, in fact, a dream job. A group of their employees, led by Bob Barton and Joel Erdwinn, had recently completed a compiler for the Burroughs 220 computer, their new machine, and it was a spectacular achievement. It ran maybe ten times faster than any other compiler that had ever been written, and it produced better machine language instructions too! The chief reason for its success was that it was the first piece of commercial software to use list processing, an efficient type of data structure that didn't become widespread until many years later. This compiler, called BALGOL, had impressed me greatly when I saw it at Case just before coming west. So naturally I asked to see the code, as soon as I'd arrived at the Burroughs plant in Pasadena. I wanted to know the secret of its success. Well, they agreed to show me the listing, I mean the program details as written in assembly language. But they apologized because the listing contained very few comments. "No problem," I said, because I'd already read lots of badly documented compiler listings.

Thus it turned out that my first task as a consultant was to write comments on the listing of the BALGOL compiler. (Later I was to learn that my written comments had in fact served as an implicit textbook for Stanford's first students of programming languages.) The BALGOL compiler was the second truly great program that I'd ever had the opportunity to read, following my experience with Poley's SOAP II in 1957. And not only did I have a chance to read it; Burroughs paid me $5.00 per hour to do that! As I said, it was a dream job.

The product planning department was just finishing its design of a really far-out computer, completely different from anybody else's machine, called the Burroughs B5000. It was based on a radical philosophy that sounded real good at the time, but is now out of fashion and probably deservedly so. The idea was to build a computer specifically designed to run high-level languages, languages like ALGOL or FORTRAN. The machine language would be so close to an algebraic language that very little translation would be necessary. Hardware engineers were devising tools for design automation, by which it was becoming possible to build computers that were much more complex in their internal logical structure than ever before. So now the Burroughs team wanted to do as much in hardware as we had previously done in software. Bob Barton's former BALGOL group had therefore gone over to the product planning division — except for its chief programmer, Joel Erdwinn, who had decided to join Fletcher Jones at Computer Sciences Corporation, one of the first big software companies.

(Incidentally, I never met Fletcher Jones. But years later I received my main academic appointment as Stanford's Fletcher Jones Professor of Computer Science, after he had died tragically in a plane accident. A foundation was set up in his memory, and it supported endowed professorships at Stanford and a few other universities.)

Back to my story. Most of the people who had worked on BALGOL were now my colleagues, and I could spend a lot of time with them because I wasn't married yet. I was spending my first year of grad school as a bachelor, and I spent many hours in restaurants eating meals with those outstanding programmers. I got to know them quite well, also visiting them in their homes, and I certainly got to know the B5000 well.

That led to my next main assignment as a consultant. The engineers who actually had to build the B5000 were in a bind, because that machine was so radical in its concepts. "We don't have models of any other machines that look like this, how are we supposed to make one?" They had been given the written specifications, which were supposedly complete, but the specs didn't really explain the philosophy behind the machine. So I could do something that Burroughs had no other way to achieve. As a consultant I could greatly increase the communication between the people on the main floor who had designed the machine and the people in the basement who were building it.

The hardware engineers downstairs reported to their boss, who reported to his boss, who reported to some vice-president in Detroit; the product planners upstairs reported to their boss, who reported to his boss, who had the same connection in Detroit. There were no direct links in the organizational chart between the engineers and the designers, other than going up three levels of management and down again. However, I knew both groups, because I was a consultant who could cross company lines. I could walk both upstairs and downstairs on the stairway. In retrospect, I may have been worth a million dollars to Burroughs, as a communication channel between two groups of people who really didn't understand what the people at the other end were doing.

My job eventually boiled down to this: I would work with the engineers and look at their wiring diagrams, how they were putting the machine together, so that I could verify that it really would work as the planners had intended. Conversely, their experiences with the hardware logic suggested improvements to the design, which I could clear with the people upstairs. Eventually the hardware engineers ran their detailed plans for the machine through a step-by-step simulator, until they thought it was working. Then I became the "second simulator," by trying to defeat their design as if I were debugging a computer program. It turned out that I caught more than 200 errors in this way, allowing them to correct the logic before actually building a prototype and having to do expensive modifications afterward.

That was the way I earned my salary at Burroughs during those first two or three years. Still, there was no connection between my computer consulting and my academic work. At the university I did pure mathematics. I never really used mathematical techniques in my consulting; I never really used computing techniques in my mathematics. I lived in two different worlds at that time.

Well, there was actually an exception to that rule; I've already told you about my curiosity with respect to Chomsky's language theory. Some people had found that you could use some of Chomsky's ideas for linguistics and apply them to computer languages. I was intrigued by this because Chomsky's theory looked like mathematics, but it was also tied to computing. Wow, here was something where I could be doing both at the same time! Therefore, as I told you a couple weeks ago, I took a copy of Chomsky's book on syntactic structures along on my honeymoon, to read in odd moments as we crossed the ocean and back. I set out to solve the so-called ambiguity problem: Given a context-free grammar, does it define a language in which all sentences can be parsed in exactly one way? I learned later that this problem had already been proved to be unsolvable, that there was no way to solve it. But I didn't know anything about unsolvability; I just thought it was an interesting problem that was mathematical, yet also close to my interests in programming.

I presented context-free grammars and the ambiguity problem as the topic for my oral examination at Caltech. Math grad students were supposed to present some piece of original research, and the work that I presented was based on Chomsky's theory. Of course, I didn't solve the ambiguity problem that I'd started out to tackle. But I was able to solve some simple cases, and my partial results were of sufficient interest to become the subject of that oral exam.

DK: Your life changed when you became a married man.

DEK: Yes, Jill and I got married in '61 and we spent our summer in Europe on our honeymoon, as you know. Then we started to set up house in California, renting a small apartment for three months until finding a house that we were able to buy in November. Our first real home was in a little town called Sierra Madre, just east of Pasadena and quite near Burroughs. And our home-ownership began with an adventure: The day after we'd signed the contract for that house, big forest fires broke out suddenly in the mountains, right above Sierra Madre! We still lived in Pasadena, and the police wouldn't allow us to go anywhere near our new house because we hadn't moved any belongings and we weren't officially residents of Sierra Madre as yet. All we could do was look out the window and see that the flames were coming closer and closer. It was pretty frightening, because we'd just put all our savings into the down payment of this house and then the whole mountain went up in flames. Fortunately the fire was contained, although not until it had come within two blocks of our street.

So we moved into our new house in December, and then in January a man came out to see me and take me to lunch. He was an editor for Addison–Wesley. He said, "Don, how would you like to write a book about how to write compilers?" A prominent numerical analyst named Richard Varga, who was a consulting editor to Addison–Wesley, had heard that I knew how to write compilers and so he'd suggested that they approach me. Although I was just a second-year graduate student, just turned 24, they had heard that I'd finished a couple of compilers that weren't too bad.

Well, our meeting was just like, I don't know what, like a north pole magnet meeting a south pole magnet. It was just a perfect match. My immediate reaction was, "Yeah, I'd love to write a book, writing is something that I've always enjoyed." As I went home from Caltech that day I was all excited about what kind of a book I could write. I jotted down a list of 12 chapters that I thought such a book should have. I still have this piece of paper where I jotted those chapter titles down. I already knew that the title would be *The Art of Computer Programming*.

My original plan for 12 chapters is still intact today, almost 35 years later. But the ordering of chapters has changed, and of course only six of the chapters have been published so far because so many other things have come up in my life. I might not ever write the final versions of Chapters 11 and 12, if that material has already been written down satisfactorily by somebody else by the time I'm ready to return to those topics. But I definitely hope to complete the other ten chapters. Chapters 1 through 10 are going to take me through Volume 5, and those five volumes will cover the core of computer science (or at least the core concepts that were already known in 1962). Specialized topics that relate only to compilers are discussed in Chapters 11 and 12, as applications of the basic techniques in the core.

I completed a draft of all twelve chapters, amounting to more than 3000 handwritten pages, before starting to type any of it at the end of 1965. Since the opening chapters dealt with core issues of computer science, I could actually sketch out some ideas for the book while consulting at Burroughs; obviously the Burroughs employees were interested in computer science, too.

One of the things I could do for Burroughs was to give lectures about software to their hardware people. Caltech also gave me a chance to use some of my notes from *The Art of Computer Programming* and teach an experimental course. Therefore, even before getting my PhD degree, I was teaching students about compilers and sorting techniques and some other aspects of programming.

Going back a little bit, to the summer of '62, I took time off from both Caltech and Burroughs, to write a FORTRAN compiler for the Univac Solid State computers. This summer job was arranged by friends of mine from Case, who had discovered that Univac needed such a compiler, and they figured that I could do it in three months. Not me alone, but with Bill Lynch, another friend of mine from Case, who was now a grad student at the University of Wisconsin in Madison. Thus Bill and I, between the two of us, agreed to write a FORTRAN compiler. For delivering that program I received $12,500, which was considered an incredible summer salary — more than an assistant professor could make in nine months.

Bill and I worked 16 hours a day in order to accomplish our task. We rented an apartment in Madison for two months, then another apartment in Philadelphia for the third month. (We had to debug our programs at the Univac plant in Philadelphia.) Although we were working solidly, we knew that we'd soon be done with the job, so it wasn't going to go on and on. The work certainly wasn't boring, but there was lots to do; we had almost no time left for R&R.

Still, I did take off one day during that summer to enjoy myself doing mathematical research. The reason was that our compiler needed what's called a symbol table or a dictionary look up routine; when a person writes a FORTRAN program and has a variable named TOTAL or something, the compiler needs to look up those letters and find out which variable it is. The standard way to do it, which I'd learned from Poley's assembler (and which I still use in TEX) is called "hashing." The compiler I was writing used a variant of hashing called "linear probing," and I knew that it was a pretty good method but there was no mathematical theory of how good it was. I'd heard rumors that some students of Professor Feller, the leading probability theorist at Princeton, had looked at this problem and had given up on it. But as I was writing the part of the program that does the hashing, I started to think about how one might actually solve this problem and figure out exactly how long the method of linear probing usually takes to do a lookup.

Luckily, I came up with the answer.* That was the second time in my life when I'd combined mathematics and computer science successfully. Computer programming was its own world apart from mathematics; but here I was using some ideas from the mathematics of counting,

---

* The six pages of notes that I typed up for myself concerning this work a year later (22 July 1963) can now be found in Philippe Flajolet's *Research News* for November 1997, http://algo.inria.fr/AofA/Research/11-97.html.

and I could actually apply them to a computer programming problem about dictionary lookup. Today that seems obvious, in retrospect, but at the time it came as a big surprise to me.

Well, this experience changed my life very profoundly, because it led to what I now consider to be my main life's work, "the analysis of algorithms." I now knew exactly how good the method of hashing with linear probing was expected to be, and I knew that it had been fun to find the answer. And I also realized that millions of other problems of a similar nature were still waiting to be analyzed. If you write any kind of computer program, then you can ask the question, "How good is it? Exactly how fast does it run?"

In 1962, such questions had hardly been asked, except in one field called queuing theory. I'd heard about some studies of queuing, about analyses of processes where people line up for service at counters and we want to understand the bottlenecks that tend to build up. Queuing problems were less discrete than the computer-science-type of problem that I'd encountered with respect to hashing; but they were analyses of a certain kind of algorithm, they were quantitative studies of procedures. I realized that there were scads and scads of other algorithms out there that could be analyzed, too. Therefore I could see no end to the interesting and enjoyable kind of research that I'd begun during my day off from writing a FORTRAN compiler.

Then I got back to school and had a chance to teach some computer-related classes at Caltech. I had to finish my thesis in '63, but I began to write *The Art of Computer Programming* in earnest during June and July of that year. I started to write about sorting, and that's when I really did a lot of analyses of algorithms. I began to learn many more techniques of analysis as I explored the methods that had been invented for sorting, for putting numbers and words into order.

And before we finish today, I have one more story to tell about the name "analysis of algorithms," although it didn't take place until later.

At the end of '67 I was attending a conference in Santa Barbara. One day at mealtime the man sitting next to me introduced himself, then asked, "And what are you interested in? What's your main field?"

It struck me that there was no name for what I was doing. I said, "Well, I'm an associate professor of mathematics at Caltech. But I'm really most interested in computer science, this newfangled subject that's been started at a few universities."

"Oh, computer science. Artificial intelligence?" he said.

"Well, no, I'm not really doing artificial intelligence."

He smiled. "Numerical analysis?"

"No, I'm not really into numerical analysis either."

"Ah, OK, you must be a language man."

At that time computer science was really divided into three parts. You either were doing research in artificial intelligence, numerical analysis, or programming languages. There was nothing else. So I had to reply, "Well, it's true that I've worked on programming languages. But that's not really my main interest."

After that night, I started to think that I really need a name for what I do. I knew that Richard Bellman was famous for inventing a new field that he called "dynamic programming." I figured that if he could make up a new name, so could I. Therefore I chose the term "analysis of algorithms," even though I didn't know exactly what that term meant. For the next few years, my working definition was very simple, but also very vague:

$$\text{analysis of algorithms} \;=\; \text{what interests me.}$$

Finally, however, I was able to articulate what algorithmic analysis really means, and I promoted the term when giving invited talks at international conferences in Nice (1970) and in Ljubljana (1971). Both of those talks were entitled "Analysis of Algorithms." I explained what that term had come to mean, as my work had begun to crystallize, namely that it refers to quantitative studies of the efficiency of computational methods. And I'm pleased to see that Analysis of Algorithms is now one of the main categories that are named when the subfields of computer science are listed.

Chapter 15

Conversations, 1996: Programming and Languages

[Recorded 13 September 1996.]

DK: Let's talk about programming today. (I'm trying to become more daring and get you into areas that I don't know much about.)

DEK: I think we talked before about the empirical fact that about 2% of all people are apparently born to be great programmers. Then there are the other 98% who have to live with computers. Some of them can do programming, with difficulty, but most of them will never be comfortable trying to write programs. The difference has nothing to do with intelligence; natural-born programmers just have a different way of looking at things, so that computers seem transparent to them.

For example, my wife is extremely smart and capable, but I don't think that she will ever enjoy programming. She is good at creating macros for a text editor, sometimes impressing me with subtle tricks that I didn't think of; but macro writing is quite different from the creation of what we call "recursive procedures" or even "while loops." She's friendly to programmers, but won't ever want to write code herself. Conversely, she is able to do all sorts of things with her mind and with her hands that are way beyond my own abilities.

An analogy with automobiles is often suggested: Almost everybody in our society needs to know how to drive a car, but comparatively few need to know how to repair one. Even fewer are needed to design them. In other words, there are some people who are great mechanics, and other people like me who would never be able to take an engine apart and put it back together again without causing a big fire or some kind of explosion. So the analogy is appealing.

But I think the things that we try to do with computer programs are a lot more complicated than the things that we try to do with automobiles. Thus the difference between the tasks you can perform with prefabricated program components, compared to what you can achieve if you are a really good programmer, is much greater than the difference between the best car that Ford can build with prefabricated parts versus the best car that Ford's employees can build with custom-made parts. I mean, people who aren't good at the whole process are able to do a lot more than they could before if we give them lots of plug-in components; yet the ability to write your own programs is almost infinitely better than the ability to incorporate plug-in components into somebody else's program. As a real programmer, I could never be happy if I had to live my life confined to using tools that are found on pull-down menus instead of implementing my own algorithms. I suspect that a real mechanic wouldn't mind so much working with a good factory-made tool that he hadn't built by himself.

On the other hand, even for a born programmer, there's a tremendous difference between high-level programming and low-level programming. At the lowest level, I'd have to construct my programs in binary notation, zeros and ones, as the computer sees them. That's very far from the way I conceive of those programs in my head. Therefore programmers work with languages that are intended to match our thought processes; we write programs in "higher-level" languages, and our code is mechanically translated by compilers into an equivalent low-level form.

"Assembly language" is one level above the lowest level of zeros and ones. It is geared to a specific machine; every new computer design needs a new assembly language. If you know what the computer can do, if you know all of its basic instructions, and if you want to tell the computer exactly what to do, you can express those instructions symbolically in assembly language. This task is considerably easier and less error-prone than an attempt to create the binary notation directly, because an assembly program translates your symbolic code into the desired zeros and ones.

When computers were smaller and slower, assembly language was of significant importance, because many programs would not run fast enough unless you chose every instruction carefully and controlled every step of the process. For example, I once did such a thing in 1968 when I was working in cryptanalysis. I was writing a program that I knew was going to be executed a trillion times. It was a very short program, only about twenty instructions; but those twenty instructions were going to be executed a million million times. Therefore if I could shorten the time to execute the instructions by only 100 nanoseconds, which is a ten-millionth of a second, I would save more than a day of computer time overall. That meant one-plus days saved for every secret code that we wanted to break. In those days 100 nanoseconds was the machine's clock rhythm; so I knew that the intellectual effort needed to eliminate every unnecessary clock pulse from the machine's operations in my program would definitely be worthwhile. (That was before the era of large-scale computer chips; nowadays the government could just buy a million or so chips. However, secret codes have also gotten much harder to break.)

The point is that there are times when you want something to be extremely efficient, and that's when you use assembly language. But I hardly ever need to do that any more. The next level up is to write programs in an algebraic language, which doesn't depend on the design of any particular machine. A "compiler" is a piece of software that translates such programs from the algebraic language into zeros and ones (or sometimes first into assembly language). The main programming problem that fascinated me when I was an undergraduate student, and for several years later, was the problem of how to write a compiler. My friends and I wrote several compilers, and that's why I was asked to write *The Art of Computer Programming* in the first place.

Compiler technology is now quite advanced, but it still never reaches the kind of efficiency that is achievable with assembly language. The main reason is that, when you write a program to solve a problem, you can express your ideas in many different ways; I mean, many different programs correspond to the same method of solution. Yet you present only one of those programs to the compiler. You know in your head that certain numbers are going to be small and others are going to be large. You know that certain calculations can be done in a different order, and that certain cases will never occur or will happen only rarely, and so on. But you don't tell the compiler any of this. One of the possible versions of your program will ask whether a certain number is greater than zero; another version will ask whether or not that number is nonzero. You may know that those two questions are interchangeable, because the number in question cannot be negative; but the compiler won't know this, so the compiler can explore only a few of the many alternatives.

In other words, the compiler can only produce the best program that corresponds to the one and only version that you wrote down. The best program you could have constructed in assembly language is usually much better, because of all the other options that you actually know about. Some of the hundreds of ways that you could have written your program will match the machine's capabilities much better than others.

Starting in 1960 or so, compilers have been said to be "90% efficient," meaning that if you were to use assembly language instead of the compiler then your program would only run 10% faster. That statistic was always false; I've almost never seen a program that I couldn't make run five or ten times as fast as the compiled version, by studying the code carefully and using an assembler.

Still, as I said, I rarely use assembly language any more, because I hardly ever need extreme efficiency. Today's computers are so fast, I don't mind if my compiler is only 10% efficient.

The early ideas of algebraic languages have been refined and extended so that they now come in different flavors. For example, some algebraic languages are "object oriented," others are "functional," and so on, representing different people's intuitions about how algorithms are most naturally understood.

Extensive libraries of subroutines have been developed to accomplish tasks that are frequently needed. Many programmers now have a pretty dull life because their jobs consist almost entirely of calling on programs written by somebody else. They simply have to keep a dozen books open so that they can write down magic incantations to invoke appropriate library routines, being careful to list the parameters in the proper order. I haven't yet seen a library package that was pleasant to use, except for necessary subroutines that do various kinds of input and output.

Algebraic languages are greatly enhanced by what I like to call "literate programming." As you know, that was the subject of the first of several books about my work, which you have so kindly offered to publish. Literate programming allows me to express my programs in ways that match my mental images much more closely than ordinary algebraic languages do, because I can use English and technical illustrations, in addition to algebra. Furthermore I can decompose my program into small parts that are easily comprehended; and I can arrange those parts in any way that I like, for greater understanding by myself and by whoever else looks at them.

At higher levels yet we have programming languages for special kinds of computations, like number crunching, matrix algebra, symbolic formula manipulation, statistical analyses, linear optimization, list processing, database searching, and so on. Efficiency is much less important than ease of programming in such cases.

Chapter 16

Conversations, 1996: Artificial Intelligence, Students, Retirement

[Recorded 20 September 1996.]

DK: In our last conversation we talked about programming and computer languages. Today I thought I'd ask you what your thoughts are about AI [artificial intelligence].

DEK: OK, but I'm not sure in which connection: AI covers a huge number of subspecialties. There are AI expert systems, AI methods for automatic program synthesis, AI programs to play chess, AI programs to try to understand languages, and so on; what aspects are you thinking about?

DK: We can start with expert systems and perhaps move on to theoretical AI, the culture of AI, and claims made in its name.

DEK: Well, I don't pay much attention to the claims; I tend to look at what a subject is, not what it's supposed to be in the future. Predictions are cheap, and anyway people have short memories. So my opinions, for what they're worth — I'm mostly an outsider with respect to AI — are based on the past. In general, I'm really thankful for all the contributions that AI research has made to mainstream CS [computer science].

Before getting into more details, I can't resist telling a little joke. Doug Hofstadter once said, after considering the question of how people conceptualize symbols that appear in many forms, "The most difficult problem in all AI research is to understand the letter 'A'." To which I naturally replied, "And the second-most difficult problem is to understand the letter 'I'."*

---

*See his papers "Metafont, metamathematics, and metaphysics," *Visible Language* **16** (1982), 309–338; "On seeing 'A's and seeing As," *Stanford Humanities Review* **4**, 2 (1995), 109–121.

165

From very early on, the quest for AI has been the most ambitious goal in the minds of many of the world's best computer programmers. Interested people joined forces and were challenged to write more sophisticated programs than they would have if they hadn't had such a challenge. And the things they tried to do went way beyond the realm of traditional algorithms; working in AI was a different experience and at a higher level than anything that had previously been attempted with computers. As a result, a great number of the most important tools that programmers in all fields use today first emerged in the AI community. The AI people had to think harder, so they came up with better methods.

For example, sophisticated data structures for representing information inside a machine began in the AI world. These methods, which underlie all kinds of modern programs for graphics, for music synthesis, for automated reasoning, and for virtually any complex application, can trace their roots to early AI programs.

Thus I've always found AI a fertile source of ideas and methods. I never thought that their research was actually going to succeed, in the sense of getting to the end and having a machine that really passes the Turing test for intelligence. At least not for a hundred years, say. On the other hand I don't believe with [Roger] Penrose that such an event is somehow impossible, that human abilities could never ever be matched by machines. I see a huge chasm between what machines can do now and the cognitive processes that actually take place inside human brains, yet I don't believe that cognition is forever beyond the reach of automation.

There's certainly a tremendous gulf between what AI researchers have been able to achieve and what they want to achieve. Still, I like the fact that they're working on it. The more they work, the more they learn about intelligence and psychology and so on. I agree with George Forsythe that the best way to learn any subject is to try to explain it to a computer, to try to automate it. So they're making progress, and I cheer them on even though I don't believe they're going to get to the end of the road. Maybe a lot of them don't believe it either; and that doesn't matter to me. I've told you often that I think a good journey is more important than reaching a destination.

I tend to read a lot of AI literature for its techniques that relate to combinatorial searching, especially, because those techniques are directly related to Volume 4 of *The Art of Computer Programming*. The subject of that book, combinatorial algorithms, involves searching through huge mazes of possibilities, with heuristics that help to cut down the number of places where we need to look for fruitful alternatives. Such techniques have actually been developed independently in three different communities: some of them in artificial intelligence, some in electrical engineering, and some in operations research. In the early days the researchers of each community were unaware that other groups were working on the same thing, because they had different words for the concepts. The electrical engineers didn't know that their methods were also, in disguise, being discussed in operations research departments, and a third way in AI departments. I found it very interesting that each of those three groups came up with something about shortest-path searching that the other two groups didn't know. Many concepts were common to all three, expressed in different words; yet each group found something extra of importance, because their individual viewpoints led them in different directions. So in Volume 4, I'll be able to draw on all three traditions, enriching each one with the help of the others and with additional insights from theoretical computer science.

Actually Volume 1 already owes much to the AI community, because the basic idea of list processing goes back to two early AI languages, IPL and LISP. I told you the other day about the BALGOL compiler that I encountered when I came to Burroughs in 1960. That was the compiler that ran thirty times faster than its competitors, yet took less space and produced better output. The main genius behind BALGOL, Joel Erdwinn, had been reading AI papers, and he realized that the techniques used inside of IPL for AI work were ideally suited also to writing a compiler.

Almost everybody in those days thought that list processing was a complicated process that could only be done in a high-level language such as IPL or LISP, or with a complex library of subroutines. Joel, however, realized that it was easy to do list processing from scratch in *any* language, using only a few lines of code. After reading his program, I learned how nice this method was, so I naturally stressed it in the chapter about data structures in my Volume 1.

Probably the most radical thing about Volume 1, when it came out, was its "revelation" that list processing isn't exotic, it's a simple tool for everybody. Many universities adopted Volume 1 as a text in those days, because there was nothing else like it at the time. Thus the AI-spawned idea of list processing became widespread, and I think the quality of programming went up tremendously in the next ten years because this message got out.

DK: I have to confess that there was some prejudice in my question.

DEK: What was your prejudice?

DK: I'm a bit suspicious of some of the claims made in the name of AI.

DEK: Well, I'd say the only mistake they made was to predict that they were going to revolutionize everything and that it wouldn't take long. But who am I to complain about people who can't estimate the amount of time that will be needed to complete a complex project?

Some AI researchers think that if they keep the same techniques they have, but if they just could introduce a critical mass of information into their system, then all of a sudden their algorithms would begin "thinking." Just as in movies like *The Forbin Project*. I'm skeptical about that, but how will we ever know?

I don't think there's any chance of accumulating that much information anytime soon, because I don't imagine there will be enough people willing to devote their lives to the boring task of accumulating such a critical mass in usable form. Doug Lenat is trying, but he doesn't have the temperament of a James Murray, who worked relentlessly on the Oxford English Dictionary for so many decades. I told you the other day that I can resist boredom; I can keep myself from being bored while doing busywork for maybe six weeks at a time. But not year after year. Until such a mass of data is gathered, however, we'll never know whether to believe the hypothesis that it will suddenly begin to jell.

Anyway, I've read many parts of the *Handbook of Artificial Intelligence* carefully, but skimmed over other parts that seem to relate less to computer science in general. Therefore I don't know a great deal about expert systems.

I do know that expert systems have been extremely useful in certain problem areas, but they get flaky near the boundary of those domains. For instance, I definitely wouldn't trust them to control a nuclear weapon. The way they work is by compiling together a huge number of rules that say, "If you see such and such, then do such and such." Collections of order-dependent rules like that are notoriously difficult for humans to understand, when there are lots of them. When you work with such rules and they fail, then you must add another rule; but then, you know, something else might go wrong. That is just so different from the way trustworthy systems are created.

There are hundreds of expert systems that are doing valuable things for people. However, I don't believe they will ever be reliable. If you have a non-critical task where you can say, "If the computer does a good job, I'll be happy, but if it does a bad job then I'll still be alive," then an expert system might be just the thing for you. On the other hand, I don't want an expert system to be flying the plane when I'm aboard.

DK: I find the designation of expert system a little pretentious. Isn't "expert system" just another way of saying "computer program"?

DEK: My understanding is that the term "expert system" refers to a program of a very particular type, composed of so-called production rules with the if-then form that I just mentioned. And, well, it's OK to have a little hype sometimes, unless you can think of a better word.

In fact the name "expert system" turns out to be quite suitable, once you realize that experts disagree in the world. Take any controversial issue. If, say, Ted Koppel interviews four experts, you usually get four different opinions; if he interviews twenty experts, there will be twenty different opinions. I first learned this in 1962, when I was in a room with dozens of Caltech faculty who were discussing the Cuban missile crisis. I couldn't find any points of agreement between them, yet I knew they were among the smartest people in the world.

Perhaps I'm exaggerating, as usual. But if you ask ten doctors to make a diagnosis, you're almost sure to get at least two different diagnoses. Maybe they will split seven to three, or something like that. In that sense, an expert system can be considered reliable, because it might agree with the seven. But the three might be right.

Experts can give you the current prevailing wisdom. As long as you define "expert" in a way that doesn't mean "infallible," then expert systems are fairly well named. But if you assume that "expert" means "one hundred percent accurate," you'll be misled by the name.

Let me come back to my main point. If you want to study the human mind, the best way I know is to try to automate as much as you can about the way humans behave. Maybe the people who are going to spend their entire careers in such studies need to believe that they will some day succeed in making an artificially intelligent creature. But if I were in their shoes, I'd be quite happy with a much more modest goal, in any subject area: "Let me see how much I can automate, so that I can understand more about the territory."

DK: In your defense of AI, you suggested that some of the discoveries in computer science would have not been made, had it not been for this kind of vision and this kind of pursuit.

DEK: Well, the discoveries would probably have been made, but I think it would have taken a lot longer. I'm glad that the process was speeded up. People like [Allen] Newell, [Marvin] Minsky, and [John] McCarthy had this great idea: "Let's get a whole bunch of brilliant people together, put them into a room and stir, and see what comes out." And they got funding to make this happen. So a lot of very creative individuals formed a working subculture that had good fermentation, good things happening. Of course there also was a lot of dead wood, but you have to allow that in the mixture while you're stirring; you never know in advance when the cream's going to rise. The basic ideas that I'm celebrating didn't just arise spontaneously; a larger group was needed to get the ball rolling so quickly.

The world is also indebted to the early AI community for people like Bill Gosper, who is one of the great experimental mathematicians of our day. He too was nourished by this culture.

As an outsider I can, of course, also find things to criticize. For example, I saw a couple of research proposals that were written so cleverly that it was impossible for the project to fail. You know, the way they were written, the proposers could declare the project a success as long as they got money, no matter what else they did. This is, I think, why a lot of people started to resent what was going on. Why should we admire people who take no risks?

I'll be traveling to Japan soon, and that fact reminds me of the so-called Fifth Generation Computer Project, a massive investment by the Japanese government during the past decade or so, earmarked for the development of new hardware and software intended to advance AI. The project had noble goals, but I think it failed for reasons similar to what I've already said: The planners thought that AI would be just around the corner, if they could only build faster machines and improve the Prolog language, while compiling a critical mass of data about knowledge in general and about languages in particular.

That project developed large grammars of English and Japanese, but their work never came anywhere near their hopes for automatic language translation. Again they ran into the huge gulf that separates computational methods from the mysterious thing called intelligence.

On the other hand I've personally been waiting for something else to appear — what might be called "intentionally bad translation," or rather "brute-force mechanical translation," "unintelligent translation." I long for a program that would take a Japanese text and render it literally in a Japanese-flavored dialect of "pidgin English." I mean, imagine a word-for-word translation from a Japanese document into something that wouldn't really be very good English at all, although I think I could learn that dialect of English in a week. I could learn the peculiarities of the word order, and I could learn the ambiguities, if I had something English-like to work with instead of having to learn thousands of characters and do tedious dictionary lookups. That task is much too formidable for me as things stand now, because I want the same not only for Japanese but also for Chinese languages, for Indian languages, for Czech, Swedish, Russian, French, Spanish, Greek, Hebrew, and so on.

Brute-force translation would be really useful, but people who work in the field give such projects short shrift because word-for-word rendering doesn't meet their quality standards. I think they're trying to do something that's basically impossible, and the intelligence they try to add actually makes my task harder because the flaws of their fancy methods are difficult to understand. I say, please take me 90% of the way to my destination, in as simple a way as possible, and I'll supply the rest. I can learn another dialect of English real fast; I can learn a guy's peculiar habits of speech.

DK: Have you seen some of these translation programs? They do exist.

DEK: Oh, good!

DK: At CSLI Publications we have one that does French, for example.

DEK: Oh, OK. Come to think of it, I did see the demonstration of an interesting system when I visited St. Petersburg a couple years ago. I think it was called ProText, and it worked with Russian, German, and English. It wasn't quite what I just described, but it did provide translations in a dialect that I think I could have learned quickly. Of course it's useful only when I already have an electronic file containing the text to be translated. I don't have time to sit there and key everything in.

DK: OK, I guess I've picked your brains enough about AI, which is often in the news but outside your main field of interest.

Let's talk a little about your experiences working with graduate students over the years. I know a few of them personally because of their work on typography, but you must have advised many others.

DEK: Some weeks ago I think I mentioned that I've had 28 PhD students, with 28 different personalities.

To a mathematician, 28 is a very special number, called a "perfect number": It's the next number after 6 that's equal to the sum of its divisors. I mean, $6 = 3 + 2 + 1$, where 3, 2, and 1 are the numbers that divide evenly into 6. Similarly, $28 = 14+7+4+2+1$. Such numbers were considered to have mystical properties during Renaissance times; in fact the lore of perfect numbers was one of the few aspects of mathematics that survived the Dark Ages. Therefore I now can easily remember the number of students that I supervised, and I'm happy that it has turned out to be perfect in more ways than one.

Of course I also served on the committees of many other students, and helped with their dissertations. (In fact I once delayed the PhD of one now-prominent French computer scientist by a year, because I insisted that he live up to his potential rather than dashing off an unpolished piece of work.) One of the greatest joys of my career has been the opportunity to work with so many brilliant computer scientists as they were beginning to find their own voices.

Each student naturally had his own profile of strengths and weaknesses. I could therefore tell you 28 interesting stories. But I don't want to do that, because it would be impossible to discuss them in any even-handed way. I also know that many of them would be embarrassed to see how I praise their talents. Instead, I think it's best to tell only one of those stories, which in fact is the only one to have an unhappy ending — indeed, a tragic ending, forever etched in my memory.

Before I start, however, I should say something about the PhD degree, because most people outside of universities don't really understand the nature of that degree. A PhD is awarded for research, meaning that the student has contributed to the state of the world's knowledge. That's quite different from a bachelor's degree or a master's degree; those degrees are awarded for a mastery of *existing* knowledge. (In some non-science fields, like Art, a master's degree is more akin to a PhD; but I'm speaking now about the situation in mathematics and in the sciences.)

My point is that it's a mistake to think of a PhD as a sort of next step after a BS or MS degree, like advancing further in some academic straight line. A PhD diploma is another animal entirely; it stands for a quite different kind of talent, which is orthogonal to one's ability to ace an examination. A lot of people who are extremely bright, with straight A^+ grades as undergraduates, never get a PhD. They're smart in a way that's different from "research smart." I think of my parents, for example: I don't believe either one of them would have been a good PhD candidate, although both were extremely intelligent.

It's extremely misleading to rank people on an IQ scale with the idea that the smarter they are, the more suitable they are for a PhD degree; that's not it at all. People have talents in different dimensions, and a talent for research might even have a *negative* correlation with the ability to tie your own shoes.

Consequently I've encountered several students who were enormously talented, yet challenged in the research dimension. One of them was Clark Crane, the subject of my story. He came to Stanford from the Air Force Academy, with Graduate Record Exam scores in the 99th percentile. He was very quick, very friendly, and also instilled with military discipline. He came to me and said, in essence, "I'd like to do research with you. Teach me how to do research. I've done lots of preparation and passed all my exams. Now all I have to do is be creative, so tell me how to be creative. I'll do it. Anything you say, sir, I will do." He was a nice guy, and I soon was able to get him to call me "Don."

I started his apprenticeship by giving him mini-research problems to tackle. I mean, I asked him to answer some questions that had never been answered before, but which I suspected could be resolved after thinking about them seriously for a week or so. One by one, I'd give him a little problem like that, and a week later he'd come back either with a solution or with some partial progress. "Great," I thought, "these lessons are working."

I kept giving him problems that were a little bit harder, and a little bit harder still, and suddenly this approach clicked: About six months later, he came to me with a brand new idea, something I hadn't asked him anything about, something that definitely advanced the state of *The Art of Computer Programming*. He added some more ideas in the same vein and wrote a very fine PhD thesis. I recall seeing textbooks in Norway in the 70s that featured his work, discussing "Crane trees" named after him, because he'd invented this elegant new concept.

I counted this experience as a victory for being able to teach a student how to do research. But it was more like teaching a dog to stand up on its hind legs; research wasn't really part of Clark's nature, not a gut thing with him. It was something that he was sort of being forced to do by the system.

He got a job as an assistant professor at UCSD, and moved down there with his wife. But when he found out that he couldn't really sustain research with the big shots at La Jolla, I think he began to feel unhappy. He was a good teacher, but I don't think he was comfortable working with the senior professors. After a year of teaching he decided to go to medical school and get an MD in addition to his PhD. His new goal was to use his computer skills to improve medical care. Six years after his graduation from Stanford, I wrote a letter to "Clark Crane, M.D." at a hospital in San Diego, answering a question that he'd asked about recent experiments with interactive cable TV; he was interested in new ways to teach doctors about programming.

Suddenly however I learned from mutual friends that his marriage had broken up. That was a big surprise to me, because I'd met his wife and thought of them as a nice couple, with two small children. I have no idea what led to the breakup, but afterward he got very despondent and began to drink. I was told that he had access to pure alcohol in the hospital where he worked.

And, alas, he sort of went out of his mind. For several years Jill and I would occasionally get phone calls in the middle of the night: Clark was calling, wanting to talk to us and tell us how much he loved us. He would repeat that refrain over and over, with classical music playing in the background so loudly that we could hear it plainly. We learned that he was also making similar calls to the Air Force Academy, his alma mater. He must have become a textbook case of some sort of mania. We knew he was a Lutheran, so we tried to get him some help through his pastor in San Diego. Sometimes he would be OK for a while, and then he would relapse again. He died at age 41, about five years after his marriage had broken up. At the end I suspect that he was unable to think a logical thought whatsoever.

He was certainly naïve in the world, and if he hadn't had that access to the liquor cabinet he might very well have gotten through it all. But he had this easy way to drink himself into oblivion for a while. And I think that ruined his mind. I don't know if there were any other kind of drugs involved, but I certainly know that alcohol was a factor.

The brilliant achievements in his thesis remain. Although new methods have been discovered, his ideas about balanced trees and so-called "leftist trees" will probably always be noteworthy. Yet I can't help wondering whether I should have advised him not to strive for a PhD in the first place. He gave excellent lectures; should I have steered him toward a teaching career? He was one of my very first students, and I really had no good reason to deny his dream to do research. Unfortunately he had decided in advance what his life should be, without understanding his own strengths.

DK: Have you seen the movie called *Tunes of Glory*, with Alec Guinness and John Mills? Your student's story reminds me of it.

DEK: Well, that movie has some common elements, like the military discipline, the drunkenness, and a person's inability to live up to his own expectations. Still I think Clark's story was quite different.

Thank goodness there were 27 stories with happy endings, in addition to this one exceptionally sad tale.

DK: Did you ever do research with undergraduate students?

DEK: Yes, a little, but I'm not sure exactly what you mean. In the spring of 1987 I led a project with nine undergrads working on the preliminary stages of what became *The Stanford GraphBase*. We would meet as a group every Tuesday night for several hours; then they would work on their own, gathering data and writing literate programs.

There was another case where three undergraduates came to me and said, "We want to take a reading course with you. We want to read Volume 2 of *The Art of Computer Programming*, and it's not taught in any other classes, so please meet with us once a week." That worked out nicely too.

I had dreams of maybe going to one of the Stanford Overseas campuses and working with undergrads there. But that never panned out, I never had the time to do it.

DK: Do you miss teaching, now that you've been retired for several years?

DEK: Yes indeed, but I have the Computer Musings to keep me happy. The next of these will be coming up in two or three weeks.

As you know, I retired early so that I could work essentially full time on completing *The Art of Computer Programming* and other book projects. Unofficially I retired at age 53, at the beginning of 1990, followed by two years' leave of absence; officially I retired at age 55.

A key part of those retirement plans was an arrangement by which I could give public lectures that would be offered to the community free of charge, on any subjects that I thought would be worth talking about. To quote my webpage: "No tuition is charged, no attendance is taken, no credit is given. Each talk is independent of the others, and pitched at an audience of non-specialists. Sometimes I talk about difficult technical issues, but I try to minimize the jargon and complications by stressing the motivation and the paradigms and the high-level picture, without sweeping the details entirely under the rug."

I launched that series of talks in January of 1992, and gave five "musings" during the first half of that year. Altogether there have been about two dozen up till now, sometimes occurring only two weeks apart, although the schedule is quite irregular. There's been only one so far in 1996, but two more are planned.

In general I like to talk about whatever I've learned recently that I think other people will also enjoy hearing about. Often the topic is something that updates a topic in *The Art of Computer Programming*. I find that the act of explaining it to an audience almost always makes me understand it much better myself, thereby enhancing the material I've been writing.

In Japan, it looks like I'll be giving eight different lectures in five different cities. Three of those lectures will be about typography and/or calligraphy. One of my talks at Tohoku University will be a warmup for the Computer Musing that I'll be giving at Stanford in December.

DK: Were these talks arranged by the prize committee?

DEK: No, just the first two. For the others, I wrote to people that I knew from previous correspondence, and said "If you want me to talk, I'll be available; we can try to work something out." That way I'll get to connect faces to places.

By the way, speaking of the Kyoto prize, my first talk is nontechnical, to be given at the plenary session. I'm supposed to say something that every housewife in Japan would appreciate.

DK: I read it.

DEK: Already? Good! I think we should probably use it as the first chapter of the *Digital Typography* book, just to have a gentle introduction to the whole topic. I don't think it repeats too much stuff that's in the other chapters. The only glitch is that I won't have the illustrations ready for you until I get back.

DK: What do you think about the Web? In terms of acquiring knowledge or getting information it seems to me there is nothing there that I can't find in a library, although I grant that the Web is more convenient.

DEK: No, I disagree. The Web is completely different from a traditional library, because people are able to search it by content instead of just by author or title. At the moment, very few books are available in electronic form. But some day, when the whole library is electronic, when all of the world's great books have been put online, I think we'll have powerful database searching methods and it will be a completely new ball game.

Indexes to content used to be available for only a few books, like the Bible and the works of Shakespeare and Chaucer. A person could become an expert on an author like Voltaire, say, only by spending a lifetime reading the works and compiling their own private index. When Voltaire's works go electronic, anybody will be able to find what's inside.

Just to give you a simple example: Late in January, I learned HTML, the low-level language by which webpages are specified. Then during February I set up a collection of "home pages," telling about various aspects of my life. For example, there's a page about frequently asked questions, a page about why I no longer use email, a page about errata to my books, and so on. A minute ago I quoted from the page about Computer Musings. (In fact, I started with 28 webpages, a perfect number!)

Well, on one page I put the names of people whose address I don't know, or people whose middle names I don't know, and I just said, "If anybody knows these people, please tell me." Already I've gotten many, many replies to these queries; it's amazing. I'm getting letters that say, "a colleague noticed my name on this webpage, so I know that you wanted to reach me." Yesterday a man told me that one of the people I listed had been his college teacher.

I don't think these people found my list of names by first going to my home pages and exploring from there. In most cases I bet they found it after searching by content, saying, "What webpages have the following name on it?" For example, everybody looks for their own name, to see whoever might have mentioned them or to discover if somebody else happens to have the same name as they do. Then they'll stumble across my page, which they never would have done in a library.

Now people have a way to say, "Tell me everything in this huge mass of information that includes the following words in it." That's brand new, and it's fantastic.

DK: I like to browse in a library almost at random, finding things by serendipity.

DEK: You can still have serendipity in the Web too. I'm not saying that libraries are obsolete; I'm saying that we now have a great enhancement of what we had before. The Web takes us to a whole new level.

I'm also beginning to notice that the Web is allowing many people to find others who share their special interests. The world is composed of thousands of "subcultures," by which I mean groups of people who collect certain things or who are fans of certain authors or who play unusual games or who build crazy machines, etc. Most of these subcultures consist of fewer than a hundred people, and they previously had no good way to communicate. Now, with the Web, they discover each other.

DK: There's an overabundance of information coming to us from the Web. What do you think of this aspect?

DEK: Yes, it's more fun to discover information when it's underabundant; then you feel like you've done something. By contrast, when it's overabundant, you feel guilty if you don't succeed, instead of proud if you do. As the Web grows, we'll have to learn new ways to discipline ourselves when we search for new information.

DK: On our way to lunch, you spoke about being angry last week while working on a problem. I'd like to ask you about that, because it's hard for me to imagine you getting angry.

DEK: I get impatient when an unexpected obstacle arises. Last week while reading the ACM *Journal* I learned that one of the famous papers from the 1970s that I'm citing in *The Art of Computer Programming* contains an error. But nobody had ever corrected the error. So I had to put everything else on hold, and work out a way to patch the erroneous proof. I couldn't quote an incorrect result.

Well, I sat there hour after hour, saying "Gol-darn it, this blankety-blank formula isn't simplifying." I couldn't find a short cut, and that made me madder and madder. Of course I should have remained calm, since that would have been conducive to solving the problem. Finally, thank goodness, I did succeed.*

Maybe my North-European ancestry has something to do with the fact that I don't get angry very often. But computers can make me mad too. One of my pet peeves occurs when a failure of some sort is accompanied by beautiful graphics. Designers should restrain themselves unless they are sure that the user is happy.

DK: What do you mean?

DEK: I don't know if I can explain it satisfactorily, but I'll try. Ordinarily, when a computer program is working properly, I love it if its developers have enhanced it with some kind of cute animation or some special graphic effect. But when the machine crashes or fails to do the right thing, every cute icon or beautiful graphic makes me much more angry than in the old days when there were no graphical interfaces at all.

Incidentally, I did get extremely angry at an ATM machine the first time that I ever tried to use one, but the reason was entirely different. When ATMs were brand new and their software was pretty pathetic, I got my first bank card on a Friday. On the next day, Saturday, I received a substantial royalty check, and I wanted to get two more days' worth of interest. The bank was closed, but I thought, "Aha, I can use my new bank card, this will be great."

OK, I put the card in the slot, and the machine asked me to type something or other. Unfortunately I didn't type it exactly right — so the machine ate the card! It said "I'm sorry, come back on Monday to retrieve your card." [laughs]

Well at this point I was filled with rage. How dare the computer tell me this and hold on to my card, after I had been trying my best to follow its instructions? I looked everywhere on that thing for a sign that said "punch here." I had to take my frustration out on something. I was incensed that that stupid machine would not trust me, after I'd simply made an innocent mistake. Furthermore I'd wasted a lot of time in order to go out in my car and get to the machine.

So I let another fifteen years go by before I tried to use an ATM machine again.

DK: [laughs] It's hard to imagine you angry, because I can see you annoyed; I can see you upset, but I always imagine you walking away from, let's say, "angry situations." Your attitude seems to be "I'm not going to waste my time by getting angry."

---

* See exercise 5.3.3–24 in the second edition of *Sorting and Searching* (1998).

DEK: Well, that's the usual mode, but I have to take out aggressions somehow, too. Maybe that's why I play the organ.

DK: How often do you play the organ?

DEK: I haven't played it now for about two weeks, three weeks. I played piano last Sunday, though, for three hours. That was fun.

DK: That reminds me, I never asked you how you got started with organ playing.

DEK: I mentioned that my father had been an organist. For example, five years before I was born, he had played at the Chicago World's Fair. In fact, he eventually ended up purchasing an electronic organ for our home (but only after I'd gone off to college).

I took a year of organ lessons from my piano teacher when I was 12 years old, but never did anything more until I was 25. The organist at our church in Pasadena suddenly came down with a detached retina, in 1963, and I was asked to fill in for him for several months while he recovered. At that time several of the top organists in the country lived in the Pasadena area, so I got to hear fine music and was inspired to do a lot of practicing and to join the American Guild of Organists.

I've continued to play occasionally ever since 1963. For example, I played for the service when my son was baptized in 1965, because my father had once done the same for me.

During my year in Princeton [1968–1969] I took weekly lessons at Westminster Choir College, and I did the same during my year in Boston [1985–1986]. I've never gotten extremely good, but with practice I can play a few pieces fairly well.

The nicest thing is that opportunities to play on wonderful instruments keep arising, because the word has gotten out that I love organ music. When I visit another city, anywhere in the world, my host usually knows somebody to knows the local organ expert; so I often am invited to fool around. Fortunately I don't have to give a great performance, because I'm only a computer scientist after all. I can just relax and enjoy the thrill of making a well-designed organ sing. Often the churches are impressive too, from a musical standpoint, with great reverberation. And it's fun to climb up into the lofts in order to see behind the scenes.

Chapter 17

Conversations, 1996: Accidents, Planning, Naming

[Recorded 24 October 1996.]

DK: While we were driving to the restaurant, you were telling about the time when you broke your arm in a bike accident.

DEK: Right. It was in the early 60s; let's see, I can date it because I was working on chapter ten of *The Art of Computer Programming*. We were living in Sierra Madre at the time, a suburb of Pasadena. It was the summer of '64, and I had just gotten my Moulton bike — the bike with little wheels — which was later stolen. The bike was brand new then. We lived in a very hilly area, a few blocks from undeveloped land that extended all the way up to Mount Wilson.

On that particular day I went riding to try out my new bike. Coming down the hill, the bike started going faster and faster. I put on the brakes for the first time, and they didn't work! They had actually been mounted backwards: The brake was a piece of rubber held by a metallic sort of three-sided box, which was attached the wrong way. The motion of the bike is supposed to force the rubber into the box; but being mounted the other way, the rubber came right out, and I lost the brakes. There were no brakes at all! And I was going faster and faster downhill.

I've always had a tendency to panic when I'm out of control, when I'm going fast. If I'm skiing too fast I lose my head. So I didn't think of jumping off the bike. I just thought, "The brake isn't working, the brakes are gone, so I'll try to turn the corner and do something after turning." The option of getting off the bike, before it started going too fast, didn't occur to me until after I was going really fast.

Fortunately there were no cars coming. I jumped the curb, smashed up on some concrete, and fell hard on somebody's driveway. The bike was badly damaged and my right wrist was broken. So I had to be a lefty for awhile.

That turned out to be, as these things are, a blessing in disguise. The fracture was quite unusual, so my doctor thought that I should see a specialist, an orthopedist. Thus I met a doctor who really loved bones, Dr. Burschinger, who had done his training at County Hospital in Los Angeles; at that hospital he saw more smashed bones from motorcycle accidents and so on than any normal doctor would see in a lifetime. He was fascinated by my broken wrist, and told me that I had "Barton's fracture." He said it was rare— "You see these in textbooks" — and he wanted a picture of it for his files. But the only way to fix it, he explained, was non-obvious: to twist the wrist in a certain way, like this [demonstrates]. And he had to put it in a cast, twisted into this awkward position, because it involved the wrist bones, which are very complicated. He really knew his stuff and really loved his work; and he loved doing it well, too.

The main reason my accident turned out to be a blessing was that Dr. Burschinger also knew a lot of other really good doctors. At the time, Jill and I had been having trouble having children. He recommended a gynecologist to us, and then we had our kids in '65 and '66. Still later, when I had ulcers in '67, the gynecologist recommended a very good gastroenterologist; and that's the doctor who recommended our doctor up in Menlo Park when we came to Stanford. So we found out that doctors are like everybody else, some are better than others. Not all of them get A^+ in their college courses; some of them are really B students and maybe C. But the good ones seem to know each other, so it was nice to get into that network. And I did that through the broken arm.

While my arm was broken, I had to write left-handed. My left-handed handwriting is terrible, but I did write some sections of *The Art of Computer Programming*, which of course I was working on during every spare minute. (When I start revising that part of the manuscript, I'm going to have fun puzzling out my handwriting from those days; it will be pretty weird.) My sister Paula was visiting us that summer, and her visit led to a sort of bonding experience: I needed her to help me with proofreading, and also with writing, since I couldn't write very fast. So she began to help me on technical work. You know how brothers and sisters usually don't talk to each other about technical things; they usually stick to general conversation, or maybe play games against each other. Now, for the first time, we sort of became colleagues, and she turned out to be a wonderfully intelligent helper during that month while I was disabled and couldn't write. She had no experience with computers or anything, but she picked up the ideas very quickly and we got to know each other a lot better.

This wasn't my first time wearing a cast. I'd had a lot of broken bones when I was young, because I was tall and grew fast; my bones weren't very strong. I broke my arm once when I was on a trampoline trying to do a flip, trying to flip over: Yikes, I'd jumped badly and was flipping just halfway over, falling with my head straight down! I must have decided that, instead of breaking my neck, I'd break my arm instead. So I stuck out my arm and it got broken, and my arm was in a cast for quite awhile during seventh grade.

The first broken bone I'd had was actually, I think, when I was two years old. I fell off the slide in a park. You know how kids are supposed to climb up the steps and slide down a long, sloping slide. Well, for some reason I seemed to think you could also try to slide down the steps instead: be faster, more fun. Broke my collarbone when I was two.

But the worst one was when sledding at Christmas time. I think it was seventh grade, again. There's a great big hill in Milwaukee next to the river bank, near the TV station. It's a pretty flat area, but the Milwaukee River comes through and carves out a little valley, making a nice hill where you could take your sled down. My mom and dad and Paula and I went out, and they showed me how to steer the sled. There was a little crossbar in the front, and if you turned it sharply it was supposed to bend the rails enough to turn you to the left or the right. OK, I took off and got going pretty fast. At the foot of the hill there was a tree, and I was going right towards that tree. I steered, but the sled didn't turn! Again I didn't think of jumping off. All I could think was, "It's supposed to turn, it's supposed to work," so I kept trying to steer the sled but it keep going straight. I finally smashed right into the tree and broke my leg. The leg didn't heal for a long time; it was some kind of a strange fracture, and my thigh got all swollen up.

So as you can see I had a long history of broken bones when I was young. Luckily, none lately! [laughs]

DK: In the car while driving here, we were also talking about all the major decisions that you had to make in 1967, like choosing the university where you'd teach.

DEK: Yes, right. I think I mentioned that I wrote to Bob Floyd, asking him where he would like to end up.

The two of us decided to come to Stanford, as you know. At a party last Sunday I met a man who said he'd always wanted to say hello, because he was on Stanford's advisory board, the committee that's the last hurdle before the trustees sign off on a new appointment. He said that the board had read my papers very carefully, and it looked like a good risk to appoint me as full professor in spite of my youth (I was 29). Finally I met him now, almost thirty years later.

I've also met a man who was on Harvard's faculty appointment board at the same time, and he told me later that he thought it was a good case, too. The story about how I met him is more interesting: It happened during 1986, the year we lived in Boston.

I started to work on the book *3 : 16* that year, and was in the process of inviting the calligraphers who would do the illustrations. One of the invitees, Jean Evans, lived in the Boston area; we knew her a little bit through mutual friends in the type design world. She's designed some fonts and worked with Bitstream, worked with Matthew Carter. In fact, he's the one who recommended her as being a real good person to invite for the book. After I wrote to her, she told me she'd heard that I played the piano, and she said that her husband played the clarinet. So she asked Jill and me to come to their house and have an evening of piano, clarinet, and dinner.

We went to meet them, and it turned out that they lived just two blocks from Harvard Square. I learned that her husband was a professor at Harvard, not just a clarinet player. He was in the chemistry department, and he'd been on the faculty committee that had offered me a professorship fifteen years earlier; no, I guess it was almost twenty years earlier. They served us a great meal. We talked about a variety of things, but there were a couple of references to a time that they'd been in Sweden. Well, it turned out that he was Bill Lipscomb, the 1976 Nobel laureate in chemistry! We had gone to see them because his wife was such a great calligrapher; later we learned that she was also a former tennis champion, though he's the one who was in the newspapers more often. He was a good clarinet player, too.

At the end of the meal we went back to playing, because we'd played only short time before dinner. I put a table fork in my pocket — so that I could use it again for dessert — and moved over to the piano. That night when we got back to our apartment, I noticed that I still had their fork in my pocket. We called them the next morning and said, "Next time you invite the Knuths, be sure to count the silverware."

Anyway, going back to deciding where to teach, offers came in from Berkeley, Harvard, Stanford, and Caltech. Stanford was the winner for several reasons: First and foremost — I told you that I didn't want to move twice, so I wanted to resolve the issue of location once and for all — one of the big reasons was being able to live right on campus, within biking distance. I knew that by coming here I'd never have to commute, the rest of my life. Forty years of not commuting meant a lot to me.

Living on the Stanford campus also meant that we could be close to San Francisco, close to culture. We didn't actually want to live in the city itself, because life in a big city can be hectic.

By the way, I had declined feelers from Cornell, which is more remote from large cities, because we wanted to live in a place where people would come and visit us instead of us having to go to them; we expected to save a lot of time just by being in an accessible place. (I didn't realize that there would also be visitors coming by that you sort of have to take time off to see, what Mike Flynn calls the Visiting Polish Professor syndrome: Every week there is somebody who's going to be here only one time in his life, and you shouldn't miss any of them, so you're always interrupting your schedule.) We also figured that everybody important in computer science would be visiting Stanford regularly, maybe coming by once every three years or so.

The point was that, at Stanford, I got to meet almost everybody without having to travel myself. And that has worked well for me. Also, the shopping was good. The schools were good. So we liked Stanford because of its location, location, and location.

And to top things off, Stanford also had the best computer science department of any place in the world, and I wanted to be part of this group. At Harvard, I would have had to work hard trying to argue for the importance of computer science, in order to build up their relatively small faculty, which did not have much credibility with Harvard's mathematicians and physicists at that time.

DK: Another member of the Stanford community, the novelist Albert Guerard, once said that he found life on campus despite all its advantages was also limiting. I thought he felt the isolation didn't help his work as a novelist or literary critic.

DEK: Well, novelists sort of have to live an awful life, so they can describe awful parts of the world, right? I mean, that's a paradox, but they have to be like Hemingway or something. I don't have to write bedroom scenes or crime scenes very often.

DK: Anyway, you were talking about the group that was present at the time when you made the decision to come to Stanford.

DEK: Yes, George Forsythe was the great leader, the great visionary. He sought out people who had a clear idea what computer science could be, and I think he's really the founding father of computer science. He also took care of nitty gritty. I mean, he would give faculty tips on how much chalk to bring to the classrooms. At every level, he was a model leader by his example and his attitude, and also just by giving advice all the time. His wisdom was wonderful; I mean, he was incredibly energetic, working day and night. That's why Stanford was tops from the very beginning.

We had three large groups. One was numerical analysis, which he'd been involved with; one was artificial intelligence, which was led by John McCarthy and Ed Feigenbaum; and then there was the software or programming languages group that included Jerry Feldman, Niklaus Wirth, and David Gries. The latter two had to leave because Floyd and I were coming — we were their replacements. Niklaus Wirth went to a professorship in Zurich, in his native Switzerland, and David Gries went to Cornell, where he's had a distinguished career: He's been chairman and so on there.

DK: Who were your main contacts in the field of computer science, before coming to Stanford?

DEK: I was good friends with Klaus [Wirth]. I'd visited him several times on our trips to Stanford and stayed at their house; likewise, he had come down to Caltech several times to visit us, and we'd talked about lots of stuff and wrote letters back and forth. He was one of my closest computer science friends in those days, besides Bob Floyd.

The others were Tony Hoare and Edsger Dijkstra, whom I met at conferences and had a lot of deep discussions with in the late 60s. In 1970 I got to know them really well, because all three of us were speaking at an international summer school that's held annually at the University of Newcastle upon Tyne. Incidentally, I went to the 25th reunion of that summer school two or three years ago.

I used to go to conferences in the 60s and knew most of the leading contributors, the people who published the most articles. I was editor of the programming languages department of two of ACM's publications, while at Caltech, and I was corresponding with lots and lots of people.

I don't know if I told you about my experiment: When I started to be a journal editor, I reviewed a certain paper and decided that it wasn't worth publishing. But I also thought it would be interesting as a calibration of reviewers. So I made 25 copies of it and I sent it out to 25 different people, to see what they would say. How many of them would believe that it should be published? How many wouldn't understand it at all?

I probably was being unethical when I did that; but, well, I'm admitting it now. I already had written a referee report to the author, and had given advice about how to revise and improve the paper. The only thing unethical I guess would be that I was wasting the time of

25 potential referees, not telling them the truth about the fact that I had already rejected the paper. Anyway, I got to know people's qualities that way; I could see who were going to be my good referees, and I understood some of their strengths and weaknesses. This experiment also enabled me to learn better techniques, because some of the referee reports were naturally better than my own. Others, well, I thought they were lousy; that too was to be expected. It's like doctors, and lawyers, and politicians: There are many levels of quality, and no filter has ever been invented that lets only the good people through. We've always got to figure out some way to cope with the mixture of talents in the world.

I was in correspondence with people from all over, but computer science was pretty small in those days and you could know everybody who was in the field.

DK: It wasn't referred to as computer science then, was it?

DEK: Well, in America that name caught on real quick. It didn't take hold everywhere else: Russians at that time called it cybernetics; the German name was *Informatik*. I don't recall the British view. In Norway, where I lived in '72, computer science was still called EDB, '*Elektronisk Databehandling*' — in other words, electronic data processing. In Denmark, it had the name *datalogi*, which was pretty good. Peter Naur put a lot of thought into that name. (Peter was another friend that I met in '67. You might recall that Jill and I encountered him in Trondheim during our trip to Norway in that year.) Peter invented the word '*datalogi*' and gave it a very precise definition; I've quoted his definition of data in the index to Volume 1.

Sweden had the best name for a computer, namely 'dator', D-A-T-O-R. Somebody in Sweden associated with one of the biggest newspapers in Stockholm said, "Look, Elektronisk Databehandling Maskin or EDB-Maskin is too much of a mouthful. Let's call it a Dator." The circulation of that paper was sufficiently strong that within a month everybody in Sweden knew what a dator was. Swedish is the only language in the world that has such a nice name; I like it because computers don't just deal with numbers, they deal with all kinds of data.

Anyway, computer science had a name that everybody knew in America, and that name prevailed because of sheer inertia. I like it more than the German *Informatik* or the equivalent French *informatique*; I'm not quite comfortable with those terms because they talk about the stuff that computers deal with but not about the dealing. The basic thing about algorithms is that they need data to work on, information to work on, but computer science stands for more than that. It's not just

information; information sounds to me a lot more like library studies —
you know, classifying information, but not actually changing information
or processing data. So I like the term computing. Another name like
"algorithmic science" would be even better, but too much to hope for.

There are lots of fields whose name is wrong, like "context-free languages" in linguistics. Well, I guess context-free languages are languages,
but they certainly have context. I mean, it's really not a good name, on
intuitive grounds or anything else: It's a weird oxymoron for a concept
that involves a certain kind of context, yet calls itself context-free! What
is a beginner to think? (Roughly speaking, if you have a left parenthesis
in a context-free language, then you've got to have a matching right
parenthesis. Everything between them is in the context of those parentheses. Yet we call this "context-free," because there's another kind of
grammar called "context-sensitive" in which context can be prominent
to an extreme degree.)

How did the term 'context-free' become standard? In the early 1960s
there were four or five different, competing names for the same concept,
only one of which was understood by everybody. If you said "context-
free language," everybody knew what you meant, in spite of the fact that
the term was conceptually bad. If you used one of the other names, some
people wouldn't catch on; you'd also have to say "which, by the way,
is what other people call a context-free language." The inappropriate
name therefore caught on by default, because it took less explanation.
Perhaps 'computer science' won out for similar reasons.

Eventually a name becomes a label that's detached from its meaning.
For example, people have forgotten what the word 'mathematics' meant
when that term was first coined. Etymologically speaking, what did
those syllables actually signify, when they were originally put together?
The ancient Greek meaning (namely, "science" or "knowledge") is irrelevant to us today, because everybody has grown up associating the word
'mathematics' with its contemporary significance (namely, the study of
relationships between quantities).

Actually Andy Gleason of Harvard's math department introduced
my favorite definition, a few years ago: "Mathematics is the science of
patterns."

DK: Since we're talking about terminology, were you happy with the
designation of 'artificial intelligence', when it took hold?

DEK: I never thought about that. I sometimes think facetiously that
it should be renamed 'superficial intelligence' because, well, we have to
discuss what 'intelligence' really means. By now we've gotten computers

to do everything that people normally say requires thinking, but we've made almost no advances to emulate the things that people do *without* thinking. Much remains to be done.

I believe that a big part of intelligence is what we do subconsciously—what we do without planning, without mental effort. But I don't really pretend to know much about intelligence.

The main thing is that a rose would smell as sweet by any other name, and so we just have to have a label for things. I try to help get good names going, if it's still early enough that I might have an influence. I've written lots of letters to people saying, "Wouldn't it be better to think of another name, or to use such-and-such? There's a possible conflict with so-and-so. Let's choose a good term while we can."

But once the battle is lost, I don't go on trying to fight it again. Just now I'm preparing new editions of *The Art of Computer Programming*, and I'm changing several words that were used in the previous editions, because I know that the old words are no longer current. The bad guys won, but they've won; I conform to the will of the majority.

DK: Can you give me a couple of examples, one where you won, one where you lost?

DEK: Well, I might be winning the battle of the heap and the battle of the multiset.

Let's consider heaps first. An important data structure was invented in 1963 by a man named Williams in England; he called it a heap. His concept of heap had a precise mathematical meaning, as a one-dimensional array of numbers: The value in position k is always less than or equal to the values in positions $2k$ and $2k + 1$, whenever those values don't lie outside the bounds of the array. For example, if there are eight elements in the array, we have

$$x_1 \leq x_2, \quad x_1 \leq x_3, \quad x_2 \leq x_4, \quad x_2 \leq x_5, \quad x_3 \leq x_6, \quad x_3 \leq x_7, \quad x_4 \leq x_8.$$

It follows, for example, that the first number in the heap is the smallest.

Williams showed how to use heaps to sort numbers into order, and that heaps have many other uses as well. Furthermore, 'heap' was a nice, short word; naturally I adopted it when I wrote about *Sorting and Searching*.

But in the middle 70s some other computer scientists, who had never heard of Williams's heaps, decided to use that same word to stand for what my friends and I had always been calling a 'pool'—an area of computer memory that was sort of free for sharing in variable-size blocks. My book on *Fundamental Algorithms* described how to take things from the pool, reserve them, use them, and maybe restore them to the pool again afterwards. Alas, for some reason these other people started calling *that* the 'heap'. Maybe it makes some sense; if you live on a farm, you know, maybe you don't go near the water very often, you might think of the shared working area as a heap of stuff instead of a pool. But anyway, the latecomers didn't know that the word 'heap' was already used in hundreds of papers about another data structure, and there was a conflict.

I looked recently at several dozen dictionaries of computer science, and only two of them mention 'heap' in that other sense now. But there was a wave of papers in the late 70s that made me begin to worry that I couldn't use 'heap' any more, because somebody else would unknowingly spoil this perfectly nice concept.

Another case in which I think I've picked the winning horse — I don't really look at this as a personal triumph; what I mean is that standard terminology is moving in a direction that pleases me — is the word 'multiset'. I knew for a long time, and certainly it became clearer and clearer as I was writing my books, that mathematicians needed a name for a concept that is like an ordinary set, except that its elements could be repeated more than once.

Consider, for instance, the set of three things, {dog, cat, rabbit}, together with another set of elements, {cat, mouse}. The traditional way to take the union of those two sets gives us just four elements, not five, namely {dog, cat, mouse, rabbit}, because all elements of a set are supposed to be different.

But in many parts of mathematics, and especially in computer science, you need the case where an element can be present twice, or any number of times. For example, what we now call the "multiset union" of those two sets is a five-element multiset: {dog, cat, cat, mouse, rabbit}. This way a cat gets in there twice.

That sounds like a very simple idea, and it's quite important in mathematics; it goes back, for instance, to one of the most fundamental questions, the roots of a polynomial equation. A quadratic equation has two roots, and an equation of the nth degree has n roots. The fundamental theorem of algebra, as it's called, says that every polynomial of degree n has n complex roots. But it doesn't always have n complex roots that are distinct; the n roots form a multiset, not always a set, because some of the roots can occur over and over again. Similarly, we often need to work with the multiset of prime factors of an integer, not the set of prime factors: 12 is 2 times 2 times 3.

Amazingly, there was no word for this concept, although people would speak informally of a "set with repeated elements." Not only was there no decent word; there was no notation for the multiset union of two multisets.

More and more people were becoming aware of the need for such a term and such a notation, and each of them was inventing a new name in the papers that they would write, leading to incompatible terminology.* I discussed this with my friend Dick de Bruijn, a professor from the Netherlands who I have to talk to you more about, because he's been a significant mentor; I want to dedicate my book of discrete-math papers to him. (I had a letter from him a couple of months ago, and he's certainly still very vigorous.) Anyway I asked his advice about the need for a good name, in 1968, and he wrote back saying "Let's call it a multiset," a new word that he had just coined. I liked it immediately, and included it in my book *Seminumerical Algorithms* (1969). I also tried to spread the word around, in letters to colleagues, and I think that it has been widely adopted by now in spite of the fact that many other terms had once been floated.

The only serious competitor, in some parts of the world, is the term 'bag'. I think that word is dying out, as a name for sets with repeated elements, but still I get surprised every year or so by seeing it again. I don't think I could ever be comfortable using that word in my books, partly because a bag is a container rather than a collection of elements, but mainly because it also sounds awful. I mean, it's a terrifically unaesthetic English word. (Think of "bag lady" and "biting the bag," etc.)

I expressed this opinion in some letters to my former student Lyle Ramshaw, and he wrote a very eloquent discussion in reply. But unfortunately he didn't like 'multiset', because it is three syllables long! He was writing a paper where he needed the concept quite often, and he needed other prefixes to go in front of it: He wanted to make compound words, like 'hypermultiset', so he wanted a one-syllable equivalent. Lyle did agree, however, that 'bag' was a loser.

So we went to Roget's *Thesaurus*, and I proposed a set of twenty words, although I said "I still think 'multiset' is the big winner." His choice, on the other hand, was 'suite', a sweet-sounding term that also has a good connotation. A suite is, like, different rooms or a collection of musical pieces that go together. Unfortunately for him, however, that proposal has a fatal flaw: French people could never live with it,

---

* *Note, 30 April 2011:* By strange coincidence, I now happen to be reading a long-forgotten paper by A. B. Kempe, "A memoir on the theory of mathematical form," *Philosophical Transactions* **177** (1886), 1–70, in which §45 proposes the term 'heap' for the multiset concept!

because they *already* use the word *suite* for 'set'! They would be left out in the cold if English mathematicians began to distinguish suites from sets. Lyle's choice would be quite satisfactory, leading to pleasant combinations like 'subsuite' and so on, except for that French connection.

Before finishing my story about 'multiset' I must tell you about Gian-Carlo Rota, a very prominent mathematician, called Gianco by his friends. Gianco is editor of *The Encyclopedia of Mathematics* and of several leading mathematics journals, and quite a wonderful book reviewer and critic. His reviews are full of poignant, sharp remarks about everything in mathematics. He proposed in the middle 60s to use the word 'list' for the multiset concept.

Well, computer science couldn't possibly live with that; I mean, a list is very basic for us and we all know what a list is. John McCarthy's LISP language was based on lists, and programmers have got lists all over the place. How could we let a mathematician tell us what a list is, after we'd already spent considerable time developing a completely different theory? So I wrote several letters to him and said "Look, you can't use 'list'; you are too influential a person. You gotta understand that this is going to cause endless problems if you do."

Rota had also written another book about a mathematical theory that's popularly called matroid theory — M-A-T-R-O-I-D, sort of analogous to the word 'matrix' — but he himself didn't like the word matroid at all, he had scrupulously avoided it in his book. Instead, he wrote about 'combinatorial geometries.' And in fact, his notion of a combinatorial geometry was more general than what we call a matroid; a matroid is equivalent to a nondegenerate combinatorial geometry.

In 1968 I wrote to Gianco about de Bruijn's term 'multiset', and he agreed to make a deal: He promised to use 'multiset' instead of 'list' in his papers, if I would promise not to use 'matroid' but to say 'combinatorial geometry' instead. Here we were, wheeling and dealing now; this is the way science happens, I'm told. And he lived up to his part of the bargain. No mathematician now misuses the word 'list', as far as I know. Furthermore, the ratio of people using 'multiset' to 'bag' is at least a thousand to one, and growing. I mean, this aspect of terminology is stabilizing in the right way.

But I'm going to renege on my part of the agreement, because I don't need to write about matroid theory until Volume 4. Meanwhile the rest of the world has completely jumped on the bandwagon to call the concept a matroid, and there's a million to one saying 'matroid' over 'combinatorial geometry'. Clearly I won't have to live up to my part of the agreement, because that would be stupid. The battle's lost and he would be the first to admit it. When I do write Volume 4, I'll say of course that a combinatorial geometry is a more general concept than a matroid — it's the nondegenerate case; but that's as far as I'll go.

OK, the terms 'heap' and 'multiset' are coming out to my liking. In what cases did I lose? Well, the terminological issue that has affected my books the most relates to a word that signifies a certain kind of opponent. When we're trying to prove that a computer algorithm is always going to be efficient, we have to imagine some opposing force that tries to make the algorithm run as slowly as possible.

For example, if I want to prove that my algorithm will always finish pretty fast, I have to explain to you what it's going to do in every circumstance. Going the other way, somebody who wants to prove that no algorithm can be fast must explain how to present serious obstacles to any possible algorithm.

That kind of opposing force is now called an adversary. I needed a name for it, when I first wrote Volume 3. And I decided to use the term 'oracle', because the Oracle of Delphi gave answers to questions that a pilgrim (or algorithm) might ask.

But later I realized that many computer scientists were using the term 'oracle' in quite another sense: An oracle would help you, not compete with you. If you wanted to know the answer to some question, you asked the oracle, and the oracle would reveal the truth. Think of having an oracular subroutine in your program; then you can say, "I have to do so-and-so much work, including so-and-so many times when I'll need to ask the oracle for help."

Therefore in the second printing of Volume 3 (1975), I changed the word from 'oracle' to 'demon'. But again I guessed wrong. Twenty more years have gone by, and theoretical computer scientists have definitely converged on the word 'adversary' for this concept. In the new edition that I'm preparing, Section 5.3.2 will speak only of adversaries, not of oracles or demons.

It's vital to have good names for the things we deal with. Whole cultures have realized the power of names; as you know, there often are strict taboos against using the name of God, because it's too sacred. Knowing somebody's name is thought to mean having power over them, in many parts of the world.

Names are also important when developing a software product. Before the product has a decent name, it doesn't jell; afterwards, it magically comes together. I noticed this effect very strongly when I chose the name TEX, and later when Bob Filman suggested the name META-FONT. A subtle, psychological effect changed my whole attitude to those programs. I don't know exactly why, but I do know that the names proved to be very powerful, from the moment they were chosen.

And the same thing happens in the world of computer science. I need good definitions and good terminology, or else my discussion is just wishy-washy. So I always try to choose a good name, and a good notation, whenever possible.

I also try to choose one that doesn't conflict with other names. The biologists carry this to extremes; they have huge, long words to name everything, usually based on Greek roots. Computer scientists like me try to realize the power of names, but we don't name things just for the joy of making up new words, we try to have systematic names that form some kind of a family, so that you can predict what another name would mean. Of course biologists and organic chemists do this too; I guess they have many more things to name, so they're forced to have long ones.

Furthermore, scientists try to have names that are intuitive, and therefore easy to remember. From a logical point of view, any name would do; but from a psychological point of view, only a few names actually work well.

We try not to proliferate names more than necessary, but when writing a paper we don't usually expect that a new term introduced in that paper is going to take over the world. Bad names usually get going because an author didn't think very hard before proposing it; a nonce word was created for convenience without realizing that it was going to be carried forward.

I was guilty of this bad tendency in one of my earliest and still best-known papers, where I decided arbitrarily to define something called L-R-of-k grammars, 'LR(k)'. Such grammars correspond to artificial languages that are especially efficient for computers to deal with. I never gave any thought to this terminology; I just wrote it down because my algorithm was reading characters from left to right, so that's LR; and it was looking k steps ahead, that was k. I called it LR(k) with no consideration whatsoever about whether there might be a better term. By now, however, maybe tens of thousands of papers have been written about aspects of LR(k).

I could have probably come up with a much better name; in fact, in 1967 I was already trying to rescue this terminology. My paper about LR(k) was written in the beginning of '65, and my lectures of '67 that I told you about, given in Denmark, introduced another theory called 'LL(k)'. I wanted to come up with some reason why L-R-of-k might have made sense, so I worked out a hokey way in which all four of the combinations LR, LL, RL, and RR could be technically meaningful. My introduction of 'LL(k)' tended to mask the arbitrariness of the earlier 'LR(k)'; but it still was pretty weak. Ex post facto, I might say, "Well, it's a good thing that LR was introduced in the early days," but that would be false. Anyway LR and LL are standard terminology now, not necessarily the best.

You don't need a new name for something unless it's going to be used over and over again, unless it's an important combination of concepts. When a field is pretty rich, its terms do tend to crystallize and get picked up by many other researchers. There's an art to it; you don't want to overdo or under-do naming.

In the social sciences, I don't like the 'isms' that identify philosophies with some label or other. They certainly degrade all the political arguments going on now, with the election coming; we have to know which 'isms' we subscribe to. I suppose those tags help a little bit to identify points of view; without any 'isms' at all, we probably wouldn't be able to organize our thoughts as well. But mostly I think political and philosophical labels are carried too far, so that we're losing track of real subject matter and just playing a game, with pointless points won by one side or another.

Chapter 18

Curriculum Vitæ

Biographical and Personal Information

Donald Ervin Knuth, born 10 January 1938 in Milwaukee, Wisconsin. Chinese name 高德纳 (pronounced G⁻aoDénà or Ko Tokuno).

Married to Nancy Jill Carter of Fostoria, Ohio, on 24 June 1961.

Children: John Martin (born 21 July 1965); Jennifer Sierra (born 12 December 1966).

Academic History

Case Institute of Technology, September 1956–June 1960; B.S., summa cum laude, June 1960; M.S. (by special vote of the faculty), June 1960.

California Institute of Technology, September 1960–June 1963; Ph.D. in Mathematics, June 1963. Thesis: *Finite Semifields and Projective Planes.*

Employment Record

Consultant, Burroughs Corp., Pasadena, California, 1960–1968.

Assistant Professor of Mathematics, California Institute of Technology, 1963–1966.

Associate Professor of Mathematics, California Institute of Technology, 1966–1968.

Professor of Computer Science, Stanford University, 1968–.

Staff Mathematician, Institute for Defense Analyses — Communications Research Division, 1968–1969.

Guest Professor of Mathematics, University of Oslo, 1972–1973.

Professor of Electrical Engineering (by courtesy), Stanford University, 1977–.

197

Fletcher Jones Professor of Computer Science, Stanford University, 1977–1989.
Professor of The Art of Computer Programming, Stanford University, 1990–1992.
Professor of The Art of Computer Programming, Emeritus, Stanford University, 1993–.
Visiting Professor in Computer Science, University of Oxford, 2002–2006, 2011–2014.
Honorary Distinguished Professor, Cardiff School of Computer Science and Informatics, 2011–2016.

Professional Societies

American Mathematical Society, 1961–.
Committee on Composition Technology, 1978–1981.
Association for Computing Machinery, 1959–.
Chairman, subcommittee on ALGOL, 1963–1964.
General technical achievement awards subcommittee, 1975–1979.
National Lecturer, 1966–1967.
Visiting Scientist, 1966–1967.
Mathematical Association of America, 1959–.
Society for Industrial and Applied Mathematics, 1965–.
American Guild of Organists, 1965–.

Honorary Societies

Pi Delta Epsilon, 1958–.
Tau Beta Pi, 1958–.
Blue Key, 1959–.
Sigma Xi, 1960–.
American Academy of Arts and Sciences (Class I, Section 5), 1973–.
National Academy of Sciences (Class III, Section 33), 1975–.
The British Computer Society, Distinguished Fellow, 1980–.
National Academy of Engineering, 1981–.
Institute of Electrical and Electronics Engineers, Honorary Member, 1982–.
l'Académie des Sciences, Paris, Associé Étranger, 1992–.
Det Norske Videnskaps-Akademi, Utenlandsk medlem, 1993–.
Bayerische Akademie der Wissenschaften, Korrespondierendes Mitglied der Mathematisch-naturwissenschaftlichen Klasse, 1998–.

Royal Society of London for Improving Natural Knowledge, Foreign Member, 2003–.

Pi Mu Epsilon, 2007–.

Russian Academy of Sciences [Российская Академия Наук], Foreign Member, 2008–.

Upsilon Pi Epsilon, 2011–.

Honorary Doctorates

Doctor of Science, honoris causa, Case Western Reserve University, 1980.

Doctor of Science, honoris causa, Luther College, 1985.

Doctor of Science, honoris causa, Lawrence University, 1985.

Doctor of Science, honoris causa, Muhlenberg College, 1986.

Doctor of Science, honoris causa, University of Pennsylvania, 1986.

Docteur honoris cause, Université Paris–Sud (Orsay), 1986.

Doctor of Science, honoris causa, University of Rochester, 1986.

Doctor of Science, honoris causa, State University of New York at Stony Brook, 1987.

Doctor of Science, honoris causa, Valparaiso University, 1988.

Doctor of Science, honoris causa, University of Oxford, 1988.

Doctor of Science, honoris causa, Brown University, 1988.

Doctor of Science, honoris causa, Grinnell College, 1989.

Doctor of Science, honoris causa, Dartmouth College, 1990.

Doctor of Science, honoris causa, Concordia University, Montréal, 1991.

Honorary Doctor of Technology, Royal Institute of Technology, Stockholm, 1991.

Почётный Доктор, Saint Petersburg University, 1992.

Doctor of Science, honoris causa, Adelphi University, 1993.

Docteur honoris causa, Université de Marne-la-Vallée, 1993.

Doctor Scientiæ Mathematicæ, honoris causa, Masaryk University, Brno, 1996.

Doctor of Science, honoris causa, Duke University, 1998.

Doctor of Science, honoris causa, St. Andrews University, Scotland, 1998.

Doctor of Letters, honoris causa, University of Waterloo, Canada, 2000.

Επίτιμος Διδάκτωρ, Athens University of Economics and Business, 2001.

Doctor of Science, honoris causa, Eberhard Karls Universität Tübingen, 2001.

Doctor Philosophiæ honoris causa, Universitetet i Oslo, 2002.

Doctor honoris causa in de Wetenschappen, Universiteit Antwerpen, 2003.

Doctor of Science, honoris causa, Harvard University, 2003.

Επίτιμος Διδάκτωρ, University of Macedonia, 2003.

Doctor of Science, honoris causa, Université de Montréal, 2004.

Honorary Doctor, National Academy of Sciences, Republic of Armenia, 2005.

Doktor der Wissenschaften, honoris causa, Eidgenössische Technische Hochschule Zürich, 2005.

Honorary Doctor of Letters, Concordia University Wisconsin, 2006.

Docteur honoris causa, Université Bordeaux I, 2007.

Doctor of Science, honoris causa, University of Glasgow, 2011.

Honors and Awards

Case Honor Key, 1959.

Woodrow Wilson Fellow, 1960.

National Science Foundation Fellow, 1960.

Grace Murray Hopper Award (first recipient), Association for Computing Machinery, 1971. ($1000)

John Simon Guggenheim Fellow, 1972–1973.

Alan M. Turing Award, Association for Computing Machinery, 1974. ($1000)

Lester R. Ford Award, Mathematical Association of America, 1975. ($100, for paper P63.)

California Institute of Technology Distinguished Alumni Award, 1978.

National Medal of Science, 1979.

W. Wallace McDowell Award, IEEE Computer Society, 1980. ($1000)

Priestley Award, Dickinson College, 1981. ($1000)

IEEE Computer Pioneer Award (charter recipient), 1982.

Golden Plate Award, American Academy of Achievement, 1985.

ACM SIGCSE Award, 1986. ($500)

ACM Software Systems Award, 1986.

Steele Prize for Expository Writing, American Mathematical Society, 1986. ($4000)

The New York Academy of Sciences Award, 1987. ($5000)

Benjamin Franklin Medal, Franklin Institute, Philadelphia, 1988.

J. D. Warnier Prize, 1989. ($3000)

Gold Medal Award, Case Alumni Association, 1990.

Computer Language productivity award, 1992. [Awarded for *Literate Programming*.]

Lester R. Ford Award, Mathematical Association of America, 1993. ($250, for paper P137.)

Best New Book: Computer Science, Association of American Publishers, 1994. [Awarded for *The Stanford GraphBase.*]

ACM Fellow (charter recipient), 1994.

Adelsköld Medal, Royal Swedish Academy of Sciences, 1994.

IEEE John von Neumann Medal, 1995. ($10,000)

Harvey Prize, Technion, 1995. ($35,000)

Memorial Medal, Mathematics and Physics Faculty, Charles University, Prague, 1996.

Cum Deo Award (charter recipient), Milwaukee Lutheran High School, 1996.

Kyoto Prize for Advanced Technology, The Inamori Foundation, 1996. (¥50,000,000)

Fellow of The Computer History Museum, 1998–.

Minor planet "(21656) Knuth" [http://sunkl.asu.cas.cz/~asteroid/planetky/21656/eng.htm], named in 2001.

Honorary Fellow, Magdalen College, Oxford University, 2005–.

Gold Commemorable Medal, State Engineering University of Armenia, 2006.

Gold medal from Yerevan State University, 2006.

Electronic Design's Engineering Hall of Fame, 2007.

SIAM Fellow (charter recipient), 2009.

Katayanagi Prize for Research Excellence, 2010 ($10,000).

ABACUS Award, Upsilon Pi Epsilon, 2011 ($5,000).

2010 Frontiers of Knowledge Award in Information and Communication Technologies, BBVA Foundation, 2011 (€400,000).

IET Faraday Medal, 2011.

Ausbildungs- und Beratungszentrum für Informatikunterricht Platinum Gold Medal of Eidgenössische Technische Hochschule Zürich for Computer Science and Computer Science Education, 2012.

Principal Invited Lectures

ACM National Convention, Syracuse, 1962; see paper Q5.

NATO Summer School, Denmark, 1967; see paper P48.

Britannica Scholar, Chicago, 1968.

International Symposium on Teaching of Programming, Newcastle upon Tyne, 1970.

International Congress of Mathematicians, Nice, 1970; see paper P44.

IFIP Congress, Ljubljana, 1971; see paper P46.

International Congress on Logic, Methodology, and Philosophy of Science, Bucharest, 1971; see paper P56.

Mathematical Association of America, San Francisco, 1974.

The Computer Science Lecture, Carnegie-Mellon University, 1974.

ACM National Convention, San Diego, 1974; see paper P68.

Symposium on Computational Systems, Monterrey, Mexico, 1975.

Chaire Aisenstadt, Université de Montréal, 1975; see *Mariages Stables*.

American Association for the Advancement of Science, Boston, 1976; see paper P82.

Gibbs Lecture (American Mathematical Society), Atlanta, 1978; see paper P91.

Gillies Lectures, University of Illinois, 1979.

Hitchcock Professor, University of California, 1979.

Ritt Lecture, Columbia University, 1980.

International Colloquium on Automata, Languages, and Programming, Epidaurus, Greece, 1985; see paper Q82.

4th SIAM Conference on Discrete Mathematics, San Francisco, 1988.

IFIP Congress, San Francisco, 1989 (keynote address); see paper P138.

Organick Memorial Lectures, University of Utah, 1990.

Donegall Lectures in Mathematics, Trinity College, Dublin, 1992.

International Symposium on Teaching of Programming, Newcastle upon Tyne (25th Anniversary Year), 1992.

Chaim Weizmann Memorial Lectures, Weizmann Institute of Science, 1992.

ACM–SIAM Symposium on Discrete Algorithms, Austin, 1993; see paper P127.

ATypI Congress, San Francisco, 1994.

Unicode Conference, San José, 1995.

Commemorative lecture for Fiftieth Anniversary of Mathematisch Centrum, Amsterdam, 1996.

Commemorative lecture for Kyoto Prize, Kyoto, 1996; see paper R59.

SIAM Annual Meeting, Stanford, 1997.

God and Computer Lectures, MIT, 1999; see *Things a Computer Scientist Rarely Talks About*.

Pascal Lectures, University of Waterloo, 2000.

Strachey Lecture, Oxford University, 2001.

Pi Mu Epsilon J. Sutherland Frame Lecture, San José, 2007.

BCS/IET Turing Lectures, 2011.

Dan E. Christie Lectures, Bowdoin College, 2011.

Editorial Boards

ACM Transactions on Algorithms, 2004–.
Acta Informatica, 1970–.
Advances in Mathematics, 1971–1979.
Applied Mathematics Letters, 1987–2000.
Communications of the ACM, 1966.
Combinatorica, 1985–1998.
Computers and Mathematics with Applications, 1973–2008.
Discrete Applied Mathematics, 1979.
Discrete and Computational Geometry, 1986–.
Discrete Mathematics, 1970–1978.
Electronic Journal of Combinatorics, 1994–.
Fibonacci Quarterly, 1964–1979.
Historia Mathematica, 1972–1979.
Human-Computer Interaction, 1985–1995.
IEEE Transactions on Software Engineering, 1975–1979.
Information Processing Letters, 1970–1979.
Japan Journal of Industrial and Applied Mathematics, 1997–.
Journal of Algorithms, 1979–2004.
Journal of Computer and Information Sciences, 1969–1979.
Journal of Computer and System Sciences, 1969–.
Journal of Computer Science and Technology, 1989–.
Journal of Experimental Algorithmics, 1996–.
Journal of Graph Algorithms and Applications, 1996–.
Journal of Graph Theory, 1975–1979.
Journal of the ACM, 1964–1967.
Journal on Statistical Planning and Inference, 1975–1979.
Mathematica Journal, 1990–.
The Mathematical Intelligencer, 1978–1979.
Random Structures & Algorithms, 1990–2007.
SIAM Journal on Computing, 1973–1979.
Software — Practice & Experience, 1979–2007.
Software Concepts & Tools, 1994–2000.
Structured Programming, 1989–1993.
Theory of Computing, 2004–.
Utilitas Mathematica, 1970–1972.

Publications

See Chapter 19 (books), Chapter 20 (papers), and Chapter 21 (alphabetical index of titles).

Patents

U.S. Patent 3422405 (with Roger E. Packard) Digital computers having an indirect field length operation (14 January 1969).

U.S. Patent 3454929 (with Donald P. Hynes) Computer edit system (8 July 1969).

U.S. Patent 3548174 Random number generator (15 December 1970).

U.S. Patent 3626167 (with LeRoy R. Guck, Lawrence G. Hanson) Scaling and number base converting method and apparatus (7 December 1971).

U.S. Patent 5305118 (with Stephen N. Schiller) Methods of controlling dot size in digital halftoning with multi-cell threshold arrays (19 April 1994). European patent 96108227.8-2202 (17 July 1996).

Ph.D. Students

Wayne Theodore Wilner: "Declarative Semantic Definition," 1971.

Clark Allan Crane: "Linear Lists and Priority Queues as Balanced Binary Trees," 1972.

Isu Fang: "FOLDS, A Declarative Formal Language Definition System," 1972.

Michael Lawrence Fredman: "Growth Properties of a Class of Recursively Defined Functions," 1972.

Vaughan Ronald Pratt: "Shellsort and Sorting Networks," 1972.

Richard Lee Sites: "Proving that Computer Programs Terminate Cleanly," 1974.

Gary Don Knott: "Deletion in Binary Storage Trees," 1975.

Edwin Hallowell Satterthwaite, Jr.: "Source Language Debugging Tools," 1975.

Robert Sedgewick: "Quicksort," 1975.

Leonidas Ioannis Guibas: "The Analysis of Hashing Algorithms," 1976.

Mark Robbin Brown: "The Analysis of a Practical and Nearly Optimal Priority Queue," 1977.

Richard Eric Sweet (joint supervision with Cordell Green): "Empirical Estimates of Program Entropy," 1977.

John Fredrick Reiser: "Analysis of Additive Random Number Generators," 1977.

Bernard Marcel Mont-Reynaud: "Hierarchical Properties of Flows, and the Determination of Inner Loops," 1977.

Luis Isidoro Trabb Pardo: "Set Representation and Set Intersection," 1978.

Lyle Harold Ramshaw: "Formalizing the Analysis of Algorithms," 1979.

Christopher John Van Wyk: "A Language for Typesetting Graphics," 1980.

Jeffrey Scott Vitter: "Analysis of Coalesced Hashing," 1980.

Michael Frederick Plass: "Optimal Pagination Techniques for Automatic Typesetting Systems," 1981.

Ignacio Andrés Zabala Salelles: "Interacting with Graphic Objects," 1982.

Daniel Hill Greene: "Labelled Formal Languages and Their Uses," 1983.

Franklin Mark Liang: "Word Hy-phen-a-tion by Com-put-er," 1983.

Andrei Zary Broder: "Weighted Random Mappings," 1985.

John Douglas Hobby: "Digitized Brush Trajectories," 1985.

Scott Edward Kim: "Viewpoint: Toward a Computer for Visual Thinkers," 1987.

Pang-Chieh Chen: "Heuristic Sampling in Backtrack Trees," 1989.

Ramsey Wadi Haddad: "Triangularization: A Two-Processor Scheduling Problem," 1990.

Tomás Feder: "Stable Networks and Product Graphs," 1991.

Addendum

The webpage

http://www-cs-faculty.stanford.edu/~knuth/vita.html

contains further information about published biographical information, audio recordings, and video recordings, as well as other developments that occurred after the listing above was prepared in the spring of 2011.

Chapter 19

Books and their Translations

The Art of Computer Programming

- *Fundamental Algorithms*, Volume 1 of *The Art of Computer Programming.*

First edition. (Reading, Massachusetts: Addison–Wesley, 1968), xxii + 634 pages.

Second edition, completely revised. (Reading, Massachusetts: Addison–Wesley, 1973), xxii + 634 pages.

Romanian translation by Adrian Davidoviciu and Adrian Petrescu, edited by Smaranda Dimitriu and Paul Zamfirescu, *Tratat de programarea calculatoarelor*, Volumul 1, *Algoritmi fundamentali* (Bucharest: Editura tehnică, 1974), 676 pages.

Russian translation by Галина П. Бабенко and Ю. М. Баяковский, edited by К. И. Бабенко and В. С. Штаркман, *Искусство программирования для ЭВМ*, Том 1: *Основные алгоритмы* (Moscow: Mir, 1976), 735 pages.

Japanese translation, under direction of 島内剛一 [Takakazu Simauti], in two volumes: Chapter 1, by 広瀬健 [Ken Hirose], 基本算法 / 基礎概念 [*Kihon Sampō / Kiso Gainen*] (Tokyo: Saiensu-Sha, 1978), 22+331 pages; Chapter 2, by 米田信夫 [Nobuo Yoneda] and 筧捷彦 [Katsuhiko Kakehi], 基本算法 / 情報構造 [*Kihon Sampō/ Jōhō Kōzō*] (Tokyo: Saiensu-Sha, 1978), 8 + 373 pages.

Chinese translation by 管纪文 [Guan JiWen] and 苏运霖 [Su Yunlin], 计算机程序设计技巧 [*Ji Suan Ji Cheng Xu She Ji Ji Qiao*], 第一卷 [Di 1 Juan], 基本算法 [*Ji Ben Suan Fa*] (Beijing: Defense Industry Publishing, 1980), 14 + 573 pages.

Spanish translation by Michel Antscherl Harlange and Joan Lluis i Biset, under direction of Ramón Puigjaner i Trepat, *El arte de programar ordenadores*, Volumen 1: *Algoritmos fundamentales* (Barcelona: Editorial Reverté, 1980), xxiii + 672 pages.

207

Indian Student Edition, with an introduction by P. C. P. Bhatt (New Delhi: Narosa Publishing House, 1985).

Hungarian translation by András Gyárfás, G. Zoltán Szabó, László Székely, and Tamás Turán, under direction of Miklós Simonovits, *A számítógép-programozás művészete* 1. *Alapvető algoritmusok* (Budapest: Műszaki Könyvkiadó, 1987), 654 pages.

Third edition, completely revised. (Reading, Massachusetts: Addison–Wesley, 1997), originally xx + 650 pages; xx + 652 pages since 2011.

Russian translation by С. Г. Тригуб, Ю. Г. Гордиенко [Гордієнко], and И. В. Красиков, edited by С. Н. Тригуб, under direction of Ю. В. Козаченко, *Искусство программирования*, Том 1: *Основные алгоритмы* (Moscow: Vil'iams, 2000), 713 pages.

Romanian translation by Mihaela Târpa, *Arta programării calculatoarelor*, Volumul 1, *Algoritmi fundamentali* (Bucharest: Editura Teora, 2002), 616 pages.

Chinese translation by 苏运霖 [Su Yunlin], 计算机程序设计艺术 [*Jisuanji Chengxu Sheji Yishu*], 第1卷 [Di 1 Juan], 基本算法 [*Jiben Suanfa*] (Beijing: National Defense Industry Press, 2002), xx + 625 pages.

Polish translation by Grzegorz Jakacki, *Sztuka programowania*, Tom 1: *Algorytmy podstawowe* (Warsaw: Wydawnictwa Naukowo-Techniczne, 2002), xxiv + 679 pages.

Japanese translation by 青木孝 [Takashi Aoki], 筧一彦 [Kazuhiko Kakehi], 鈴木健一 [Ken-Ichi Suzuki], and 長尾高弘 [Takahiro Nagao], supervised by 有澤誠 [Makoto Arisawa] and 和田英一 [Eiiti Wada] (Tokyo: ASCII Corporation, 2004), xxii + 632 pages.

Korean translation by 류광 [Ryu Gwang], 컴퓨터 프로그래밍의 예술 [*Keompyuteo peurogeuraemingui yesul*], 1: 기초 알고리즘 [*Gicho algorijeum*] (Seoul: Hanbit Media, 2006), 793 pages.

Czech translation by David Krásenský, *Umění programování*, 1. díl, *Základní algoritmy* (Brno: Computer Press, 2008), xx + 649 pages.

German translation (Heidelberg: Springer), in preparation.

Macedonian translation (Skopje: Prosvetno Delo), in preparation.

MIX (Reading, Massachusetts: Addison–Wesley, 1971), 48 pages.

Volume 1, Fascicle 1: *MMIX: A RISC Computer for the New Millennium* (Upper Saddle River, New Jersey: Addison–Wesley, 2005), v + 134 pages.

Romanian translation by Ioan Bledea, *MMIX: Un calculator RISC pentru noul mileniu* (Bucharest: Editura Teora, 2005), ix + 149 pages.

Japanese translation by 青木孝 [Takashi Aoki], supervised by 有澤誠 [Makoto Arisawa] and 和田英一 [Eiiti Wada] (Tokyo: ASCII Corporation, 2006), vii + 134 pages.

Russian translation by Ю. Г. Гордиенко [Гордієнко], edited by С. Н. Тригуб, *MMIX — RISC-компьютер для нового тысячелетия* (Moscow: Vil'iams, 2007), 151 pages.

Polish translation by Grzegorz Jakacki, *MMIX — komputer na nowe tysiąclecie* (Warsaw: Wydawnictwa Naukowo-Techniczne, 2008), xii + 146 pages.

Hungarian translation by Péter Burcsi and Zoltán Csörnyei, under direction of Antal Iványi, *MMIX: RISC számítógép a következő évezredre* (Budapest: Antoncom Infokommunikációs, 2009), 168 pages.

- *Seminumerical Algorithms*, Volume 2 of *The Art of Computer Programming*.

First edition. (Reading, Massachusetts: Addison–Wesley, 1969), xii + 624 pages.

Russian translation by Галина П. Бабенко, Э. Г. Белага, and Л. В. Майоров, edited by К. И. Бабенко, *Искусство программирования для ЭВМ, Том 2: Получисленные алгоритмы* (Moscow: Mir, 1977), 724 pages.

Second edition, completely revised. (Reading, Massachusetts: Addison–Wesley, 1981), xiv + 689 pages.

Romanian translation by Florian Petrescu, Ioan Georgescu, and Rolanda Predescu, edited by Paul Zamfirescu, *Tratat de programarea calculatoarelor*, Volumul 2, *Algoritmi seminumerici* (Bucharest: Editura tehnică, 1983), 722 pages.

Japanese translation, under direction of 島内剛一 [Takakazu Simauti], in two volumes: Chapter 3, by 渋谷政昭 [Masaaki Sibuya], 準数値算法 / 乱数 [*Jun Suchi Samp¯o/ Rans¯u*] (Tokyo: Saiensu-Sha, 1982), ii + 259 pages; Chapter 4, by 中川圭介 [Keisuke Nakagawa], 準数値算法 / 算術演算 [*Jun Suchi Samp¯o/ Sanjutsu Enzan*] (Tokyo: Saiensu-Sha, 1986), xii + 536 pages.

Hungarian translation by Fiala Tibor, Róbert Freud, János Gerlits, Gábor Hanák, and Tibor Nemetz, under direction of Miklós Simonovits, *A számítógép-programozás művészete 2. Szeminumerikus algoritmusok* (Budapest: Műszaki Könyvkiadó, 1987), 690 pages.

Chinese translation by 管纪文 [Guan JiWen] and 苏运霖 [Su Yunlin], under direction of 陆汝钤 [Lu Ruqian], 计算机程序设计技巧 [*Ji Suan Ji Cheng Xu She Ji Ji Qiao*], 第二卷 [Di 2 Juan], 半数值算法

[*Ban Shu Zhi Suan Fa*] (Beijing: Defense Industry Publishing, 1992), 10 + 622 pages.

Third edition, completely revised. (Reading, Massachusetts: Addison–Wesley, 1997), originally xiv + 762 pages; xiv + 764 pages since 2011.

Russian translation by Л. Ф. Козаченко, В. Т. Тертышный, and И. В. Красиков, edited by С. Н. Тригуб, under direction of Ю. В. Козаченко, *Искусство программирования*, Tom 2: *Получислен-ные алгоритмы* (Moscow: Vil'iams, 2000), 830 pages.

German translation of Chapter 4, by Rüdiger Loos, *Arithmetik* (Heidelberg: Springer, 2001), xiii + 538 pages.

Romanian translation by Mihaela Tărpa, Cora Radulian, and Mihai Iosif, *Arta programării calculatoarelor*, Volumul 2: *Algoritmi seminumerici* (Bucharest: Editura Teora, 2002), 663 pages.

Chinese translation by 苏运霖 [Su Yunlin], 计算机程序设计艺术 [*Jisuanji Chengxu Sheji Yishu*], 第2卷 [Di 2 Juan], 半数值算法 [*Ban Shuzhi Suanfa*] (Beijing: National Defense Industry Press, 2002), xii + 760 pages.

Polish translation by Adam Malinowski, *Sztuka programowania*, Tom 2: *Algorytmy seminumeryczne* (Warsaw: Wydawnictwa Naukowo-Techniczne, 2002), xviii + 820 pages.

Japanese translation by 斎藤博昭 [Hiroaki Saito], 長尾高弘 [Takahiro Nagao], 松井祥悟 [Shogo Matsui], 松井孝雄 [Takao Matsui], and 山内斉 [Hitoshi Yamaushi], supervised by 有澤誠 [Makoto Arisawa] and 和田英一 [Eiiti Wada] (Tokyo: ASCII Corporation, 2004), xvi+ 725 pages.

Korean translation by 류광 [Ryu Gwang], 컴퓨터 프로그래밍의 예술 [*Keompyuteo peurogeuraemingui yesul*], 2: 준수치적 알고리즘 [*Junsuchijeog algorijeum*] (Seoul: Hanbit Media, 2007), 933 pages.

Czech translation by David Krásenský, *Umění programování*, 2. díl, *Seminumerické algoritmy* (Brno: Computer Press, 2010), xii + 763 pages.

Spanish translation, *El arte de programar ordenadores*, Volumen 2: *Algoritmos seminuméricos* (Barcelona: Editorial Reverté), in preparation.

Macedonian translation (Skopje: Prosvetno Delo), in preparation.

• *Sorting and Searching*, Volume 3 of *The Art of Computer Programming*.

First edition. (Reading, Massachusetts: Addison–Wesley, 1973), xii + 722 pages + foldout. Printings after 1974 have also page 723.

Romanian translation by Rodica Boconcios, A. Davidoviciu, P. Dimo, Fl. Moraru, A. Petrescu, and I. Sipoș, edited by Smaranda Dimitriu, *Tratat de programarea calculatoarelor*, Volumul 3: *Sortare și căutare* (Bucharest: Editura tehnică, 1976), xii + 736 pages + foldout.

Russian translation by Надежда И. Вьюкова, В. А. Галатенко, and А. Б. Ходулев, edited by Ю. М. Баяковский and В. С. Штаркман, *Искусство программирования для ЭВМ*, Том 3: *Сортировка и поиск* (Moscow: Mir, 1978), 844 pages + foldout.

Spanish translation by Jaime de Argila y de Chopitea and Ramón Puigjaner Trepat, under direction of Ramón Puigjaner Trepat, *El arte de programar ordenadores*, Volumen 3: *Clasificación y búsqueda* (Barcelona: Editorial Reverté, 1980), xxiii + 672 pages + foldout.

Chinese translation by 管纪文 [Guan JiWen] and 苏运霖 [Su Yunlin], under direction of 陆汝钤 [Lu Ruqian], 计算机程序设计技巧 [*Ji Suan Ji Cheng Xu She Ji Ji Qiao*], 第三卷 [Di 3 Juan], 排序和查找 [*Pai Xu He Cha Zhao*] (Beijing: Defense Industry Publishing, 1985), viii + 645 pages + foldout.

Hungarian translation by György Elekes, Péter Erdős, János Gerlits, László Hárs, Antal Iványi, and Vera Oláh, under direction of Miklós Simonovits, *A számítógép-programozás művészete 3. Keresés és rendezés* (Budapest: Műszaki Könyvkiadó, 1988), 761 pages + foldout.

Second edition, completely revised. (Reading, Massachusetts: Addison–Wesley, 1998), originally xiv + 780 pages + foldout; xiv + 782 pages + foldout since 2011.

Romanian translation by Mihaela Târpa, *Arta programării calculatoarelor*, Volumul 3: *Sortare și căutare* (Bucharest: Editura Teora, 2002), 680 pages + foldout.

Russian translation by В. Т. Тертышный and И. В. Красиков, edited by С. Н. Тригуб, under direction of Ю. В. Козаченко, *Искусство программирования*, Том 3: *Сортировка и поиск* (Moscow: Vil'iams, 2000), 823 + 4 pages.

Japanese translation by 石井裕一郎 [Yuichiro Ishii], 伊知地宏 [Hiroshi Ichiji], 小出洋 [Hiroshi Koide], 高岡詠子 [Eiko Takaoka], 田中久美子 [Kumiko Tanaka], and 長尾高弘 [Takahiro Nagao], supervised by 有澤誠 [Makoto Arisawa] and 和田英一 [Eiiti Wada] (Tokyo: ASCII Corporation, 2006), xvi + 741 pages + foldout.

Chinese translation by 苏运霖 [Su Yunlin], 计算机程序设计艺术 [*Jisuanji Chengxu Sheji Yishu*], 第3卷 [Di 3 Juan], 排序与查找 [*Paixu Yu Chazhao*] (Beijing: National Defense Industry Press, 2002), x + 779 pages.

Polish translation by Krzysztof Diks and Adam Malinowski, *Sztuka programowania*, Tom 3: *Sortowanie i wyszukiwanie* (Warsaw: Wydawnictwa Naukowo-Techniczne, 2002), xviii + 838 pages + foldout.

Korean translation by 류광 [Ryu Gwang], 컴퓨터 프로그래밍의 예술 [*Keompyuteo peurogeuraemingui yesul*], 3: 정렬 과 검색 [*Jeonglyeol gwa geomsaeg*] (Seoul: Hanbit Media, 2008), 939 pages + foldout.

Macedonian translation (Skopje: Prosvetno Delo), in preparation.

Czech translation (Brno: Computer Press), in preparation.

• *Combinatorial Algorithms*, Part 1, Volume 4A of *The Art of Computer Programming*.

Volume 4, Fascicle 2: *Generating All Tuples and Permutations* (Upper Saddle River, New Jersey: Addison–Wesley, 2005), v + 127 pages.

Romanian translation by Cora Radulian, *Generarea tuturor tuplurilor și permut ̆arilor* (Bucharest: Editura Teora, 2005), vii + 144 pages.

Japanese translation by 小出洋 [Hiroshi Koide], supervised by 有澤誠 [Makoto Arisawa] and 和田英一 [Eiiti Wada] (Tokyo: ASCII Corporation, 2006), viii + 129 pages.

Russian translation by Ю. Г. Гордиенко [Гордієнко], edited by С. Н. Тригуб, *Генерация всех кортежй и перестановок* (Moscow: Vil'iams, 2007), 146 pages.

Polish translation by Adam Malinowski, *Generowanie wszystkich krotek i permutacji* (Warsaw: Wydawnictwa Naukowo-Techniczne, 2007), xiv + 137 pages.

Hungarian translation by Zoltán Kása and Csaba István Sidló, under direction of Antal Iványi, *Permutációk és n-esek előállítása* (Budapest: Antoncom Infokommunikációs, 2008), 160 pages.

Volume 4, Fascicle 3: *Generating All Combinations and Partitions* (Upper Saddle River, New Jersey: Addison–Wesley, 2005), v+150 pages.

Russian translation by И. В. Красиков, edited by С. Н. Тригуб, *Генерация всех сочетаний и разбиений* (Moscow: Vil'iams, 2007), 200 pages.

Hungarian translation by László Szalay, Mihály Szalay, and Lajos Lóczi, under direction of Antal Iványi, *Kombinációk és partíciók előállítása* (Budapest: Antoncom Infokommunikációs, 2008), 176 pages.

Japanese translation by 筧一彦 [Kazuhiko Kakehi], supervised by 有澤誠 [Makoto Arisawa] and 和田英一 [Eiiti Wada] (Tokyo: ASCII Corporation, 2008), viii + 154 pages.

Volume 4, Fascicle 4: *Generating All Trees; History of Combinatorial Generation* (Upper Saddle River, New Jersey: Addison–Wesley, 2006), vi + 120 pages.

Russian translation by И. В. Красиков, edited by С. Н. Тригуб, *Генерация всех деревьев; История комбинаторной генерации* (Moscow: Vil'iams, 2007), 156 pages.

Hungarian translation by János Virágh, under direction of Antal Iványi, *Fák előállítása; Kombinatorikus előállítások története* (Budapest: Antoncom Infokommunikációs, 2008), 160 pages.

Japanese translation by 筧一彦 [Kazuhiko Kakehi] and 小出洋 [Hiroshi Koide], supervised by 有澤誠 [Makoto Arisawa] and 和田英一 [Eiiti Wada] (Tokyo: ASCII Corporation, 2010), viii + 118 pages.

Volume 4, Fascicle 0: *Introduction to Combinatorial Algorithms and Boolean Functions* (Upper Saddle River, New Jersey: Addison–Wesley, 2008), xii + 216 pages.

Japanese translation by 和田英一 [Eiiti Wada] (Tokyo: ASCII Corporation, 2009), xii + 206 pages.

Chinese translation under direction of 黄林鹏 [Lin Peng Huang] (Beijing: China Machine Press, 2010), xii + 432 pages.

Hungarian translation by Zsuzsanna L'ang, András Hajdu, Katalin Pásztorné Varga, Magda Várterész, and Gabor Alagi, under direction of Antal Iványi, *Bevezetés a kombinatorikai algoritmusokhoz és Boole-függvényekhez* (Budapest: Antoncom Infokommunikációs, 2011), 272 pages.

Macedonian translation (Skopje: Prosvetno Delo), in preparation.

Volume 4, Fascicle 1: *Bitwise Tricks & Techniques; Binary Decision Diagrams* (Upper Saddle River, New Jersey: Addison–Wesley, 2009), viii + 260 pages. Later printings had page 261, then page 262.

Japanese translation by 和田英一 [Eiiti Wada] (Tokyo: ASCII Corporation, 2011), x + 256 pages.

Hungarian translation by Csaba Bánsághi, Rita Csákány, Endre Daróczy-Kiss, Lehel Kovács, László Domozslai, Péter Ligeti, Mónika Makai, and Dániel Szisz, under direction of Antal Iványi, *Bittrükkök és bitmódszerek; Bináris döntési diagramok* (Budapest: Antoncom Infokommunikációs, 2011), 311 pages.

First edition of the hardcover Volume 4A. (Upper Saddle River, N. J.: Addison–Wesley, 2011), xvi + 883 pages.

Russian translation (Moscow: Vil'iams), in preparation.

Chinese translation (Beijing: Posts & Telecommunications Press), in preparation.

Computers & Typesetting

Tau Epsilon Chi: A System for Technical Text (Providence, Rhode Island: American Mathematical Society, 1979), ii + 200 pages.

$\TeX$ *and* METAFONT: *New Directions in Typesetting* (Providence, Rhode Island: American Mathematical Society, and Bedford, Massachusetts: Digital Press, 1979), xi + 45 + 201 + 105 pages.

- *The* $\TeX$*book*, illustrated by Duane Bibby, Volume A of *Computers & Typesetting*.

First paperback edition. (Reading, Massachusetts: Addison–Wesley, 1984), x + 483 pages.

First hardcover edition. (Reading, Massachusetts: Addison–Wesley, 1986), x + 483 pages.

Japanese translation by 鷺谷好輝 [Yoshiteru Sagiya] and 斎藤信男 [Nobuo Saito], $\TeX$ブック [$\TeX$bukku]: コンピュータによる組版システム [*Konpyuuta ni yoru sohan sisutemu*], illustrated by Duane Bibby (Tokyo: ASCII Corporation, 1989), xix + 657 pages.

Russian translation by М. В. Лисина, edited by С. В. Клименко and С. Н. Соколов, *Все про* $\TeX$, illustrated by Duane Bibby (Protvino, Moscow: AO RDT$\TeX$, 1993), xvi + 575 pages.

Russian translation by Л. Ф. Козаченко, edited by Ю. В. Козаченко, *Все про* $\TeX$, illustrated by Duane Bibby (Moscow: Vil'iams, 2003), 549 pages.

French translation by Jean-Côme Charpentier, *Le* $\TeX$*book: Composition informatique*, illustrated by Duane Bibby (Paris: Vuibert Informatique, 2003), xiv + 555 pages.

Polish translation by Piotr Bolek, Włodzimierz Bzyl, and Adam Dawidziuk, $\TeX$: *Przewodnik użytkownika*, illustrated by Duane Bibby (Warsaw: Wydawnictwa Naukowo-Techniczne, 2005), xviii + 541 pages.

- $\TeX$: *The Program*, Volume B of *Computers & Typesetting* (Reading, Massachusetts: Addison–Wesley, 1986), xvi + 594 pages.

- *The* METAFONT*book*, illustrated by Duane Bibby, Volume C of *Computers & Typesetting*.

First paperback edition. (Reading, Massachusetts: Addison–Wesley, 1986), xii + 361 pages.

First hardcover edition. (Reading, Massachusetts: Addison–Wesley, 1986), xii + 361 pages.

Japanese translation by 鷺谷好輝 [Yoshiteru Sagiya], METAFONTブック [*METAFONTbukku*], illustrated by Duane Bibby (Tokyo: ASCII Corporation, 1994), xvi + 451 pages.

Russian translation by Мустафа Р. Саит-Аметов, advised by Ю. В. Козаченко, *Все про* METAFONT, illustrated by Duane Bibby (Moscow: Vil'iams, 2003), 375 pages.

- METAFONT: *The Program*, Volume D of *Computers & Typesetting* (Reading, Massachusetts: Addison–Wesley, 1986), xvi + 560 pages.

- *Computer Modern Typefaces*, Volume E of *Computers & Typesetting* (Reading, Massachusetts: Addison–Wesley, 1986), xvi + 588 pages.

Collections of Selected Papers

クヌース先生のプログラム論 [*Kunuusu Sensei no Program-Ron*, Professor Knuth's Programming Discipline], an anthology of Japanese translations edited by 有澤誠 [Makoto Arisawa] (Tokyo: Kyoritsu-Shuppan, 1991), v + 199 pages.

- *Literate Programming* (Stanford, California: Center for the Study of Language and Information, 1992), xvi + 368 pages. (CSLI Lecture Notes, no. 27.)

Japanese translation by 有澤誠 [Makoto Arisawa], 文芸的プログラミング [*Bungeiteki Programming*] (Tokyo: ASCII Corporation, 1994), 463 pages.

- *Selected Papers on Computer Science* (Stanford, California: Center for the Study of Language and Information, and Cambridge, England: Cambridge University Press, 1996), xii + 274 pages. (CSLI Lecture Notes, no. 59.) Printings made after 2003 have xii + 276 pages, because a new chapter was added.

- *Digital Typography* (Stanford, California: Center for the Study of Language and Information, 1999), xvi + 685 pages. (CSLI Lecture Notes, no. 78.)

Russian translation by Роман М. Кузнец, Олга А. Маховая, Николаи В. Третяков, and Юрии В. Тюменцев, edited by Ирина А. Маховая, *Компьютерная Типография* (Moscow: Mir, 2003), 669 pages.

- *Selected Papers on Analysis of Algorithms* (Stanford, California: Center for the Study of Language and Information, 2000), xvi + 621 pages. (CSLI Lecture Notes, no. 102.) Printings made after 2006 have xvi + 622 pages, because the index has gotten longer.

- *Selected Papers on Discrete Mathematics* (Stanford, California: Center for the Study of Language and Information, 2003), xvi + 812 pages. (CSLI Lecture Notes, no. 106.)

- *Selected Papers on Computer Languages* (Stanford, California: Center for the Study of Language and Information, 2003), xvi + 594 pages. (CSLI Lecture Notes, no. 139.)

- *Selected Papers on Design of Algorithms* (Stanford, California: Center for the Study of Language and Information, 2010), xvi + 453 pages. (CSLI Lecture Notes, no. 191.)

- *Selected Papers on Fun and Games* (Stanford, California: Center for the Study of Language and Information, 2011), xvii + 741 pages. (CSLI Lecture Notes, no. 192.) Later printings have xvii+742 pages.

French translations by Patrick Cégielski, of selections from all eight *Selected Papers* volumes:

Éléments pour une histoire de l'informatique (Paris: Société mathématique de France, and Stanford, California: Center for the Study of Language and Information, 2011), xvi+371 pages. (CSLI Lecture Notes, no. 190.)

Algorithmes (Paris: Société mathématique de France, and Stanford, California: Center for the Study of Language and Information, 2011), xiv + 510 pages. (CSLI Lecture Notes, no. 194.)

- *Companion to the Papers of Donald Knuth* (Stanford, California: Center for the Study of Language and Information, 2011), xiii + 440 pages. (CSLI Lecture Notes, no. 202.)

Textbooks

- (with Daniel H. Greene) *Mathematics for the Analysis of Algorithms.* First edition. (Boston, Massachusetts: Birkhäuser Boston, 1981), 107 pages. (Progress in Computer Science and Applied Logic, Volume 1.)

Second edition, with new appendices. (Boston, Massachusetts: Birkhäuser Boston, 1982), 123 pages.

Russian translation by Б. Б. Походзей, edited by Юри В. Матиясевич, *Математические методы анализа алгоритмов* (Moscow: Mir, 1987), 120 pages.

Third edition, with additional appendices. (Boston, Massachusetts: Birkhäuser Boston, 1990), viii + 132 pages.

Reprinted in the Modern Birkhäuser Classics series, as a paperback and eBook (Boston, Massachusetts: Birkhäuser, 2008), x + 132 pages.

Japanese translation (Kindai Kagaku Sha), in preparation.

- (with Ronald L. Graham and Oren Patashnik) *Concrete Mathematics: A Foundation for Computer Science.*

First edition. (Reading, Massachusetts: Addison–Wesley, 1989), xiii + 625 pages.

Chinese translation by 賴飛羆 [Fei-Pei Lai], 具體數學 [*Chü T'i Shu Hsüeh*] (Taipei: Dong Hua Publishing, 1990), xv + 731 pages.

Chinese translation by 陳衍文 [Yen-Wen Chen], 具體數學 [*Chü T'i Shu Hsüeh*] (Taipei: Ru Lin Publishing, 1991), xii + 695 pages.

Chinese translation by 庄心谷 [Zhuang Xingu], 具体数学：计算机科学基础 [*Ju Ti Shu Xue: Ji Suan Ji Ke Xue Ji Chu*] (Xian: Xian Electronic Technology University Publishing, 1992), xii + 539 pages.

Italian translation edited by Giovanni Monegato, *Matematica Discreta: Principi matematici per l'informatica* (Milan: Editore Ulrico Hoepli, 1992), xviii + 607 pages.

Japanese translation by 有澤誠 [Makoto Arisawa], 安村通晃 [Michiaki Yasumura], 萩野達也 [Tatsuya Hagino], and 石畑清 [Kiyoshi Ishihata], コンピュータの数学 [*Konpyuuta no Sūgaku*] (Tokyo: Kyoritsu-Shuppan, 1993), xvi + 606 pages.

Second Edition, extensively revised. (Reading, Massachusetts: Addison–Wesley, 1994), xiii + 657 pages.

Portuguese translation by Val'eriade Magalh˜aesIorio, *Matemática Concreta: Fundamentos para a Ciência da Computação* (Rio de Janeiro: Livros Técnicos e Científicos Editora, 1995), xii + 477 pages.

Polish translation by Piotr Chrząstowski, A. Czumaj, L. Gąsieniec, and M. Raczunas, *Matematyka konkretna* (Warszawa: Polskie Wydawnictwa Naukowe, 1996), 718 pages.

Hungarian translation by Sándor Fridli, János Gonda, Attila Kovács, László Lakatos, and Csabáné Láng, *Konkrét Matematika: A számítástudomaány alapja* (Műszaki Könyvkiadó, 1998), xvi + 647 pages.

French translation by Alain Denise, *Mathématiques concrètes: Fondations pour l'informatique* (Paris: International Thomson Publishing, 1998), xiv + 688 pages.

Russian translation by А. Б. Ходулев and Б. Б. Походзей, *Конкретная математика: Основание информатики* (Moscow: Mir, 1999), 704 pages.

Greek translation by Χρήστος Α. Καπούτσις, edited by Ευστάθιος Ζάχος, *Συνκριτά Μαθηματικά: Μια θεμελίωση για την Επιστήμητων Υπολογιστών* (Athens: Kleidarithmos Publications), in preparation.

Chinese translation by 张明尧 [Zhang Mingyao] and 张凡 [Zhang Fan], 具体数学—计算机科学基础 [*Ju Ti Shu Xue—Ji Suan Ji Ke Xue Ji Chu*] (Beijing: China Machine Press), in preparation.

Spanish translation (Addison–Wesley Spain and Universidad Autonoma de Madrid), in preparation.

Croatian translation (Zagreb: Golden Marketing), in preparation.

- (with Tracy L. Larrabee and Paul M. Roberts) *Mathematical Writing* (Washington, D.C.: Mathematical Association of America, 1989), iii + 115 pages. Page 116 appeared in later editions.
Japanese translation by 有澤誠 [Makoto Arisawa], with additional illustrations and notes by the translator, クヌース先生のドキュメント纂法 [*Kunuusu Sensei no Dokyumento Samp¯d*] (Tokyo: Kyoritsu-Shuppan, 1989), x + 194 pages; second edition, 1993.

Other Works

- *Surreal Numbers*, illustrated by Jill C. Knuth (Reading, Massachusetts: Addison–Wesley, 1974), vi + 119 pages.
Czech translation by Helena Nešetřilová, *Nadreálná čísla*, in *Pokroky Matematiky, Fyziky a Astronomie* **23** (1978), 66–76, 130–139, 187–196, 246–261.
Japanese translation by 好田順治 [Junji Koda], illustrated by Jill C. Knuth, 超現実数 [*Chogen Jis Su*] (Tokyo: Kaimei Sha Ltd., 1978), 179 pages.
German translation by Brigitte and Karl Kunisch, illustrated by Jill C. Knuth, *Insel der Zahlen: Eine zahlentheoretische Genesis im Dialog* (Braunschweig: Friedr. Vieweg & Sohn, 1979), 124 pages.
Japanese translation by 好田順治 [Junji Koda], illustrated by Jill C. Knuth and 高橋正輝 [Masaki Takahashi], 超現実数 [*Chogen Jis Su*], published in eight monthly installments in *Basic Sūgaku* (August 1978 through March 1979).
Spanish translation by Lluc Garriga, illustrated by Jill C. Knuth, *Números Surreales* (Barcelona: Editorial Reverté, 1979), 101 pages.
Hungarian translation by János Virágh and Zoltán Ésik, illustrated by Zoltán Tardos, *Számok valóson innen és túl* (Budapest: Gondolat, 1987), 136 + ii pages.
Portuguese translation by Jorge Nuno Silva, illustrated by Jill C. Knuth and José Bandeira, *Números Surreais* (Lisbon: Gradiva, 2002), 113 pages.
Japanese translation by 松浦俊輔 [Shunsuke Matsuura], illustrated by サイトウユウスケ [Yusuke Saito] and Jill C. Knuth, 至福の超現実数 [*Shifuku no Chogen Jis Su*], (Tokyo: Kashiwa Shobo, 2005), 174 pages.
Chinese translation by 高博 [Bo Gao], illustrated by Jill C. Knuth, 研究之美 [*Yan Jiu Zhi Mei*] (Beijing: Publishing House of Electronics Industry), in preparation.

- *Mariages stables et leurs relations avec d'autres probl`emes combinatoires: Introduction à l'analyse mathématique des algorithmes.*
Première édition. (Montréal: Les Presses de l'Université de Montréal, 1976), 106 pages.
Édition revue et corrigée. (Montréal: Les Presses de l'Université de Montréal, 1981), 106 pages.
English translation by Martin Goldstein, *Stable Marriage and Its Relation to Other Combinatorial Problems: An Introduction to the Mathematical Analysis of Algorithms* (Providence, Rhode Island: American Mathematical Society, 1997), xiii + 74 pages. (CRM Proceedings & Lecture Notes, Volume 10.)
Russian translation by Едуард Лернер and Олга Кашина, *Устойчивость супружеских пар и гругие комбинаторные задачи (Введение в математический анализ алгоритмов)* (Moscow: Moscow Center for Continuous Mathematical Education), to appear.

- *3:16 Bible Texts Illuminated.*
First printing. (Madison, Wisconsin: A-R Editions, 1990), iii+268 pages.
Second printing, revised. (Madison, Wisconsin: A-R Editions, 1992), iii + 268 pages.

- *Axioms and Hulls* (Heidelberg: Springer-Verlag, 1992), ix + 109 pages. (Lecture Notes in Computer Science, Volume 606.)

- (with Silvio Levy) *The CWEB System of Structured Documentation.*
First edition. (Reading, Massachusetts: Addison–Wesley, 1993), iv + 227 pages.
Version 3.6, with hypertext support. (Reading, Massachusetts: Addison–Wesley, 2001), ii + 237 pages.

- *The Stanford GraphBase: A Platform for Combinatorial Computing.*
First edition. (New York: ACM Press, and Reading, Massachusetts: Addison–Wesley, 1994), viii + 576 pages.
Paperback edition, revised. (New York: ACM Press, and Reading, Massachusetts: Addison–Wesley, 2009), viii + 576 pages.

- *MMIXware: A RISC computer for the third millennium* (Heidelberg: Springer-Verlag, 1999), vii + 550 pages. (Lecture Notes in Computer Science, Volume 1750.)
Japanese translation by 滝沢徹 [Tooru Takizawa], *MMIXware:* 第三千年紀のための *RISC* コンピュータ [*Dai sanzen nenki no tame no RISC konpyuuta*] (Tokyo: SiB access, 2002), viii + 550 pages.

- *Things a Computer Scientist Rarely Talks About* (Stanford, California: Center for the Study of Language and Information, 2001), xi + 257 pages. (CSLI Lecture Notes, no. 136.)

Japanese translation by 滝沢徹 [Tooru Takizawa], 牧野祐子 [Yuko Makino], and 富澤昇 [Noboru Tomizawa], コンピュータ科学者が めったに語らないこと [*Konpyuuta Kagakusha ga Mettanī Kataranaī Koto*] (Tokyo: SiB access, 2003), x + 260 pages.

Addendum

The webpage

```
http://www-cs-faculty.stanford.edu/~knuth/vita.html
```

contains uptodate information about books that were published after the spring of 2011, when the listing above was prepared.

Chapter 20

Annotated List of Papers

The papers of Donald E. Knuth are grouped here in three series: P, Q, and R. Series P contains the major journal publications. Series Q contains secondary works such as reviews, letters to the editor, statements of problems or solutions to problems, transcripts of talks, forewords to books, and other items that typically were published without extensive screening by referees. Series R contains works of limited circulation, such as technical reports, often published locally. Each paper has a serial number — for example #P1, #P2, ..., #Q1, ... — which was assigned when the author first included it in his own records.

An asterisk signifies a paper that was almost entirely written by one or more of the co-authors listed, not by Knuth himself; such works do not appear among the volumes of his collected papers. But most of the papers (except in series R) have been reprinted, often with amendments that correct errors and/or supply further context. In such cases the corresponding page numbers are shown at the end of the bibliographic entry, preceded by a two-letter code that identifies the relevant volume:

AA = *Selected Papers on Analysis of Algorithms;*
CL = *Selected Papers on Computer Languages;*
CP = *Companion to the Papers of Donald Knuth;*
CS = *Selected Papers on Computer Science;*
DA = *Selected Papers on Design of Algorithms;*
DM = *Selected Papers on Discrete Mathematics;*
DT = *Digital Typography;*
FG = *Selected Papers on Fun and Games;*
LP = *Literate Programming.*

The bibliographic details for most papers of the P series, and for many of the Q series, are followed here by brief annotations in italic type, added in 2011 as sort of a postscript to explain the general context or to tell a related story.

221

P1. The potrzebie system of weights and measures. *MAD Magazine* **1**, 33 (June 1957), 36–37. (Illustrated by Wallace Wood.) Reprinted in *Like, MAD* (New York: Signet Pocket Books No. S1838, 1960), 139–145. Page 36 reprinted in *Completely MAD* by Maria Reidelbach (Boston, Massachusetts: Little, Brown, 1991), 191. *Starting at the summit with this work as technical publication number 1, my œuvre could not help but go downhill from here.* [FG 1–8]

P2. RUNCIBLE — Algebraic translation on a limited computer. *Communications of the ACM* **2**, 11 (November 1959), 18–21. *This paper describes a compiler for the IBM 650 that was written by a team of undergraduates at Case Institute of Technology. Everybody now recognizes that its spaghetti-like unstructured methods should be shunned in software engineering; but it did work, and it was used extensively at the time.* [CL 457–469]

P3. An imaginary number system. *Communications of the ACM* **3** (1960), 245–247. Errata, *Communications of the ACM* **4** (1961), 355. *This exploration of new ways to represent complex numbers was actually carried out before I entered college, at the same time as P1 was written.* [DM 271–276]

P4. (with R. C. Bose* and I. M. Chakravarti) On methods of constructing sets of mutually orthogonal latin squares using a computer. Part I: *Technometrics* **2** (1960), 507–516. Part II: *Technometrics* **3** (1961), 111–117. *Professor Bose was a charismatic teacher who visited Case Institute of Technology during my senior year. His lectures inspired me to write a computer program in which I confronted an instance of a challenging task that I would know later as the "maximum clique problem." He kindly decided to include my name as a coauthor of this pair of papers, although I didn't know it at the time. In fact, due to a curious set of circumstances, I never have actually read either paper! Of course I'm curious to see what's in there; yet I know that if I do peek inside, I'll never again be able to claim at dinner parties that I've never actually read all of my own works.*

P5. Minimizing drum latency time. *Journal of the ACM* **8** (April 1961), 119–150. *This was the first substantial research paper that I worked on diligently and submitted to a major journal. It describes a practical solution to a problem that is no longer of practical interest, namely to arrange data and instructions optimally on a rotating drum. If that problem had remained important, I still believe that the methods of this paper would be the best way to deal with it.* [DA 397–436]

P6. (with Jack N. Merner) ALGOL 60 *Confidential*. *Communications of the ACM* **4** (1961), 268–272. *A well-meaning, but irreverent and* *somewhat impertinent critique of the ALGOL 60 programming language in its original form.* [CL 103–114]

P7. (with G. A. Bachelor, J. R. H. Dempster, J. Speroni) SMALGOL-61. *Communications of the ACM* **4** (1961), 499–502. *A committee-designed subset of ALGOL 60 designed to be readily implementable on small computers.* [CL 115–122]

P8. Euler's constant to 1271 places. *Mathematics of Computation* **16** (1962), 275–281. *What I did while first learning about multiprecision division techniques and the wonders of Bernoulli numbers.* [DA 373–382]

P9. Evaluation of polynomials by computer. *Communications of the ACM* **5** (1962), 595–599. *Sort of a first draft of what was to become Section 4.6.4 of The Art of Computer Programming.* [DA 383–395]

P10. A history of writing compilers. *Computers and Automation* **11**, 12 (December 1962), 8–18. Reprinted in *Compiler Techniques*, edited by Bary W. Pollack (Princeton: Auerbach, 1972), 38–56. French translation by Patrick Cégielski in *Éléments pour une histoire de l'informatique* (see Chapter 19), 179–198. *My first attempt to trace the early history of software. I learned later, while writing paper P83, that an extensive prehistory of unpublished work — unknown in 1962 to youngsters like me — had actually been brewing in many parts of the world, long before any of the events described here. Proper channels of communication were still being established.* [CL 439–456]

P11. Computer-drawn flowcharts. *Communications of the ACM* **6** (1963), 555–563. *Advocates a method of documentation that I'd found useful when writing commercial software. This work had a strong influence on the way algorithms would subsequently be presented in The Art of Computer Programming.* [CL 471–493]

P12. Length of strings for a merge sort. *Communications of the ACM* **6** (1963), 685–688. *This paper, my first published work about what would later be called the analysis of algorithms, studies the behavior of the "replacement selection" technique, widely used as the first stage of programs that sort large amounts of data with magnetic tapes.* [AA 205–214]

P13. Transcendental numbers based on the Fibonacci sequence. *Fibonacci Quarterly* **2** (1964), 43–44, 52. *A cute application of the sequence 1, 1, 2, 3, 5, . . . , not quite as original as I thought at the time.* [FG 99–102]

P14. Billiard balls in an equilateral triangle. *Recreational Mathematics Magazine* #14 (January–February 1964), 20–23. *The result of my first correspondence with Martin Gardner.* [FG 63–68]

P15. (with L. L. Bumgarner, D. E. Hamilton, P. Z. Ingerman, M. P. Lietzke, J. N. Merner, D. T. Ross) A proposal for input-output conventions in ALGOL 60. *Communications of the ACM* **7** (1964), 273–283. Russian translation by М. И. Агеев in *Современное Программирование* **1** (Moscow: Soviet Radio, 1966), 73–107. *A committee report that introduced (among other things) the notion of "list procedures," a simple yet nonobvious way of specifying sequences that I believe has never yet been exploited to its full potential.* [CL 127–154]

P16. (with J. L. McNeley) SOL — A symbolic language for general-purpose systems simulation. *IEEE Transactions on Electronic Computers* **EC-13** (1964), 401–408. *Describes a language that I thought would be quite useful, until I learned about SIMULA 68 (which is better).* [CL 175–189]

P17. (with J. L. McNeley) A formal definition of SOL. *IEEE Transactions on Electronic Computers* **EC-13** (1964), 409–414. *A companion to the informal examples in P16.* [CL 191–204]

P18. Representing numbers using only one 4. *Mathematics Magazine* **37** (1964), 308–310. *The silliest way to compute 64 that you ever did see.* [FG 69–72]

P19. (with Marshall Hall, Jr.) Combinatorial analysis and computers. *American Mathematical Monthly* **72**, part 2, *Computers and Computing*, Slaught Memorial Papers No. 10 (February 1965), 21–28. *A survey paper written with my thesis advisor, covering the state of the art in a field that was just ready to blossom.* [DM 1–13]

P20. (with J. D. Alanen) Tables of finite fields. *Sankhyā*, series A, **26** (1964), 305–328. *Many combinatorial designs were being constructed by hand during these early days, using methods that are facilitated by the tables constructed in this paper.* [DM 277–304]

P21. Finite semifields and projective planes. *Journal of Algebra* **2** (1965), 182–217. Reprinted in *Neofields and Combinatorial Designs*, edited by D. Frank Hsu, *Advances in Discrete Mathematics and Computer Science* **1** (Nonantum, Massachusetts: Hadronic Press, 1984), 57–92. *The first half of my dissertation discussed finite systems of points and lines that are based on algebraic systems in which multiplication is not associative, although most of the other familiar properties do hold.* [DM 305–344]

P22. A class of projective planes. *Transactions of the American Mathematical Society* **115** (1965), 541–549. *The second half of my dissertation* *solved a longstanding open problem of combinatorics by constructing new projective planes in which the number of points per line is respectively* $2^5 + 1$, $2^7 + 1$, $2^9 + 1$, *etc.* [DM 345–355]

P23. On the translation of languages from left to right. *Information and Control* **8** (1965), 607–639. Russian translation by A. A. Мучник in *Языки и Автоматы*, edited by A. H. Маслов and Э. Д. Стоцкий (Moscow: Mir, 1975), 9–42. Reprinted in *Great Papers in Computer Science*, edited by Phillip Laplante (St. Paul, Minnesota: West Publishing, 1996), 150–173. French translation by Patrick Cégielski in *Algorithmes* (see Chapter 19), 321–356. *This paper introduced the concepts and basic algorithms related to so-called LR(k) languages and grammars, which turned out to be fundamental ingredients of compiler technology after they were developed by other researchers in later years.* [CL 327–360]

P24. Construction of a random sequence. *BIT* **5** (1965), 246–250. *Somewhat paradoxically (at least in 1965), it was possible to construct a deterministic sequence that met all of the criteria that many people had believed to be essential for randomness.* [DM 265–270]

P25. An almost linear recurrence. *Fibonacci Quarterly* **4** (1966), 117–128. *The sequence 1, 2, 4, 6, 10, 14, 20, ... whose first differences are 1, 2, 2, 4, 4, 6, 6, 10, 10, ... has interesting properties, including the asymptotic growth rate* $\ln \varphi_n \sim (\ln n)^2/4$. *(I was scooped in these results by Kurt Mahler, who had used more powerful techniques to study this sequence already in 1940.)* [DM 525–535]

P26. Oriented subtrees of an arc digraph. *Journal of Combinatorial Theory* **3** (1967), 309–314. *It is possible to count the number of oriented spanning trees of a large family of directed graphs by explicitly evaluating certain determinants. One consequence is an elementary derivation of the number of de Bruijn cycles. This material inspired Section 2.3.4.2 of The Art of Computer Programming.* [DM 203–208]

P27. (with Thomas J. Buckholtz) Computation of tangent, Euler, and Bernoulli numbers. *Mathematics of Computation* **21** (1967), 663–688. *With some effort Tom and I computed, for instance, the 294-digit number* $\lfloor B_{250} \rfloor = 1843 \ldots 1571$ *on a small computer. The same answer is now obtainable almost instantly on a smartphone; but the method we used in 1967 was far superior to the way I had computed Bernoulli numbers in paper P8.* [DA 359–372]

P28. (with Richard H. Bigelow) Programming languages for automata. *Journal of the ACM* **14** (October 1967), 615–635. *I believed that the ideas* *of this paper, which demonstrated how to prove results in the theory of computation by writing programs in an ALGOL-like language, would become quite popular among theoretical computer scientists. But those folks continue to prefer their own high-level language conventions (namely, formal mathematical definitions together with informally sketched constructions).* [CL 237–262]

P29. The remaining trouble spots in ALGOL 60. *Communications of the ACM* **10** (1967), 611–618. Reprinted in E. Horowitz, *Programming Languages: A Grand Tour* (Computer Science Press, 1982), 61–68. *The international programming language ALGOL 60 was significantly improved and clarified in 1963, after its innovative features had become better understood. But a few dark corners remain in every complex structure, and I tried in this paper to survey all of the residual glitches.* [CL 155–173]

P30. A characterization of parenthesis languages. *Information and Control* **11** (1967), 269–289. *I remember this paper chiefly because it represented the first time in my life when I was able to solve a problem after having been stumped for many days and deciding that the task was hopeless. But one morning I woke up with a new idea that cracked the parenthesis problem wide open. Unfortunately the result in this paper never turned out to be very significant, except perhaps as part of my own education.* [CL 263–284]

P31. Very magic squares. *American Mathematical Monthly* **75** (March 1968), 260–264. *Here I show that square arrays of numbers cannot have identical sums on lots of generalized diagonals unless all of the numbers are themselves identical.* [FG 73–77]

P32. Semantics of context-free languages. *Mathematical Systems Theory* **2** (1968), 127–145. Errata, *Mathematical Systems Theory* **5** (1971), 95–96. French translation by Patrick Cégielski in *Algorithmes* (see Chapter 19), 357–382. *This paper launched the idea of "attribute grammars," which turned out to be explored by many other researchers in subsequent years.* [CL 377–400]

P33. Another enumeration of trees. *Canadian Journal of Mathematics* **20** (1968), 1077–1086. *How many oriented trees on the vertices $\{a_1, \ldots, a_l, b_1, \ldots, b_m, c_1, \ldots, c_n\}$ have root a_1 and all arcs go from a to b or from b to c or from c to a? Answer: $l^{n-1}m^{l-1}n^m$. And similar formulas exist for a large class of similar problems.* [DM 209–219]

P34. (with Peter B. Bendix) Simple word problems in universal algebras. In *Computational Problems in Abstract Algebra*, edited by John Leech (Oxford: Pergamon, 1970), 263–297. Reprinted in *Automation of Reasoning*, edited by Jörg H. Siekmann and Graham Wrightson, **2** (Berlin: Springer, 1983), 342–376. French translation by Patrick

Cégielski in *Algorithmes* (see Chapter 19), 437–479. *The "Knuth–Bendix completion algorithm," introduced here and illustrated with many examples, led subsequently to a host of generalizations by other researchers and helped to spawn a general area of research known as "term rewriting systems." I wrote this paper and P32 during the busiest year of my life (1967).* [DA 275–314]

P35. The Gamov–Stern elevator problem. *Journal of Recreational Mathematics* **2** (1969), 131–137. *A paradox, about how often a down-elevator will arrive before an up-elevator, turns out to be even more paradoxical than its inventors thought.* [FG 79–86]

P36. Notes on central groupoids. *Journal of Combinatorial Theory* **8** (1970), 376–390. *A binary operator that satisfies the axiom $(ab)(bc) = b$ leads to a fascinating algebraic system that can fruitfully be studied in eight different ways, explored here. (This was the instructive axiom that led me to discover the algorithm of P34.)* [DM 357–375]

P37. (with Chandler Davis) Number representations and dragon curves. *Journal of Recreational Mathematics* **3** (1970), 66–81, 133–149. *Mathematical patterns are doubly exciting when they produce stunning visual effects as well as beautiful theorems.* [FG 571–614]

P38. Permutations, matrices, and generalized Young tableaux. *Pacific Journal of Mathematics* **34** (1970), 709–727. French translation by Patrick Cégielski in *Algorithmes* (see Chapter 19), 481–502. *By following my nose while writing Section 5.1.4 of The Art of Computer Programming, I got lucky and struck a rich vein of mathematics, now known to many researchers as the Robinson–Schensted–Knuth algorithm and its consequences.* [DM 445–464]

P39. A note on solid partitions. *Mathematics of Computation* **24** (1970), 955–961. *Two-dimensional and three-dimensional partitions of integers have many beautiful mathematical properties. The calculations reported here show that four-dimensional partitions almost surely do not. Fortunately, however, the method used in this calculation has turned out to be important for studying other questions.* [DM 483–491]

P40. Von Neumann's first computer program. *Computing Surveys* **2** (December 1970), 247–260. Reprinted in *Papers of John von Neumann on Computing and Computer Theory*, edited by William Aspray and Arthur Burks (Cambridge, Massachusetts: MIT Press, 1987), 83–96. French translation by Jean-Baptiste Yunès in *Éléments pour une histoire de l'informatique* (see Chapter 19), 53–75. *I've always been fascinated by the ways in which great ideas have been discovered. Here I hold a microscope* *up to the historic first program written for a machine that strongly resembles modern computers, and try to explain its context.* [CS 205–225]

P41. Optimum binary search trees. *Acta Informatica* **1** (1971), 14–25. Corrigenda, page 270. *Sometimes it is possible to find a data structure that is absolutely the best way to support an important algorithm. The case of binary search trees, with given frequencies on its internal and external nodes from left to right, is a particularly instructive example.* [DA 35–49]

P42. (with R. W. Floyd) Notes on avoiding 'go to' statements. *Information Processing Letters* **1** (1971), 23–31. Errata, page 177. Reprinted in *Writings of the Revolution*, edited by E. Yourdon (New York: Yourdon Press, 1982), 153–162. French translation by Patrick Cégielski in *Algorithmes* (see Chapter 19), 145–157. *During the late 1960s and early 1970s there was intense interest in the question of writing computer programs that don't jump willy-nilly from one part of the code to another. This topic was therefore one of the first things that Bob Floyd and I discussed when we became colleagues at Stanford in 1969; we wondered what kinds of programs we should really be writing, now that our old habits were coming into disrepute. Our results, summarized here, were in fact obtained partly while we were on strike protesting U.S. foreign policies, sitting next to each other and picketing campus buildings during those turbulent times.* [CL 495–505]

P43. Subspaces, subsets, and partitions. *Journal of Combinatorial Theory* **A10** (1971), 178–180. *This brief note shows that three apparently unrelated parts of mathematics are actually isomorphic to each other in a remarkably simple way.* [DM 511–513]

P44. The analysis of algorithms. *Actes du Congrès International des Mathématiciens 1970*, **3** (Paris: Gauthier-Villars, 1971), 269–274. French translation by Patrick Cégielski in *Algorithmes* (see Chapter 19), 137–144. *On this occasion — the first (and only) time that I was invited to address the International Congress of Mathematicians — I discussed the potential richness of studies relating to quantitative questions about how well algorithms can be expected to perform, and gave a name to what would prove to be my main life's work.* [AA 27–34]

P45. Examples of formal semantics. In *Symposium on Semantics of Algorithmic Languages*, edited by E. Engeler, *Lecture Notes in Mathematics* **188** (Berlin: Springer, 1971), 212–235. *This paper, a companion to P32, illustrates several more reasons to love attribute grammars.* [CL 401–422]

P46. Mathematical analysis of algorithms. *Proceedings of IFIP Congress 1971*, **1** (Amsterdam: North-Holland, 1972), 19–27. French translation by Patrick Cégielski in *Algorithmes* (see Chapter 19), 107–125. *With this paper, written a year after P44, I spoke to more than a thousand delegates at the International Congress of Information Processing (that is, of Computer Science), in a keynote address extolling the potential of algorithmic analysis. I consciously tried to define this new field and to illustrate a few of its basic paradigms, hoping that some day people would recognize "analysis of algorithms" as a noteworthy subfield of Computer Science. Happily, my dream began to be realized about a decade later, when textbooks with that title began to appear.* [AA 1–18]

P47. An empirical study of FORTRAN programs. *Software—Practice and Experience* **1** (1971), 105–133. *I believe this paper introduced a significant new approach to software engineering, in which we make a careful study of what programmers actually do and examine how to optimize things that really make a difference. It was based on a three-month summer study conducted with the help of about a dozen Stanford undergraduates.* [CL 507–543]

P48. Top-down syntax analysis. *Acta Informatica* **1** (1971), 79–110. Russian translation by Надежда И. Вьюкова in *Кибернетический Сборник* **15** (1978), 101–142. French translation by Patrick Cégielski in *Algorithmes* (see Chapter 19), 277–320. *The "bottom-up" parsing methods of P23 are complemented here by methods that go the other way. This paper was actually written in 1967, for a series of NATO summer-school lectures in Denmark whose publication was unexpectedly delayed.* [CL 285–326]

P49. (with Edward A. Bender) Enumeration of plane partitions. *Journal of Combinatorial Theory* **A13** (1972), 40–54. *Ed and I, who were office mates during the year I spent in Princeton (1968–1969), were able to resolve a decades-old combinatorial enigma: We found a simple explanation for the famous formulas that P. A. MacMahon had discovered in 1916 regarding the number of "plane partitions" — the number of ways to put n sugar cubes into the corner of a rectangular box.* [DM 465–482]

P50. (with R. L. Graham and T. S. Motzkin) Complements and transitive closures. *Discrete Mathematics* **2** (1972), 17–29. *A side effect of this work, which began as a somewhat routine investigation of the number of possible relations that can be obtained by repeatedly applying the operations of complementation and closure to a given relation, was the discovery by Motzkin of a new and basic concept, the so-called "weak components" of a directed graph.* [DM 393–404]

P51. (with N. G. de Bruijn and S. O. Rice)   The average height of planted plane trees. In *Graph Theory and Computing*, edited by Ronald C. Read (New York: Academic Press, 1972), 15–22. *If all ordered trees of n nodes are equally likely, the average distance to the deepest leaf is approximately* $\sqrt{\pi n}$. *Sharp forms of this result are derived here via the theory of complex variables, using techniques that subsequently became well known.* [AA 215–223]

P52. (with E. B. Kaehler) An experiment in optimal sorting. *Information Processing Letters* **1** (1972), 173–176. *Ted and I thought there must be a way to sort 14 elements into order by making fewer than 38 comparisons in the worst case. But no; our computer-aided explorations failed to find such a method. (Later work by Marcin Peczarski has established, in fact, that 38 comparisons is the absolute minimum.)* [AA 495–500]

P53. Ancient Babylonian algorithms. *Communications of the ACM* **15** (1972), 671–677. Errata, *Communications of the ACM* **19** (1976), 108. French translation by Patrick Cégielski in *Éléments pour une histoire de l'informatique* (see Chapter 19), 1–20. *For several weeks I immersed myself in aspects of mathematics that archæologists had discovered on old clay tablets, trying to understand the mindset of ancient scholars. Their approach to computation turned out to be both interesting and instructive; so I tried in this paper to translate it into modern language.* [CS 185–203]

P54. George Forsythe and the development of Computer Science. *Communications of the ACM* **15** (1972), 721–726. *Here's my homage to the great, foresighted man whose vision shaped Computer Science departments all over the world, especially at Stanford, thereby significantly influencing my own career.* [CS 241–259 in the first printing; CS 245–264 after 2003]

P55. (with Robert W. Floyd) The Bose–Nelson sorting problem. In *A Survey of Combinatorial Theory*, edited by Jagdish N. Srivastava (Amsterdam: North-Holland, 1973), 163–172. *Bob and I wrote many letters to each other during the 1960s concerning the construction of efficient sorting networks. This paper summarizes the principal ideas that we had come up with.* [DA 19–30]

P56. The dangers of computer science theory. In *Logic, Methodology, and Philosophy of Science* **4**, edited by Patrick Suppes, Leon Henkin, Athanase Joja, and Gr. C. Moisil (Amsterdam: North-Holland, 1973), 189–195. French translation by Patrick Cégielski in *Algorithmes* (see Chapter 19), 127–135. *One week after I presented paper P46 to an international congress in Ljubljana, I spoke to another international congress in Bucharest. The former paper extolled the virtues of computer science theories;*

this one pointed out that we should also beware of some vices. Thus I could quote myself on either side of any issue. [AA 19–26]

P57. Permutations with nonnegative partial sums. *Discrete Mathematics* **5** (1973), 367–371. *The solution to an intriguing problem that had been posed to me by Dan Kleitman at a meeting in Asilomar, California, where I met many combinatorial mathematicians for the first time.* [DM 429–432]

P58. The triel: A new solution. *Journal of Recreational Mathematics* **6** (1973), 1–7. *A controversial proof that pacifism wins, written shortly after I began a year-long visit to Norway.* [FG 209–218]

P59. (with Jill Knuth) Mathematics and Art: The dragon curve in ceramic tile. *Journal of Recreational Mathematics* **6** (1973), 165–167. *My wife and I decorated the entrance to our new home with this early instance of geek art, applying some of the ideas of P37.* [FG 615–621]

P60. (with Francis R. Stevenson) Optimal measurement points for program frequency counts. *BIT* **13** (1973), 313–322. *If we want to know how often each part of a computer program is executed, we need only place a few "counters" inside of that program. This paper explains how to insert the minimum number of counters.* [AA 43–53]

P61. Wheels within wheels. *Journal of Combinatorial Theory* **B16** (1974), 42–46. *A directed graph in which you can get from any vertex to any other always has a cyclical structure, which can be exploited to solve the "toll booth problem" posed by Tolly Holt.* [DM 387–391]

P62. The asymptotic number of geometries. *Journal of Combinatorial Theory* **A16** (1974), 398–400. *Gianco Rota asked how many generalized matroid structures are possible on n points. I found a quick way to prove that $\lg \lg g_n \sim n$ as $n \to \infty$, although the values of g_n for small n suggested otherwise.* [DM 425–427]

P63. Computer Science and its relation to Mathematics. *American Mathematical Monthly* **81** (April 1974), 323–343. A shorter form of this article, entitled "Computer Science and Mathematics," appeared in *American Scientist* **61** (1973), 707–713; reprinted in *Computers and People* **23**, 9 (September 1974), 8–11; and in *Mathematics: People, Problems, Results*, edited by Douglas M. Campbell and John C. Higgins, **3** (Belmont, California: Wadsworth, 1984), 37–47. Hungarian translation by Jószef Pelikán in *Matematikai Lapok* **24** (1973, published 1975), 345–363. Slovenian translation by Tamara Bohte in *Obzornik za Matematiko in Fiziko* **22** (1975), 129–138, 161–167. Slovak translation (abridged) by Branislav Rovan in *Pokroky Matematiky, Fiziky a Astronomie* **21**

(1976), 88–96. Russian translation by Наталья Г. Гуревич in *Совре-менные Проблемы Математики* **11**, 12 (Moscow: Znanie, 1977), 4–32. Reprinted in part in *A Century of Mathematics Through the Eyes of the* MONTHLY, edited by John Ewing (Mathematical Association of America, 1994), 285–288. French translation by Patrick Cégielski in *Algorithmes* (see Chapter 19), 1–28. *As departments of computer science began to spring up throughout the world, people wondered how my field fits in with the established disciplines. Here's my take on that question, biased of course toward my favorite topic: the analysis of algorithms. As an example, I considered problems related to hashing and "open addressing."* [CS 5–29]

P64. (with O. Amble)   Ordered hash tables. *The Computer Journal* **17** (May 1974), 135–142. *Ole Amble was the "grand old man" primarily responsible for bringing computers to Norway in the early 1950s, and I met him during my year in Oslo. He helped me translate the text of a public lecture into Norwegian (see Q32), a paper that contrasts two ways to search for data in a table, one based on ordering and one based on hashing; and he asked why nobody had tried to use both ordering and hashing at the same time. After I had first dismissed his idea as foolish, I realized that it was actually wonderful, and this paper is the result of our many discussions. The appendices contain solutions to several problems in the analysis of algorithms that were the most difficult I'd ever tackled up to that time, and I remain proud of them even though I suspect that fewer than ten people in the history of the world will ever scrutinize all of those appendices in detail.* [AA 77–99]

P65. (with Jayme L. Szwarcfiter)   A structured program to generate all topological sorting arrangements. *Information Processing Letters* **2** (1974), 153–157; erratum, **3** (1974), 64. Japanese translation by 有澤誠 [Makoto Arisawa] in *Bungeiteki Programming* (see Chapter 19), 125–133. *"An instructive example of several important general issues related to backtracking, procedures for changing recursion into iteration, manipulation of data structures, and the creation of well-structured programs."* [LP 91–97]

P66. (with Michael L. Fredman)   Recurrence relations based on mini-mization. *Journal of Mathematical Analysis and Applications* **48** (1974), 534–559. *Interesting problems of number theory arise when we study the se-quence 0, 1, 4, 8, 15, 24, 34, 47, 62, 81, 102, 124, ... defined for $n > 0$ by $M_n = n + \min_{0 \le k < n}(2M_k + 3M_{n-1-k})$, and similar sequences that arise in the analysis of recursive algorithms. For example, the numbers M_n of the given sequence are approximately $0.47n^{2.269}$.* [DM 537–564]

P67. Structured programming with **go to** statements. *Computing Sur-veys* **6** (December 1974), 261–301. Reprinted with revisions in *Current*

Trends in Programming Methodology, edited by Raymond T. Yeh, **1** (Englewood Cliffs, New Jersey: Prentice–Hall, 1977), 140–194; *Classics in Software Engineering*, edited by Edward Nash Yourdon (New York: Yourdon Press, 1979), 259–321. Japanese translation by 有澤誠 [Makoto Arisawa] in *Bungeiteki Programming* (see Chapter 19), 39–123. French translation by Patrick Cégielski in *Algorithmes* (see Chapter 19), 159–238. *This paper, which discusses the revolution in programming style that began with the work of Dijkstra and many others, was essentially written with dozens of coauthors, because I circulated it widely in draft form.* [LP 17–89]

P68. Computer programming as an art. *Communications of the ACM* **17** (1974), 667–673. French translation, with three supplementary paragraphs, in *L'Informatique Nouvelle*, No. 64 (July–August 1975), 20–27. Japanese translation by 有澤誠 [Makoto Arisawa] in *bit* **7** (1975), 434–444; reprinted in *Kunuusu Sensei no Program-Ron* (see Chapter 19), 2–19; reprinted in *Bungeiteki Programming* (see Chapter 19), 19–38. English version, reprinted with the supplementary paragraphs, in *ACM Turing Award Lectures: The First Twenty Years* (New York: ACM Press, 1987), 33–46. Russian translation by B. B. Мартынюк in *Лекции лауреатов премии Тьюринга* (Moscow: Mir, 1993), 48–64. French translation by Patrick Cégielski in *Éléments pour une histoire de l'informatique* (see Chapter 19), 345–362. *Why did I choose to write about "the art of computer programming"? Here's the answer, given when I was greatly honored by an award for the first three volumes having that title.* [LP 1–16]

P69. Estimating the efficiency of backtrack programs. *Mathematics of Computation* **29** (1975), 121–136. *This paper — an abridged form of R23, which I wrote just before coming to Stanford — explains a remarkably simple way that I'd discovered for predicting in many cases how long a combinatorial search will last.* [AA 55–75]

P70. (with Ronald W. Moore) An analysis of alpha-beta pruning. *Artificial Intelligence* **6** (1975), 293–326. *Game-playing algorithms can be analyzed too.* [AA 105–147]

P71. (with James H. Morris, Jr. and Vaughan R. Pratt) Fast pattern matching in strings. *SIAM Journal on Computing* **6** (1977), 323–350. Errata, see W. Rytter, *SIAM Journal on Computing* **9** (1980), 509–512. Reprinted in *Computer Algorithms: String Pattern Matching Strategies*, edited by Jun-ichi Aoe (Los Alamitos, California: IEEE Computer Society Press, 1994), 8–35. French translation by Patrick Cégielski in *Algorithmes* (see Chapter 19), 395–435. *The so-called Knuth–Morris–Pratt* algorithm was introduced and analyzed here, together with an analysis of other related methods. [DA 99–135]

P72. Random matroids. *Discrete Mathematics* **12** (1975), 341–358. *Many of the most efficient algorithms known for combinatorial problems apply to a general class of structures known as matroids. Dozens of important matroid families are known, yet the concept remains rather elusive. So I attempted to get more familiar with matroids by finding a way to construct them all, then to consider random paths in this construction process.* [DM 405–423]

P73. (with John F. Reiser) Evading the drift in floating-point addition. *Information Processing Letters* **3** (1975), 84–87. Errata, page 164. *When floating-point computations are rounded improperly, strange behaviors can arise. But proper rounding eliminates them.* [DA 341–348]

P74. (with Gururaj S. Rao) Activity in an interleaved memory. *IEEE Transactions on Computers* **C-24** (1975), 943–944. *Ramanujan's function $Q(n)$, which I had first encountered when analyzing the method of hashing with linear probing in 1962, turns out to apply also to a problem about memory conflicts that hardware designers had raised.* [AA 101–104]

P75. Notes on generalized Dedekind sums. *Acta Arithmetica* **33** (1977), 297–325. *I like this paper primarily because it alternates between "mathematical" and "algorithmical" ways to approach a problem in number theory that is strongly related to random number generation. The editors of a prestigious Polish journal encountered ALGOL-like language for the first time when they published this work.* [AA 149–180]

P76. (with Andrew C. Yao) Analysis of the subtractive algorithm for greatest common divisors. *Proceedings of the National Academy of Sciences* **72** (1975), 4720–4722. *The oldest nontrivial algorithm still in use today, predating Euclid by more than a century, is a procedure that finds the greatest common divisor of two given numbers via repeated subtractions. Here we show that the average number of subtraction steps is substantially more than was predicted by a continuous approximation to the expected behavior.* [AA 195–204]

P77. (with M. R. Garey, R. L. Graham, D. S. Johnson) Complexity results for bandwidth minimization. *SIAM Journal on Applied Mathematics* **34** (1978), 477–495. *How hard is it to permute the rows and columns of a matrix so that all of the nonzero elements stay as close as possible to the diagonal? The results of this paper were largely discovered by my distinguished coauthors; my job was to find a way to write up their complex constructions* *in a comprehensible manner. I decided to use biological terminology related to jellyfish in order to clarify the concepts.* [AA 505–533]

P78. (with Luis Trabb Pardo)   Analysis of a simple factorization algorithm. *Theoretical Computer Science* **3** (1976), 321–348. *Algorithms for factoring behave in a rather different way from algorithms for other tasks (like sorting) that I had studied previously. Here Luis and I discovered surprising connections between the average numbers of digits in the prime factors of n-digit numbers and the average lengths of cycles in the permutations of n objects.* [AA 303–339]

P79. Algorithms. *Scientific American* **236**, 4 (April 1977), 63–66, 69–72, 77–78, 80. Also *Scientific American Offprints*, number 360, 14 pages. Farsi translation by B. Parhami in *Bulletin of the Iranian Mathematical Society* **8** (1978), 122L–76L. French translation, "L'élaboration des algorithmes," in *L'intelligence de l'informatique* (Paris: Pour La Science, 1984), 75–86. French translation by Patrick Cégielski in *Algorithmes* (see Chapter 19), 59–87. *George Forsythe impressed on me the importance of writing papers for a general audience, instead of writing only for specialists, even though it's much more difficult to communicate with people who approach things differently than you do. I procrastinated for a few years — George died in 1972 — but kept his advice in mind; this paper, a reworking of Q32, was my first attempt in English.* [CS 59–86]

P80. (with Andrew C. Yao)   The complexity of nonuniform random number generation. In *Algorithms and Complexity*, edited by J. F. Traub (New York: Academic Press, 1976), 357–428. Russian translation by Б. Б. Походзей in *Кибернетический Сборник* **19** (1983), 97–158. *How many random bits are needed to generate random values that have different kinds of probability distributions? This paper, much of which was written while Andy and I were walking through California deserts during a week-long camping trip, explores fundamental aspects of this fascinating question.* [AA 545–603]

P81. The computer as Master Mind. *Journal of Recreational Mathematics* **9** (1976), 1–6. *I dropped everything else after receiving the game of Master Mind as a Christmas present in 1975, until I'd found a satisfying strategy. But I learned later that this was just the beginning of a story that's still ongoing.* [FG 219–229]

P82. Mathematics and Computer Science: Coping with finiteness. *Science* **194** (December 17, 1976), 1235–1242. Reprinted with corrections in *Electronics, the Continuing Revolution*, edited by Philip H. Abelson and Allen L. Hammond, AAAS publication **77-4** (Washington, D.C.: American Association for the Advancement of Science, 1977), 189–196; and in *Mathematics: People, Problems, Results*, edited by Douglas M. Campbell and John C. Higgins, **2** (Belmont, California: Wadsworth, 1984), 209–222. Bulgarian translation by Г. Чобанов and З. Докова in *Fiziko-Matematichesko Spisanie* **21** (Sofia, 1978), 58–74. German translation by Arthur Engel in *Der Mathematik-Unterricht* **25**, 6 (1979), 5–26. French translation by Patrick Cégielski in *Algorithmes* (see Chapter 19), 29–58. *My second attempt at a popular paper was an exposition of the exciting research on NP-hard problems that was blossoming in the mid-1970s.* [CS 31–58]

P83. (with Luis Trabb Pardo) The early development of programming languages. *Encyclopedia of Computer Science and Technology*, edited by Jack Belzer, Albert G. Holzman, and Allen Kent, **7** (New York: Marcel Dekker, Inc., 1977), 419–493. Reprinted in *A History of Computing in the Twentieth Century*, edited by N. Metropolis, J. Howlett, and Gian-Carlo Rota (New York: Academic Press, 1980), 197–273. French translation by Patrick Cégielski in *Éléments pour une histoire de l'informatique* (see Chapter 19), 77–178. *Luis and I had a fascinating time telling the previously unwritten story of how symbolic languages for computer programs had sprung up around the world during the 1940s and early 1950s.* [CL 1–94]

P84. (with Arne T. Jonassen) A trivial algorithm whose analysis isn't. *Journal of Computer and System Sciences* **16** (1978), 301–322. *Some problems in the analysis of algorithms have no simple answer. Arne and I proved this by finding an answer that definitely isn't simple, although the problem itself involves dealing with only three numbers at a time.* [AA 257–282]

P85. A generalization of Dijkstra's algorithm. *Information Processing Letters* **6** (1977), 1–5. *Just as regular (finite-state) languages are an extremely special case of context-free languages, this paper shows that the shortest-path problem is just a special case of a considerably more general (yet efficiently solvable) optimization problem.* [DA 209–217]

P86. Evaluation of Porter's constant. *Computers and Mathematics with Applications* **2** (1976), 137–139. *Equation 4.5.3–(42) in the first edition of my book* Seminumerical Algorithms *hypothesized a constant 1.47 that was suggested by empirical observations of the average behavior of Euclid's algorithm. A later breakthrough by J. W. Porter allowed me to express that constant 1.467078 . . . in closed form, and to evaluate it to as many decimal places as desired.* [AA 189–194]

P87. (with Michael S. Paterson) Identities from partition involutions. *Fibonacci Quarterly* **16** (June 1978), 198–212. *Amazing formulas like* $(1-x)(1-x^2)(1-x^3)(1-x^4)(1-x^5) - x^6(1-x^2)(1-x^3)(1-x^4) + x^{6+5}(1-x^3) = 1-x-x^2+x^5+x^7-x^{12}$ *follow from elementary operations on integer partitions.* [DM 493–510]

P88. (with Arnold Schönhage) The expected linearity of a simple equivalence algorithm. *Theoretical Computer Science* **6** (1978), 281–315. *Arnold and I found that a simple implementation of the basic UNION–FIND algorithm can be proved efficient by using methods of statistical mechanics that had been developed in Russia.* [AA 341–389]

P89. Deletions that preserve randomness. *IEEE Transactions on Software Engineering* **SE-3** (1977), 351–359. *This paper introduces a theoretical model for operations on data structures, and analyzes its behavior in simple cases.* [AA 283–302]

P90. The average time for carry propagation. *Indagationes Mathematicæ* **40** (1978), 238–242. *On Dick de Bruijn's 60th birthday, I showed him that I'd understood some of what he taught me, by analyzing how many times one needs to replace $x+y$ by $(x \oplus y, 2(x \,\&\, y))$ before $y = 0$, when adding two random n-bit numbers using bitwise operations.* [AA 467–471]

P91. Mathematical typography. *Bulletin of the American Mathematical Society* (new series) **1** (March 1979), 337–372. Reprinted with corrections as part 1 of TEX *and* METAFONT (see Chapter 19). Also reprinted in *Dr. Dobb's Journal of Computer Calisthenics & Orthodontia* **5**, 3 (March 1980), 5–20. Russian translation by O. A. Маховая in Компьютерная Типография (see Chapter 19), 36–78. *By an astonishing coincidence, I was asked to give a major address at the American Mathematical Society's annual meeting just at the time I had privately decided to develop a computer system for typesetting. The text of my talk, recorded here, shows the first fruits of this work. Neither I nor anybody in the audience had any inkling that the resulting TEX and* METAFONT *systems would substantially change the face of mathematics publishing during the next three decades.* [DT 19–65]

P92. (with A. V. Anisimov) Inhomogeneous sorting. *International Journal of Computer and Information Sciences* **8** (1979), 255–260. Russian translation by А. В. Анисимов in Программирование **5**, 1 (1979), 11–14. English retranslation in *Programming and Computer Software* **5** (1979), 7–10. *Yet another surprise was the fact, learned in 2005, that some leading mathematicians have found the results in this short note to be significant, although I'd actually dashed it off hastily in a few hours.* [DA 71–77]

P93. Lexicographic permutations with restrictions. *Discrete Applied Mathematics* **1** (1979), 117–125. *There's an easy, fast way to generate all permutations whose elements obey treelike ordering constraints.* [DA 79–90]

P94. Algorithms in modern mathematics and computer science. *Lecture Notes in Computer Science* **122** (1981), 82–99. Russian translation by Г. С. Цейтин in *Алгоритмы в Современнои Математике и Её Приложениях*, Часть I (Novosibirsk: Академия Наук СССР, Сибирское Отделение, Вычислительный Центр, 1982), 64–98. Revised version entitled "Algorithmic thinking and mathematical thinking," *American Mathematical Monthly* **92** (1985), 170–181. Japanese translation by 一松信 [Shin Hitotsumatsu] in *Kunuusu Sensei no Program-Ron* (see Chapter 19), 22–43. French translation by Patrick Cégielski in *Éléments pour une histoire de l'informatique* (see Chapter 19), 21–51. *What do mathematicians do? Is it different from what computer scientists do? I tried to find out by examining a random sample of some famous books.* [CS 87–114]

P95. Supernatural numbers. In *The Mathematical Gardner*, edited by David A. Klarner (Belmont, California: Wadsworth International, 1981), 310–325; reprinted with new title *Mathematical Recreations* (Dover, 1998). Russian translation by Ю. А. Данилов in *Математический цветник*, edited by И. М. Яглом (Moscow: Mir, 1983), 388–408. *Think about really big numbers: How to name them, how to guess them, how to encode them in a commafree way.* [FG 103–120]

P96. The letter S. *The Mathematical Intelligencer* **2** (1980), 114–122. Russian translation by Р. М. Кузнец in *Компьютерная Типография* (see Chapter 19), 273–292. *The hardest letter to draw properly leads naturally to an instructive problem of elementary geometry.* [DT 263–284]

P97. Deciphering a linear congruential encryption. *IEEE Transactions on Information Theory* **IT-31** (1985), 49–52. *The method most widely used to generate "random" numbers by computer isn't very good at hiding secret information.* [DA 349–358]

P98. (with Michael F. Plass) Breaking paragraphs into lines. *Software—Practice and Experience* **11** (1981), 1119–1184. Russian translation by Н. В. Третьяков and О. А. Маховая in *Компьютерная Типография* (see Chapter 19), 79–166. French translation by Patrick Cégielski in *Éléments pour une histoire de l'informatique* (see Chapter 19), 199–295. *The major advance made by TEX in comparison to previous* *methods of type composition is due to its technique of considering each paragraph as a whole before choosing the breaks between lines. This technique is based on well-known principles of dynamic programming.* [DT 67–155]

P99. Verification of link-level protocols. *BIT* **21** (1981), 31–36. *Invariant assertions can fruitfully be applied to an entire system of cooperating programs, not just to a single program.* [DA 167–173]

P100. The concept of a meta-font. *Visible Language* **16** (1982), 3–27. French translation by M. R. Delorme in *Communication et Langages* no. 55, (1983), 40–53; reprinted in *Typographie et Informatique*, proceedings of INRIA conference held 21–25 January 1985, organized by Jacques André and Patrick Sallio (Rennes, France: INRIA/IRISA – CCETT, 1985), 119–132. Russian translation by P. M. Кузнец in *Компьютерная Типография* (see Chapter 19), 296–320. *Here I illustrate the notion of parameters in font design by varying them in midsentence.* [DT 289–314]

P101. Huffman's algorithm via algebra. *Journal of Combinatorial Theory* **A32** (1982), 216–224. Russian translation by Б. Б. Походзей in *Кибернетический Сборник* **22** (1985), 159–169. *David Huffman discovered a famous algorithm that constructs codes of minimum redundancy. This paper defines the concept of a "Huffman algebra" on a linearly ordered set, and shows that Huffman's algorithm finds the smallest expressions of the algebra that can be formed from any given subset of the elements.* [DM 377–386]

P102. A permanent inequality. *American Mathematical Monthly* **88** (1981), 731–740, 798. *Starting from first principles, this expository paper explains how Egorychev proved van der Waerden's famous conjecture that the permanent of every doubly stochastic $n \times n$ matrix is $\geq n!/n^n$.* [DM 89–104]

P103. Dynamic Huffman coding. *Journal of Algorithms* **6** (1985), 163–180. *Huffman codes, which depend on the frequencies of individual letters, can be varied as those frequencies change, if the transmitting and receiving processes cooperate properly. (The method is now called the Faller–Gallager–Knuth algorithm, because it was discovered at least three times.)* [DA 51–70]

P104. An analysis of optimum caching. *Journal of Algorithms* **6** (1985), 181–199. *A clairvoyant cache memory knows what data should be kept most accessible to a running process. This paper analyzes how much improvement is possible when the access patterns are random.* [AA 235–255]

P105. (with David R. Fuchs) Optimal prepaging and font caching. *ACM Transactions on Programming Languages and Systems* **7** (1985), 62–79. *David and I faced new problems when we wanted to transmit large* *amounts of font data to a small typesetting machine. We found a practical solution by implementing a method that could be proved optimum under hypothetical conditions that were only approximately satisfied. This method was used during the summer of 1980 to typeset the second edition of* Seminumerical Algorithms. [DA 181–207]

P106. The distribution of continued fraction approximations. *Journal of Number Theory* **19** (1984), 443–448. *I've often asked Hendrik Lenstra a question that he was able to answer. This paper represents a case in which, fortunately, I was able to return the favor. The question here involves continued fractions that are eventually periodic.* [AA 181–187]

P107. An algorithm for Brownian zeros. (Originally spelled 'zeroes'.) *Computing* **33** (1984), 89–94. *Instead of generating random numbers, this algorithm generates a whole random function (although revealing only the places where that function is zero, with respect to a given resolution).* [DA 329–335]

P108. (with Michael F. Plass*) Choosing better line breaks. In *Document Preparation Systems*, edited by Jurg Nievergelt, Giovanni Coray, Jean-Daniel Nicoud, and Alan C. Shaw (Amsterdam: North-Holland, 1982), 221–242. *Michael condensed P98 and added the new concept of "kerf."*

P109. Literate programming. *The Computer Journal* **27** (1984), 97–111. Japanese translation by 黒川利明 [Toshiaki Kurokawa] in *bit* **17** (1985), 426–450; reprinted in *Kunuusu Sensei no Program-Ron* (see Chapter 19), 82–128. Japanese translation by 有澤誠 [Makoto Arisawa] in *Bungeiteki Programming* (see Chapter 19), 135–182. *I introduced the* WEB *system in a British journal, because I'd noticed that my students from Great Britain tended to be more interested in good writing than my American students were.* [LP 99–136]

P110. Lessons learned from METAFONT. *Visible Language* **19** (1985), 35–53. Russian translation by Ю. В. Тюменцев in *Компьютерная Типография* (see Chapter 19), 321–343. *A keynote presentation to the world's leading type designers, at an international workshop organized by Chuck Bigelow.* [DT 315–338]

P111. The toilet paper problem. *American Mathematical Monthly* **91** (1984), 465–470. *Paul Halmos, the journal's editor, warned me that I might not want to see a paper with this title on my resumé. People who get past the title will notice that a simple but instructive probabilistic process is examined here as it passes through a point of phase transition.* [AA 225–234]

P112. The IBM 650: An appreciation from the field. *Annals of the History of Computing* **8** (1986), 50–55. *My heartfelt homage to the machine that got me started in computing.* [CS 227–239]

P113. Semi-optimal bases for linear dependencies. *Linear and Multi-linear Algebra* **17** (1985), 1–4. *An interesting problem arose when I tried to minimize rounding errors within the calculations of* METAFONT. *A partial solution appears here, but the general question remains open.* [DA 337–340]

P114. Efficient balanced codes. *IEEE Transactions on Information Theory* **IT-32** (1986), 51–53. Reprinted in Mario Blaum, *Codes for Detecting and Correcting Unidirectional Errors* (Los Alamitos, California: IEEE Computer Society Press, 1993). *When I learned that coding theorists were interested in binary codes that have exactly as many 0s as 1s, a lucky idea came to me, for which encoding and decoding are both easy.* [DM 433–438]

P115. (with Huang Bing-Chao) A one-way, stackless quicksort algorithm. *BIT* **26** (1986), 127–130. *A young student from China discovered an interesting new way to sort, and I helped him to analyze it.* [DA 31–34]

P116. Digital halftones by dot diffusion. *ACM Transactions on Graphics* **6** (1987), 245–273. Russian translation by O. A. Маховая in Компьютерная Типография (see Chapter 19), 447–468. *This paper studies parallel alternatives to the sequential Floyd–Steinberg algorithm for rendering images as arrays of binary pixels.* [DT 449–471]

P117. Fibonacci multiplication. *Applied Mathematics Letters* **1** (1988), 57–60. *A curious new way to multiply numbers, in which the "product" of F_m and F_n is F_{m+n}.* [FG 87–92]

P118. (with Christos H. Papadimitriou* and John N. Tsitsiklis) A note on strategy elimination in bimatrix games. *Operations Research Letters* **7** (1988), 103–107. Errata, see I. Gilboa, E. Kalai, and E. Zemel, "On the order of eliminating dominated strategies," *Operations Research Letters* **9** (1990), 85–89.

P119. A Fibonacci-like sequence of composite numbers. *Mathematics Magazine* **63** (1990), 21–25. *There's a sequence a, b, $a + b$, $a + 2b$, $2a + 3b$, ... of nonprime numbers in which each number (after the first two) is the sum of its two predecessors.* [FG 93–98]

P120. (with Boris Pittel) A recurrence related to trees. *Proceedings of the American Mathematical Society* **105** (1989), 335–349. *Studies of random graphs lead to sequences that satisfy a somewhat complicated recurrence relation, studied first in P88 and reconsidered here. The "tree polynomials,"* *whose coefficients enumerate functional digraphs with a given number of components, play an important role.* [DM 565–583]

P121. (with Herbert S. Wilf)   The power of a prime that divides a generalized binomial coefficient. *Journal für die reine und angewandte Mathematik* **396** (1989), 212–219. *Herb and I were pleased to extend a well-known classical result of E. E. Kummer that had originally appeared in volume 44 of the very same journal (1852).* [DM 515–524]

P122. (with Philippe Flajolet and Boris Pittel)   The first cycles in an evolving graph. *Discrete Mathematics* **75** (1989), 167–215. This volume was also published as *Combinatorics 1988*, Proceedings of the Cambridge Conference in Honour of Paul Erdős, edited by Béla Bollobás (Amsterdam: North-Holland, 1989). *Philippe and Boris visited Stanford, and we studied the fascinating phenomena that arise when an initially empty graph or multigraph gains new edges at random. To our surprise, we could obtain precise results by manipulating bivariate generating functions $g(w, z)$ in a new way.* [DM 585–642]

P123. Efficient representation of perm groups. *Combinatorica* **11** (1991), 33–43. *Computers can deal rather well with the groups that are generated by given permutations, using the algorithms presented and analyzed here.* [DA 315–328]

P124. The errors of TEX. *Software—Practice and Experience* **19** (1989), 607–685. Japanese translation by 有澤誠 [Makoto Arisawa] in *Bungeiteki Programming* (see Chapter 19), 319–425. *For years I had preached the doctrine that we should keep track of (and learn from) our mistakes. Eventually I also began to practice what I had preached.* [LP 243–339]

P125. (with Hermann Zapf)   AMS Euler—A new typeface for mathematics. *Scholarly Publishing* **20** (1989), 131–157. Abridged version in *ABC–XYZapf*, edited by John Dreyfus and Knut Erichson (London: Wynkyn de Worde Society, 1989), 171–179. Russian translation by P. M. Кузнец in *Компьютерная Типография* (see Chapter 19), 344–368. *One of the greatest side-effects of my excursion into typographic research was the opportunity to work with the great letter artist Hermann Zapf. This paper documents the process by which he designed a typeface commissioned by the American Mathematical Society, while I served as his communication channel to a committee of mathematicians.* [DT 339–365]

P126. (with Robert W. Floyd)   Addition machines. *SIAM Journal on Computing* **19** (1990), 329–340. *Abstract computers that can add, subtract,* *and compare numbers, but which have no other built-in arithmetical capabilities, are actually able to divide x by y in $O(\log(x/y))$ steps, by using properties of the Fibonacci sequence. Exponentiation and other operations can also be done efficiently.* [DA 137–154]

P127. (with Rajeev Motwani and Boris Pittel) Stable husbands. *Random Structures & Algorithms* **1** (1990), 1–14. *If n boys and n girls rank each other at random, how many different mates will a given girl have, among all of the stable matchings defined by those rankings? The answer — roughly between $\frac{1}{2}\ln n$ and $\ln n$ — is found by applying several important general principles. (I believe that one of those solution techniques, the "principle of negligible perturbations," has not yet been sufficiently appreciated by other researchers.)* [AA 429–445]

P128. (with Richard Garfield and Herbert S. Wilf*) A bijection for ordered factorizations. *Journal of Combinatorial Theory* **A54** (1990), 317–318. *My tenuous connection to the man who later created "Magic: The Gathering" came about because both of us contributed to a problem that Herb had raised.*

P129. (with Herbert S. Wilf*) A short proof of Darboux's lemma. *Applied Mathematics Letters* **2** (1989), 139–140.

P130. (with Leonidas J. Guibas* and Micha Sharir*) Randomized incremental construction of Delaunay and Voronoi diagrams. *Algorithmica* **7** (1992), 381–413. Abbreviated version in *Automata, Languages and Programming*, edited by M. S. Paterson, *Lecture Notes in Computer Science* **443** (1990), 414–431. *I tend to be geometrically challenged, but Leo and Micha generously invited me to be a coauthor of this interesting study. I extended the algorithm slightly in Section 18 of my subsequent book Axioms and Hulls, and implemented it later as part of The Stanford GraphBase.*

P131. (with Lee Sallows*, Martin Gardner*, Richard K. Guy*) Serial isogons of 90 degrees. *Mathematics Magazine* **64** (1991), 315–324. *In this paper Lee introduced the concept of a "serial isogon," a polygon whose sides have the respective lengths 1, 2, . . . , n, in that order.*

P132. (with Arvind Raghunathan) The problem of compatible representatives. *SIAM Journal on Discrete Mathematics* **5** (1992), 422–427. *The general problem discussed here is known nowadays as "constraint satisfaction with unary and binary predicates."* [AA 535–543]

P133. A simple program whose proof isn't. In *Beauty Is Our Business*, edited by W. H. J. Feijen, A. J. M. van Gasteren, D. Gries, and J. Misra, a festschrift for Edsger Dijkstra (New York: Springer, 1990), 233–242.

At Edsger's 60th birthday celebration I exhibited a very short (and useful) program for which all known proofs are somewhat intricate. [DA 155–165]

P134. Nested satisfiability. *Acta Informatica* **28** (1990), 1–6. *A tree-structured variant of the general Boolean satisfiability problem turns out to be solvable in linear time.* [DA 91–98]

P135. Textbook examples of recursion. *Artificial Intelligence and Mathematical Theory of Computation*, papers in honor of John McCarthy, edited by Vladimir Lifschitz (San Diego, California: Academic Press, 1991), 207–229. *Some of John's favorite toy LISP programs lead to instructive problems in discrete mathematics when studied quantitatively.* [AA 391–414]

P136. A note on digitized angles. *Electronic Publishing—Origination, Dissemination, and Design* **3** (1990), 99–104. Russian translation by О. А. Маховая in *Компьютерная Типография* (see Chapter 19), 469–476. *Subtle optical effects occur when intersecting lines are converted to bitmaps.* [DT 473–480]

P137. Two notes on notation. *American Mathematical Monthly* **99** (1992), 403–422; **102** (1995), 562. *Here you'll find good reasons to like the notations for Iverson brackets and Stirling numbers that appear in my books, together with a historical discussion.* [DM 15–44]

P138. Theory and practice. *Theoretical Computer Science* **90** (1991), 1–15. Also published in *Images of Programming*, dedicated to the memory of A. P. Ershov, edited by D. Bjørner and V. Kotov (Amsterdam: North-Holland, 1991), 1–15. *Twenty years after P46, I was asked again to address an IFIP Congress. The message this time was shorter, less technical, more philosophical, and had more jokes.* [CS 149–167]

P139. Context-free multilanguages. *Theoretical Studies in Computer Science*, edited by Jeffrey D. Ullman, a festschrift for Seymour Ginsburg (San Diego, California: Academic Press, 1992), 1–13. *Just as a language is a set of words, a multilanguage is a multiset of words.* [CL 361–375]

P140. (with Svante Janson, Tomasz Łuczak, Boris Pittel) The birth of the giant component. *Random Structures & Algorithms* **4** (1993), 233–358. *My longest-ever paper was written lovingly over a period of many months. Having just finished the TEX project, and the writing of once-in-a-lifetime books such as Concrete Mathematics and 3:16, I knew that I'd never again have a chance to immerse myself in a really tough research topic, because I would soon need to concentrate fully on completing The Art of Computer Programming. My illustrious co-authors and I were able to extend the ideas of P120 and P122* *significantly further, so that we could slow down the "big bang" that occurs as a random graph evolves, measuring time by the number of complex cycles present. We now could essentially watch the graph go step by step through a double-jump phase transition as its "giant component" materialized. I tried to write this paper somewhat in the manner of Victor Hugo, by leading the reader through the process of discovery that we experienced while doing this research: pausing now and then to "smell the roses" instead of advancing the plot hastily toward the proofs of the main theorems.* [DM 643–792]

P141. Convolution polynomials. *Mathematica Journal* **2**, 4 (Fall 1992), 67–78. *A large number of important families of polynomials that I have encountered over the years all turn out to be instances of a beautiful general scheme, whose properties have been discovered independently but incompletely by many other people.* [DM 225–256]

P142. Johann Faulhaber and sums of powers. *Mathematics of Computation* **61** (1993), 277–294. *A forgotten Renaissance mathematician had a message for the 20th century.* [DM 61–84]

P143. Bracket notation for the 'coefficient-of' operator. *A Classical Mind*, essays in honour of C. A. R. Hoare, edited by A. W. Roscoe (Hemel Hempstead, Hertfordshire: Prentice–Hall International, 1994), 247–258. *Untapped advantages of notations like $[z^3 + 2z^5] f(z)$.* [DM 45–59]

P144. Mini-indexes for literate programs. *Software—Concepts and Tools* **15** (1994), 2–11. Russian translation by Ю. В. Тюменцев in Компьютерная Типография (see Chapter 19), 235–255. *How to make literate programs more accessible in books.* [DT 225–245]

P145. Two-way rounding. *SIAM Journal on Discrete Mathematics* **8** (1995), 281–290. *A corollary of this study is that spreadsheet data can always be rounded so that row and column sums both check out.* [DA 219–234]

P146. (with Inger Johanne Håland) Polynomials involving the floor function. *Mathematica Scandinavica* **76** (1995), 194–200. *Did you know that $x^3 = 3x\lfloor x\lfloor x\rfloor\rfloor - 3\lfloor x\rfloor \lfloor x\lfloor x\rfloor\rfloor + \lfloor x\rfloor^3 + 3\{x\}\{x\lfloor x\rfloor\} + \{x\}^3$?* [DM 257–264]

P147. Leaper graphs. *The Mathematical Gazette* **78** (1994), 274–297. *The chessboard knight has infinitely many exotic cousins that are able to tour suitably large boards.* [FG 541–570]

P148. The sandwich theorem. *Electronic Journal of Combinatorics* **1** (1994), article A1, 48 pages. *An introduction to the Lovász number of a graph and how to compute it.* [DM 123–176]

P149. An exact analysis of stable allocation. *Journal of Algorithms* **20** (1996), 431–442. *Surprise: When traders rate each other's goods randomly, the ranks in the unique stable allocation of those goods have the same probability distribution as the search distances of uniform hashing.* [AA 415–427]

P150. Aztec diamonds, checkerboard graphs, and spanning trees. *Journal of Algebraic Combinatorics* **6** (1997), 253–257. *A proof of Stanley's conjecture about the number of spanning trees in some remarkable bipartite graphs.* [DM 187–192]

P151. Irredundant intervals. *ACM Journal of Experimental Algorithmics* **1** (1996), article 1, 19 pages. *A literate program to implement an instructive optimization algorithm that goes beyond the traditional realm of minimax theory.* [DA 245–274]

P152. (with David J. Jeffrey*, Robert M. Corless, David E. G. Hare) Sur l'inversion de $y^\alpha e^y$ au moyen de nombres de Stirling associés. *Comptes Rendus de l'Académie des Sciences, série I*, **320** (1995), 1449–1452. *Several flavors of Stirling numbers come up when solving the equation $x = y^\alpha e^y$ for y in terms of x.*

P153. Partitioned tensor products and their spectra. *Journal of Algebraic Combinatorics* **6** (1997), 259–267. *It's often easy to compute the eigenvalues of a pleasant family of product graphs.* [DM 193–202]

P154. The Knowlton–Graham partition problem. *Journal of Combinatorial Theory* **A73** (1996), 185–189. *In volume 1 of this journal, Ron Graham published a paper about electrical wire labeling, which he told me was the most important practical result that he had devised during all the decades of his work at Bell Telephone Laboratories. Here I prove his result more simply, and sharpen it slightly, by recasting it as a matrix problem.* [DM 439–443]

P155. (with R. M. Corless*, G. H. Gonnet, D. E. G. Hare, and D. J. Jeffrey) On the Lambert W function. *Advances in Computational Mathematics* **5** (1996), 329–359. *The important function $T(z)$ that I've called the tree function in numerous works has unfortunately become known to software packages as $-W(-z)$, where $W(z)$ is the so-called Lambert function (although Lambert never knew it).*

P156. Overlapping Pfaffians. *Electronic Journal of Combinatorics* **3**, 2 (1996), paper R5, 13 pages. Reprinted in *The Foata Festschrift*, edited by Jacques Désarménien, Adalbert Kerber, and Volker Strehl (Gap: Imprimerie Louis-Jean, 1996), 151–163. *Determinants are the bipartite special case of Pfaffians; so I've gathered here all the basic facts that I could find about Pfaffians.* [DM 105–121]

P157. (with Svante Janson) Shellsort with three increments. *Random Structures & Algorithms* **10** (1997), 125–142. *The asymptotic behavior of Shellsort, a popular sorting algorithm, has resisted all attempts at analysis. Here we explore a very special case, in hopes of gaining a better understanding of this mysterious process.* [AA 447–466]

P158. Linear probing and graphs. *Algorithmica* **22** (1998), 561–568. French translation by Patrick Cégielski in *Algorithmes* (see Chapter 19), 383–393. *I first experienced the joys of algorithmic analysis in 1962, when I took a day off from compiler writing and analyzed the method of hashing that I was implementing for that compiler — an algorithm now called linear probing. Thirty-five years later, my joy was complete when I was able to replace those early brute-force calculations with a new derivation, using modern "symbolic methods" that were pioneered by Philippe Flajolet, thereby also being able to analyze higher moments of the runtime distribution. This paper was presented to Philippe on his 50th birthday.* [AA 473–483]

P159. Dancing links. *Millennial Perspectives in Computer Science*, edited by Jim Davies, Bill Roscoe, and Jim Woodcock (Houndmills, Basingstoke, Hampshire: Palgrave, 2000), 187–214. French translation by Patrick Cégielski in *Algorithmes* (see Chapter 19), 239–276. *A simple data-structure technique that facilitates undoing in backtrack algorithms leads to lots of fun. And it also suggests a new approach to proofs of correctness, using behavioral properties (which are easy to state) instead of invariant assertions (which are hopelessly complex).* [FG 437–472]

P160. (with Frank Ruskey) Efficient coroutine generation of constrained Gray sequences. In *From Object-Orientation to Formal Methods: Dedicated to the Memory of Ole-Johan Dahl*, edited by O. Owe, S. Krogdahl, and T. Lyche, *Lecture Notes in Computer Science* **2635** (Heidelberg: Springer-Verlag, 2004), 183–204. *My final homage to Ole-Johan Dahl is an amusing and thought-provoking application of recursive coroutines, one of the main concepts that I'd learned from him.* [CL 545–574]

P161. (with Fan Chung* and Ron Graham*) A symmetric Eulerian identity. *Journal of Combinatorics* **1** (2010), 29–38.

$$- * - * - * - * - * - * - * - * - * - * - * -$$

Q1. (with J. D. Alanen*) A table of minimum functions for generating Galois fields $GF(p^n)$. *Sankhyā*, series A, **23** (1961), 128.

Q2. Backus' language. *Communications of the ACM* **5** (1962), 185, abstract 62T-137.

Q3. The calculation of Easter. *Communications of the ACM* **5** (1962), 209–210.

Q4. Non-Desarguesian planes of order 2^{2m+1}. *Notices of the American Mathematical Society* **9** (June 1962), 218. *In those days it was traditional to claim priority for a new mathematical result by publishing a brief notice. Therefore, to avoid being scooped, I wrote this paragraph immediately after discovering the result that was supposed to be the cornerstone of my Ph.D. thesis (see P22).*

Q5. History of writing compilers. Digest of Technical Papers, *ACM 62 National Conference* (September 1962), 43, 126. *Subsumed by P10.*

Q6. Evaluation of polynomials by computer. *Communications of the ACM* **6** (1963), 51. *(See also P9.)* [DA 395]

Q7. Review of *Computer Applications in the Behavioral Sciences*. *Computing Reviews* **4** (May–June 1963), 120–122.

Q8. Letters on merging. *Communications of the ACM* **6** (1963), 585–587.

Q9. Addition chains and the evaluation of nth powers. *Notices of the American Mathematical Society* **11** (February 1964), 230–231, abstract 64T-140.

Q10. Non-Desarguesian planes of order 2^{2m+1}. *Notices of the American Mathematical Society* **11** (June 1964), 445–446, abstract 64T-268.

Q11. Backus Normal Form vs. Backus Naur Form. *Communications of the ACM* **7** (1964), 735–736. French translation by Patrick Cégielski in *Éléments pour une histoire de l'informatique* (see Chapter 19), 319–322. [CL 95–97]

Q12. Man or boy? *Algol Bulletin* **17** (Amsterdam: Mathematisch Centrum, July 1964) 7; **19** (January 1965), 8–9. [CL 123–125]

Q13. Teaching ALGOL 60. *Algol Bulletin* **19** (Amsterdam: Mathematisch Centrum, January 1965), 4–6. [CL 99–102]

Q14. A list of the remaining trouble spots in ALGOL 60. *Algol Bulletin* **19** (Amsterdam: Mathematisch Centrum, January 1965), 29–38.

Q15. Comments concerning PL/I language specifications as published in the IBM Manual (Form C28-6571-1). *PL/I Bulletin* **1** (January 1966), 5–14.

Q16. Problem 5264, the triangle inequality and the parallelogram law. *American Mathematical Monthly* **72** (1965), 193; solutions in **73** (1966), 211–212. [CP 1]

Q17. Additional comments on a problem in concurrent programming control. *Communications of the ACM* **9** (1966), 321–322; errata, page 878. Reprinted in *Communications of the ACM* **26** (1983), 22. [DA 175–180]

Q18. Algorithm and program; information and data. *Communications of the ACM* **9** (1966), 654. French translation by Patrick Cégielski in *Éléments pour une histoire de l'informatique* (see Chapter 19), 315–316. [CS 1–2]

Q19. (with R. W. Floyd) Improved constructions for the Bose–Nelson sorting problem. *Notices of the American Mathematical Society* **14** (February 1967), 283, Abstract 67T-228.

Q20. What is an algorithm? *Datamation* **13**, 10 (October 1967), 30–32.

Q21. Comments on programming languages. In *Simulation Programming Languages*, edited by J. N. Buxton (Amsterdam: North-Holland, 1968), passim.

Q22. Evolution of number systems. *Datamation* **15** (February 1969), 93–97; (April 1969), 307, 309; (May 1969), 229. Reprinted with corrections in Elias M. Awad, *Automatic Data Processing* (Englewood Cliffs, New Jersey: Prentice–Hall, 1970), 353–357.

Q23. Letter to the editor regarding uncrossed Knight's tours. *Journal of Recreational Mathematics* **2** (1969), 155–157. [FG 477–488]

Q24. (with Edward A. Bender) Constructive enumeration of plane partitions. *Notices of the American Mathematical Society* **16** (June 1969), 659, abstract 69T-A87.

Q25. Discussion of Mr. Riordan's paper "Abel identities and inverse relations." In *Combinatorial Mathematics and Its Applications*, edited by R. C. Bose and T. A. Dowling, University of North Carolina Monograph Series in Probability and Statistics **4** (Chapel Hill, North Carolina: University of North Carolina Press, 1969), 91–94. [DM 221–224]

Q26. Review of *Game Playing with Computers*, by Donald D. Spencer. *Journal of Recreational Mathematics* **2** (1969), 237–238.

Q27. Review of *Introduction to Combinatorial Mathematics*, by C. L. Liu. *IEEE Transactions on Information Theory* **IT-17** (1971), 119–120.

Q28. (with Michael L. Fredman) Recurrence relations based on minimization. *Notices of the American Mathematical Society* **18** (October 1971), 960, abstract 71T-B234.

Q29. (with Ronald L. Rivest) Bibliography on computer sorting. *Computing Reviews* **13** (June 1972), 283–289.

Q30. Sequences with precisely $k + 1$ k-blocks; Schröder's problem; groups. Solutions to Problems E2307, E2315, E2328. *American Mathematical Monthly* **79** (1972), 773–774, 910, 1138–1139.

Q31. The history of sorting. *Datamation* **18** (December 1972), 64, 69–70.

Q32. Søking etter noe i en EDB-maskin. (Norwegian) *Forskningsnytt* **18**, 4 (Norges Almenvitenskapelige Forskningsråd, 1973), 39–42. *I attempted to learn the Norwegian language during my year at the University of Oslo, but never got very far because everybody else wanted to practice their English. Still, I drafted this paper in Norwegian, after giving a public lecture (in English) entitled "Searching for something in a computer"; then Ole Amble helped me to correct the grammar and style; then I submitted it to the magazine that was Norway's equivalent of Scientific American. In the final publication, about 1/3 of the remaining words were mine, 1/3 were Amble's, and 1/3 were due to the magazine's editors. After a few years I retold the same technical story in English (see P79).*

Q33. A terminological proposal. *SIGACT News* **6**, 1 (January 1974), 12–18. French translation by Patrick Cégielski in *Éléments pour une histoire de l'informatique* (see Chapter 19), 331–339. *Early ideas about what to call problems that are complete for nondeterministic polynomial time were submitted to a popular vote. See Q36 for the result.* [AA 485–492]

Q34. (with Ellen Crawford and Leonard Carlitz) Problems and their solutions, submitted as a letter to the editor. *Fibonacci Quarterly* **12** (1974), 46, 79, 82. [A solution to the last problem had essentially been published earlier by David Zeitlin in *Fibonacci Quarterly* **5** (1967), 75.] *I should have submitted these to the* problem *editor instead.* [CP 1]

Q35. Review of *The Origins of Digital Computers*, by Brian Randell. *Historia Mathematica* **1** (1974), 204–207.

Q36. Postscript about NP-hard problems. *SIGACT News* **6**, 2 (April 1974), 15–16. French translation by Patrick Cégielski in *Éléments pour une histoire de l'informatique* (see Chapter 19), 341–343. [AA 493–494]

Q37. Elementary Problem E2492, some sum (binomial coefficients and mods). *American Mathematical Monthly* **81** (1974), 902; solution in **82** (1975), 855. [CP 1]

Q38. Problem 6049, cyclic permutation generators. *American Mathematical Monthly* **82** (1975), 856; solution in **84** (1977), 397. [CP 1]

Q39. Problem 6050, random maximization. *American Mathematical Monthly* **82** (1975), 856; solution in **85** (1978), 686–688. [CP 1]

Q40. (with Charles T. Zahn Jr.) Ill-chosen use of "event". *Communications of the ACM* **18** (1975), 360.

Q41. Son of *Seminumerical Algorithms*. *SIGSAM Bulletin* **9**, 4 (November 1975), 10–11.

Q42. Elementary Problem E2613, compact sets. *American Mathematical Monthly* **83** (1976), 656; solution in **84** (1977), 827–828. [CP 2]

Q43. Big Omicron and Big Omega and Big Theta. *SIGACT News* **8**, 2 (April–June 1976), 18–24. French translation by Patrick Cégielski in *Éléments pour une histoire de l'informatique* (see Chapter 19), 323–329. *Discussion of notations like* $O(n)$, $\Omega(n)$, *and* $\Theta(n)$. [AA 35–41]

Q44. Felix vs. Rover. *Journal of Recreational Mathematics* **9** (1976), 59–60.

Q45. Elementary Problem E2636, diphages and triphages. *American Mathematical Monthly* **84** (1977), 134; solution in **85** (1978), 385–386. [CP 2]

Q46. Are toy problems useful? *Popular Computing* **5**, 1 (January 1977), 1, 3–10; **5**, 2 (February 1977), 3–7. French translation by Patrick Cégielski in *Algorithmes* (see Chapter 19), 89–105. [CS 169–183]

Q47. BCS examination. *The Computer Bulletin* **2**, 9 (September 1976), 29.

Q48. The complexity of songs. *SIGACT News* **9**, 2 (Summer 1977), 17–24. Reprinted in *Communications of the ACM* **27** (1984), 344–346; errata (June 1984), 593. Reprinted in *Metafolkloristica*, edited by Franz Kinder and Boaz the Clown (Salt Lake City, Utah 84158-8183: Frank and Boaz, P.O. Box 58183), 63–65. Reprinted in *Humour the Computer*, edited by Andrew Davison (Cambridge, Massachusetts: MIT Press, 1995), 139–145. Russian translation by Андрей Б. Макуха, *RSDN Magazine* (2007), #4, 39–40. *A satire on technical writing.* [FG 33–39]

Q49. Solution to Problem 76-17, Conway's "topswaps" shuffle. *SIAM Review* **19** (October 1977), 739–741.

Q50. Organ duets. *Music* **12**, 1 (January 1978), 6.

Q51. Lewis Carroll's WORD – WARD – WARE – DARE – DAME – GAME. *GAMES* **2**, 4 (July 1978), 22–23. [FG 415–420]

Q52. BLOOD, SWEAT, and TEARS. *GAMES* **2**, 4 (July 1978), 49. [FG 421–422]

Q53. Computer-assisted indexing. *The Indexer* **11** (April 1979), 135.

Q54. Disappearances (poem). In *The Mathematical Gardner*, edited by David A. Klarner (Belmont, California: Wadsworth International, 1981), 310–325; 264; reprinted with new title *Mathematical Recreations* (Dover, 1998). Reprinted in *Mathematics: A Human Endeavor* by Harold R. Jacobs, third edition (San Francisco: Freeman, 1994), 53. Reprinted in *Kunuusu Sensei no Program-Ron* (see Chapter 19), 192–193. Russian translation by Ю. А. Данилов in *Математический цветник*, edited by И. М. Яглом (Moscow: Mir, 1983), 329. [FG 411–414]

Q55. Donald E. Knuth speaks out (interview by David H. Ahl). *Creative Computing* **6**, 1 (January 1980), 72–75.

Q56. Problem 80-6, random 2D trees. *Journal of Algorithms* **1** (1980), 109; solution in **3** (1982), 368–371. [CP 2–3]

Q57. Problem 80-11, inorder depth versus preorder depth. *Journal of Algorithms* **1** (1980), 210. Solution in Chapter 2. [CP 3, 23]

Q58. (with Christos H. Papadimitriou) Duality in addition chains. *Bulletin of the EATCS* **13** (February 1981), 2–4. [AA 501–504]

Q59. Letter to the editor re bubble sort. *Popular Computing* **9**, 1 (January 1981), 7.

Q60. Penny flipping. *Popular Computing* **9**, 4 (April 1981), 10, 12. *(See problem 1 in R45.)*

Q61. Problem 81-10, optimum caching with two page frames. *Journal of Algorithms* **2** (1981), 315. Solution in Chapter 2. [CP 4, 23–25]

Q62. A conversation with Don Knuth (interview by Donald J. Albers and Lynn Arthur Steen). *Two-Year College Mathematics Journal* **13** (1982), 2–18, 128–141. Reprinted in *Annals of the History of Computing* **4** (1982), 257–274. Reprinted in *Mathematical People*, edited by Donald J. Albers and G. L. Alexanderson (Boston: Birkhäuser Boston,

1985), 182–203. Japanese translation by 来住伸子 [Nobuko Kishi] in *bit* **16** (1985), 370–377, 506–512, 902–906, 1020–1025; reprinted in *Kunuusu Sensei no Program-Ron* (see Chapter 19), 130–167.

Q63. (with A. P. Ershov)   Editors' foreword to the proceedings of a conference on "Algorithms in Modern Mathematics and Computer Science," Urgench, Uzbek SSR, September 16–22, 1979. *Lecture Notes in Computer Science* **122** (1981), iii–v. Russian translation in *Ал-горитмы в Современнои Математике и Её Приложениях*, Часть I (Novosibirsk: Академия Наук СССР, Сибирское Отделение, Вычислительный Центр, 1982), 4–7. *A scientific pilgrimage to al-Khwārizmī country.*

Q64. Problem 82-3, late binding trees. *Journal of Algorithms* **3** (1982), 178–180; solution in **4** (1983), 385–393. [CP 4–6]

Q65. (with R. L. Graham) Elementary problem E2982, a double infinite sum for $|x|$. *American Mathematical Monthly* **90** (1983), 54; solution in **96** (1989), 525–526. [CP 7]

Q66. Fixed-point glue setting: An example of WEB. *TUGboat* **3**, 1 (March 1982), 10–27. Errata, *TUGboat* **12** (1991), 313.

Q67. A reply from the author. *Visible Language* **16** (1982), 358–359. [A response to 16 reviews of paper #P100; the reviews appear on pages 308–358.]   Also *Visible Language* **17** (1983), 417. Russian translation by Р. М. Кузнец in *Компьютерная Типография* (see Chapter 19), 318–319. [DT 312–313]

Q68. Review of *History of Binary and other Nondecimal Numeration*, by Anton Glaser. *Historia Mathematica* **10** (1983), 236–243. [DM 85–88]

Q69. TEX incunabula. *TUGboat* **5** (1984), 4–11. Russian translation by Ю. В. Тюменцев in *Компьютерная Типография* (see Chapter 19), 539–551. [DT 533–545]

Q70. My first experience with Indian scripts. *CALTIS-84*, a conference on calligraphy, lettering, typography of Indic scripts (New Delhi: February 11–13, 1984), 49. Russian translation by Р. М. Кузнец in *Компьютерная Типография* (see Chapter 19), 293–295. [DT 285–287]

Q71. Solution to Problem 83-3, a binomial double sum involving max. *SIAM Review* **26** (1984), 123–124.

Q72. Letter to the editor: Comments on quality in publishing. *TUGboat* **5** (1984), 67.

Q73. FORTRAN implementations (letter). *Annals of the History of Computing* **6** (October 1984), 402–403.

Q74. A course on METAFONT programming. *TUGboat* **5** (1984), 105–118. Russian translation by Ю. В. Тюменцев in *Компьютерная Типография* (see Chapter 19), 381–392. [DT 379–390]

Q75. Recipes and fractions. *TUGboat* **6** (1985), 36–38. Russian translation by Н. В. Третьяков in *Компьютерная Типография* (see Chapter 19), 187–191. [DT 177–180]

Q76. (with Niklaus Wirth) Programming philosophy (interviews by Ken Takara). *Computer Language* **2**, 5 (May 1985), cover, 25–35.

Q77. Problem 1234, sorted integers. *Mathematics Magazine* **59** (1986), 44; solution in **60** (1987), 46–48. [CP 7]

Q78. (with Jon Bentley) Programming Pearls: A WEB program for sampling. *Communications of the ACM* **29** (1986), 364–369. Japanese translation by 有澤誠 [Makoto Arisawa] in *Bungeiteki Programming* (see Chapter 19), 183–198. [LP 137–149]

Q79. (with Jon Bentley and M. Douglas McIlroy) Programming Pearls: A WEB program for common words. *Communications of the ACM* **29** (1986), 471–483. Japanese translation by 有澤誠 [Makoto Arisawa] in *Bungeiteki Programming* (see Chapter 19), 199–233. [LP 151–177]

Q80. Solution to problem 6480, a Catalonian sum. *American Mathematical Monthly* **93** (1986), 220.

Q81. Problem 86-2, a random knockout tournament. *SIAM Review* **28** (1986), 85–86; solution in **29** (1987), 127–129. [CP 7]

Q82. Theory and practice. *Bulletin of the EATCS* **27** (October 1985), 14–21. Greek translation by N. Κασιμάτης in *Μαθηματική Επιθεώρηση* (Bulletin of Greek Mathematical Society) τεύχος 30 (1986), 3–15. [CS 129–139]

Q83. Elementary problem E3106, a curious sum for Euler's totient function. *American Mathematical Monthly* **92** (1985), 590; solution in **94** (1987), 795–797. [CP 7]

Q84. Foreword to *The Kermit File Transfer Protocol* by Frank da Cruz (Bedford, Massachusetts: Digital Press, 1987), page xi.

Q85. (interview by G. Michael Vose and Gregg Williams) Text Processing: Computer Science considerations. *Byte* **11**, 2 (February 1986), 169–172.

Q86. Remarks to celebrate the publication of *Computers & Typesetting*. *TUGboat* **7** (1986), 95–98. [DT 555–562]

Q87. Solution to problem E3061, empty cells. *American Mathematical Monthly* **94** (1987), 189.

Q88. (with Pierre MacKay) Mixing right-to-left texts with left-to-right texts. *TUGboat* **8** (1987), 14–25. Russian translation by Р. М. Кузнец in *Компьютерная Типография* (see Chapter 19), 167–186. [DT 157–176]

Q89. Solution to problem E3062, a versatile identity. *American Mathematical Monthly* **94** (1987), 376–377.

Q90. The TEX logo in various fonts. *TUGboat* **7** (1986), 101. Russian translation by Н. В. Третьяков in *Компьютерная Типография* (see Chapter 19), 192–193. [DT 181–182]

Q91. Macros for Jill. *TUGboat* **8** (1987), 309–314. Russian translation by Н. В. Третьяков in *Компьютерная Типография* (see Chapter 19), 196–204. [DT 185–193]

Q92. Problem for a Saturday morning. *TUGboat* **8** (1987), 73, 210. Russian translation by Н. В. Третьяков in *Компьютерная Типография* (see Chapter 19), 205–206. [DT 195–196]

Q93. Fonts for digital halftones. *TUGboat* **8** (1987), 135–160. Russian translation by О. А. Маховая in *Компьютерная Типография* (see Chapter 19), 415–446. [DT 415–448]

Q94. A punk meta-font. *TUGboat* **9** (1988), 152–168. Russian translation by Ю. В. Тюменцев in *Компьютерная Типография* (see Chapter 19), 393–414. *New looks at Mona Lisa.* [DT 391–414]

Q95. Response to the Steele Prize. *Notices of the American Mathematical Society* **34** (1987), 227–228.

Q96. Exercises for *TEX: The Program*. *TUGboat* **11** (1990), 165–170, 499–511. Russian translation by Ю. В. Тюменцев in *Компьютерная Типография* (see Chapter 19), 207–234. [DT 197–223]

Q97. The difference between art and science. *Reader's Digest* (July 1987), 24. [Quoted from the profile by Bruce Schechter in *Discover* **9**, 5 (September 1984), 75.]

Q98. Printing out selected pages. *TUGboat* **8** (1987), 217. Russian translation by Н. В. Третьяков in *Компьютерная Типография* (see Chapter 19), 194–195. [DT 183–184]

Q99. N-ciphered texts. *Word Ways* **20** (1987), 173–174, 191–192. [FG 405–410]

Q100. Solution to problem E3166, a polynomial identity. *American Mathematical Monthly* **95** (1988), 662–663.

Q101. Problem 1280, a sum of floors. *Mathematics Magazine* **60** (1987), 329; solution in **61** (1988), 319–320. [CP 7]

Q102. Algorithmic themes. *A Century of Mathematics in America*, edited by Peter L. Duren, **1** (Providence, Rhode Island: American Mathematical Society, 1988), 439–445. [CS 115–122]

Q103. Introduction to *Mathematical Circus* by Martin Gardner, MAA Spectrum edition (Washington, District of Columbia: Mathematical Association of America, 1992), xi–xii.

Q104. Notes on the errors of TeX. *TUGboat* **10** (1989), 529–531. Revised version, "Learning from our errors," in *Software Development and Reality Construction*, edited by Christiane Floyd, Heinz Züllighoven, Reinhard Budde, and Reinhard Keil-Slawik (Berlin: Springer-Verlag, 1992), 28–30.

Q105. (with Barry Hayes and Carlos Subi) Elementary problem E3267, flattening an integer sequence. *American Mathematical Monthly* **95** (1988), 456–457; solution in **100** (1993), 292–294. [CP 8]

Q106. (with Ilan Vardi) Advanced problem 6581, the asymptotic expansion of the middle binomial coefficient. *American Mathematical Monthly* **95** (1988), 774; solution in **97** (1990), 629–630. [CP 8]

Q107. Typesetting *Concrete Mathematics*. *TUGboat* **10** (1989), 31–36; errata, page 342. Russian translation by O. A. Маховая in *Компьютерная Типография* (see Chapter 19), 369–380. [DT 367–378]

Q108. (with Jill C. Knuth*) TeX. *Encyclopedia of Computer Science*, third edition, edited by Anthony Ralston and Edwin D. Reilly (New York: Van Nostrand Reinhold, 1993), 1353–1355. Fourth edition, edited by Anthony Ralston, Edwin D. Reilly, and David Hemmendinger (London: Nature Publishing Group, 2000), 1756–1759. *Concise Encyclopedia of Computer Science*, edited by Edwin D. Reilly (Chichester: John Wiley & Sons, 2004), 749–751.

Q109. (with Jill C. Knuth*) METAFONT. *Encyclopedia of Computer Science*, third edition, edited by Anthony Ralston and Edwin D. Reilly (New York: Van Nostrand Reinhold, 1993), 869–870. Fourth edition, edited by Anthony Ralston, Edwin D. Reilly, and David Hemmendinger (London: Nature Publishing Group, 2000), 1154–1155.

Q110. Elementary problem E3335, a deranged recurrence. *American Mathematical Monthly* **96** (1989), 525; solution in **97** (1990), 927. [CP 8]

Q111. Solution to problem 6575, an identity involving sums and products. *American Mathematical Monthly* **97** (1990), 256.

Q112. The new versions of TEX and METAFONT. *TUGboat* **10** (1989), 325–328. Erratum, *TUGboat* **11** (1990), 12. Reprinted in *Die TEXnische Komödie* **2**, 1 (March 1990), 16–22. French translation by Alain Cousquer, "TEX 3.0 ou le TEX nouveau va arriver," *Cahiers GUTenberg*, n° 4 (December 1989), 39–45. Russian translation by Ю. В. Тюменцев in *Компьютерная Типография* (see Chapter 19), 567–575. [DT 563–570]

Q113. Virtual fonts: More fun for Grand Wizards. *TUGboat* **11** (1990), 13–23. Russian translation by Ю. В. Тюменцев in *Компьютерная Типография* (see Chapter 19), 256–272. [DT 247–262]

Q114. The genesis of attribute grammars. *Lecture Notes in Computer Science* **461** (1990), 1–12. French translation by Patrick Cégielski in *Éléments pour une histoire de l'informatique* (see Chapter 19), 297–314. [CL 423–438]

Q115. Memories of Andrei Ershov. *Programmirovanie* **16**, 1 (1990), 113–114. Russian translation by Т. М. Бульонкова in *Андрей Петрович Ершов – ыченый и человек*, compiled by М. А. Бульонков, А. А. Бульонкова, Н. А. Черемных, and И. А. Крайнева, and edited by А. Г. Марчук (Novosibirsk: Издательство Сибирского Отделения, Российской Академии Наук, Институт Систем Информатики имени А. П. Ершова, 2006), 263–265. (Several letters from Knuth to Ershov and vice-versa, from 1970, 1976, 1977, and 1978, are also translated in this volume.) [CP 37–38]

Q116. Solution to Problem 79-5, asymptotic behavior of a sequence. *SIAM Review* **22** (1980), 101–102.

Q117. Arthur Lee Samuel. *TUGboat* **11** (1990), 497–498. *From hardware design to machine learning (with checkers) to journal editing to TEX tutorials and TEXware implementations.*

Q118. The future of TEX and METAFONT. *TUGboat* **11** (1990), 489. Reprinted in *Nederlandstalige TEX Gebruikersgroep MAPS* **90.2** (May 1990), 145. Reprinted in *TEXline* **12** (London: December 1990), 1. Reprinted in *Die TEXnische Komödie* **2**, 4 (December 1990), 23–25.

French translation by Éric Picheral, "L'avenir de TEX et de META-FONT," *Cahiers GUTenberg*, n°8 (March 1991), 1–2. Russian translation by Ю. В. Тюменцев in *Компьютерная Типография* (see Chapter 19), 576–577. Reprinted in *TEX's 2⁵ Anniversary: A Commemorative Collection*, edited by Karl Berry and David Walden (Portland, Oregon: TEX Users Group, 2010), 8–11. [DT 571–572]

Q119. (with Boris Pittel) Elementary problem E3411, two sums over compositions. *American Mathematical Monthly* **97** (1990), 916–917; solution in **99** (1992), 578–579. [CP 8]

Q120. Elementary problem E3303, a binary summation. *American Mathematical Monthly* **96** (1989), 54; solution in **97** (1990), 348–349. [CP 9]

Q121. Elementary problem E3309, a binomial coefficient inequality. *American Mathematical Monthly* **96** (1989), 154; solution in **97** (1990), 614. [CP 9]

Q122. (with Philippe Flajolet) Elementary problem E3415, a hyper-generating function. *American Mathematical Monthly* **98** (1991), 54; solution in **100** (1993), 84–85. [CP 9]

Q123. Advanced problem 6649, a generalized gamma function with independent branches. *American Mathematical Monthly* **98** (1991), 168; solution in **101** (1994), 77–78. [CP 9]

Q124. (with John McCarthy) Elementary problem E3429, small pills. *American Mathematical Monthly* **98** (1991), 264; solution in **99** (1992), 684. [CP 9]

Q125. Elementary problem E3463, points in a circle. *American Mathematical Monthly* **98** (1991), 852; solution in **100** (1993), 693–694. [CP 9]

Q126. Computer programming and computer science. *Academic Press Dictionary of Science and Technology* (Harcourt Brace Jovanovich, 1992), 490. French translation by Patrick Cégielski in *Éléments pour une histoire de l'informatique* (see Chapter 19), 317–318. [CS 2–3]

Q127. (with Lee Sallows) Problem 1296, universal magic squares. *Journal of Recreational Mathematics* **16** (1984), 138; solution in **17** (1985), 145–146. [CP 10]

Q128. Introduction to *New Book of Puzzles* by Jerry Slocum and Jack Botermans (New York: W. H. Freeman, 1992), 6–7.

Q129. An interview with Donald Knuth (by Roswitha Graham and Barbara Beeton). *TUGboat* **13** (1992), 419–425.

Q130. Icons for TEX and METAFONT. *TUGboat* **14** (1993), 387–389. Russian translation by Ю. В. Тюменцев in *Компьютерная Типография* (see Chapter 19), 552–558. [DT 547–553]

Q131. $5 \times 5 \times 5$ word cubes by computer. *Word Ways* **26** (1993), 95–97. [FG 433–436]

Q132. The Stanford GraphBase: A platform for combinatorial algorithms. *Proceedings of the Fourth Annual ACM–SIAM Symposium on Discrete Algorithms* (1993), 41–43.

Q133. This Week's Citation Classic: Artistic programming. *Current Contents*, Physical, Chemical & Earth Sciences **33**, 34 (August 23, 1993), 8; also *Current Contents*, Engineering, Technology & Applied Sciences **24**, 34 (August 23, 1993), 8. [CS 261–262 in the first printing; CS 241–242 after 2003]

Q134. (with John Hershberger) Problem 85-3, on merging sequences. *Journal of Algorithms* **6** (1985), 284. Solution in Chapter 2. [CP 10, 26]

Q135. Problem 90-1, reversing the transformation from sequential representation to short codes for adjacency lists for undirected graphs. *Journal of Algorithms* **12** (1991), 183–184. Solution in Chapter 2. [CP 10–11, 26–30]

Q136. Problem 10280, a random binary operation. *American Mathematical Monthly* **100** (1993), 76; solution in **102** (1995), 561–562. [CP 11]

Q137. Problem 10298, a divisibility property of Stirling numbers. *American Mathematical Monthly* **100** (1993), 400; solution in **103** (1996), 80–81. [CP 12]

Q138. Problem 10401, a knight's surprise. *American Mathematical Monthly* **101** (1994), 682–683; solution in **104** (1997), 669. [CP 12]

Q139. ETAOIN SHRDLU non-crashing sets. *Word Ways* **27** (1994), 138. [FG 429–430]

Q140. Speech upon receiving honorary degree from St. Petersburg University. *Programming and Computer Software* **20** (1994), 290. Russian translation by Б. Б. Походзей, *Программирование* **20**, 6 (1994), 89–91; reprinted in *Компьютерная Типография* (see Chapter 19), 8–9. [CS 243–244, in printings after 2003]

Q141. Foreword to *An Introduction to the Analysis of Algorithms* by Robert Sedgewick and Philippe Flajolet (Reading, Massachusetts: Addison–Wesley, 1995), v.

Q142. The Chinese domino challenge. *Math Horizons* (April 1995), 8–9. [CP 12–13]

Q143. (with Nob Yoshigahara) Pentagon puzzle (in Japanese). *Quark Visual Science Magazine*, No. 156 (Tokyo: Kodansha, June 1995), 127. [FG 689–690]

Q144. Predictions for the year 2000, on programming. *Byte* **20**, 9 (September 1995), 110.

Q145. Foreword to $A = B$ by Marko Petkovšek, Herbert S. Wilf, and Doron Zeilberger (Wellesley, Massachusetts: A K Peters, 1996), ix.

Q146. Open letter to coordinators of TEX implementations, 13 October 1981. *TUGboat* **2**, 3 (November 1981), 5–6. Reprinted in *TEX's* 2^5 *Anniversary: A Commemorative Collection*, edited by Karl Berry and David Walden (Portland, Oregon: TEX Users Group, 2010), 4–7.

Q147. A note on hyphenation. *TUGboat* **4** (1983), 64.

Q148. It happened. *TUGboat* **8** (1987), 6.

Q149. The initial reception of *Concrete Mathematics*. *SIGACT News* **20**, 1 (Winter 1989), 48.

Q150. The Samson–Mueller (Davis–Putnam) algorithm. *SIGACT News* **9**, 1 (January–March 1977), 8–9.

Q151. Problem 10470, minimal special matrices. *American Mathematical Monthly* **102** (1995), 655; solution in **105** (1998), 771–773. [CP 14]

Q152. Problem 1479, a recursive optimization. *Mathematics Magazine* **68** (1995), 306; solution in **69** (1996), 305–307. [CP 14]

Q153. TUG'95 Questions and answers with Prof. Donald E. Knuth (edited by Christina Thiele) *TUGboat* **17** (1996), 7–22. Reprinted in *GUST* **8** (1997), 9–23. Russian translation by O. A. Маховая in *Компьютерная Типография* (see Chapter 19), 578–603. [DT 573–600]

Q154. An interview with Donald Knuth (by Jack Woehr). *Dr. Dobb's Journal* **21**, 4 (April 1996), 16–18, 20, 22.

Q155. Knuth meets NTG members (edited by Christina Thiele). *MAPS: Minutes and APpendiceS* **16** (Schagen: Nederlandstalige TeX Gebruikersgroep, 1996), 38–49. Reprinted in *TUGboat* **17** (1996), 342–355. Russian translation by O. A. Маховая in *Компьютерная Типография* (see Chapter 19), 625–650. [DT 625–653]

Q156. Questions and answers at Charles University (edited by Barbara Beeton and Christina Thiele). *TUGboat* **17** (1996), 355–367. Russian translation by P. M. Кузнец in *Компьютерная Типография* (see Chapter 19), 604–624. [DT 601–624]

Q157. Problem 10546, binomial coefficient parity. *American Mathematical Monthly* **103** (1996), 695; solution in **105** (1998), 867–868. [CP 14]

Q158. Problem 10568, subtracting square roots repeatedly. *American Mathematical Monthly* **104** (1997), 68; solution in **106** (1999), 167. [CP 14]

Q159. Problem 10576, a card-matching game. *American Mathematical Monthly* **104** (1997), 169; solution in **106** (1999), 168–169. [CP 14]

Q160. Problem 97-6, a sum over binary sequences. *SIAM Review* **39** (1997), 317; solution in **40** (1998), 372–374. [CP 15]

Q161. Crystallization of algorithms: The Art of Computer Programming. [Interview by 長尾真 [Makoto Nagao]; in Japanese.] *Computer Today* no. 77 (January 1997), 46–51.

Q162. Concerns about American technology policy. [Interview by 吉沢寿康 [Hisayasu Yoshizawa]; in Japanese.] *Nikkei Electronics* no. 683 (24 February 1997), 145–148.

Q163. Dr. Knuth meets Mitsumasa Anno. [Discussion between 安野光雅 [Mitsumasa Anno], Donald E. Knuth, and 野崎昭弘 [Akihiro Nozaki]; in Japanese.] *Sugaku Seminar* **36**, 3 (March 1997), 40–44.

Q164. Roundtable discussion with Prof. Knuth. [Discussion between 有澤誠 [Makoto Arisawa], 黒川利明 [Toshiaki Kurokawa], 来住伸子 [Nobuko Kishi], and Donald E. Knuth, with additional comments by Jill C. Knuth; in Japanese.] *bit* **29**, 4 (April 1997), 46–51.

Q165. Opinion: Harmony between theory and practice. [In Japanese.] *bit* **29**, 5 (May 1997), 3.

Q166. (with R. M. Corless* and D. J. Jeffrey) A sequence of series for the Lambert *W* function. *Proceedings of the International Symposium on Symbolic and Algebraic Computation ISSAC '97* (New York: ACM Press, 1997), 197–204.

Q167. Problem 1534, sums of ceilings of floors. *Mathematics Magazine* **70** (1997), 381; solution in **71** (1998), 390–391. [CP 15]

Q168. Problem 1539, a sharp tail inequality. *Mathematics Magazine* **71** (1998), 66; solution in **72** (1999), 65–66. [CP 15]

Q169. Problem 10593, matrices related to universal hashing. *American Mathematical Monthly* **104** (1997), 456; solution in **106** (1999), 473–474. [CP 15]

Q170. Problem 10609, a partial Abelian sum. *American Mathematical Monthly* **104** (1997), 664; solution in **106** (1999), 690–691. [CP 15]

Q171. Letter to the editor: Teach calculus with Big *O*. *Notices of the American Mathematical Society* **45** (June/July 1998), 687–688. [CP 31–34]

Q172. Biblical ladders. *The Mathemagician and Pied Puzzler*, edited by Elwyn Berlekamp and Tom Rodgers (Wellesley, Massachusetts: A K Peters, 1999), 29–34. [FG 423–428]

Q173. An interview with Donald Knuth: "A little bit of your soul in it" (interview by John Boe). *Writing on the Edge* **9** (1998), 10–25.

Q174. Solution to problem 10424, a sum of Ira Gessel. *American Mathematical Monthly* **104** (1997), 467.

Q175. An interview with Donald Knuth: Computer scientist addresses grand themes (by David I. Lewin). *Computers in Physics* **9** (1995), 248–249.

Q176. Solution to problem 97-19, three binomial convolutions. *SIAM Review* **40** (1998), 991.

Q177. (with Vaughan Pratt) Problem 10689, an algebraic definition of the real numbers. *American Mathematical Monthly* **105** (1998), 769; solution in **107** (2000), 755. [CP 16]

Q178. Problem 10691, highly variable lists. *American Mathematical Monthly* **105** (1998), 859; solution in **110** (2003), 59–60. [CP 16]

Q179. (with E. A. Lipitakis, P. Spirakis, C. Papadimitriou, and S. Gallopoulos) HERCMA 2001 — Round table discussion. In *Hellenic European Research on Computer Mathematics and Its Applications (HERCMA 2001)*, edited by Elias A. Lipitakis (Athens: LEA, 2002), 910–923.

Q180. Problem 10720, exploring all binary mazes. *American Mathematical Monthly* **106** (1999), 264; solution in **110** (2003), 60–61. [CP 16]

Q181. Problem 10726, explosive growth. *American Mathematical Monthly* **106** (1999), 362; solution in **107** (2000), 469–470. [CP 16]

Q182. (with Robert W. Floyd) Problem H-94, golden hashing. *Fibonacci Quarterly* **4** (1966), 258. [The results stated in this problem are equivalent to what was later called "Fibonacci hashing" in *The Art of Computer Programming*, §6.4.]

Q183. Problem 10832, the reciprocals of Stirling's errors. *American Mathematical Monthly* **107** (2000), 863; solution in **108** (2001), 877–878. [CP 16]

Q184. Interview: Donald E. Knuth (by Raph Levien). *TUGboat* **21** (2000), 103–110. Reprinted from the original online version, `http://www.advogato.org/article/28.html`.

Q185. Problem 10858, Fibonacci sequences with complex twists. *American Mathematical Monthly* **108** (2001), 271; solution in **111** (2004), 166–167, 922. [CP 17]

Q186. Problem 1621, Fibonacci numbers from binomial coefficients. *Mathematics Magazine* **74** (2001), 154; solution in **75** (2002), 149–150. [CP 17]

Q187. Problem 10871, balanced neighborhood squares. *American Mathematical Monthly* **108** (2001), 372; solution in **110** (2003), 161–162. [CP 17]

Q188. Problem 10875, animals in a cage. *American Mathematical Monthly* **108** (2001), 469; solution in **110** (2003), 243–245. [CP 17]

Q189. All questions answered (edited by Allyn Jackson). [Transcript of a lecture at the Technical University of Munich, 5 October 2001.] *Notices of the American Mathematical Society* **49** (2002), 318–324. Reprinted in *Mathematics Newsletter* **12** (Ramanujan Mathematical Society, 2002), 33–42.

Q190. Problem 10906, recounting the rationals. *American Mathematical Monthly* **108** (2001), 872; solution in **110** (2003), 642–643. [CP 17]

Q191. (with O. P. Lossers)   Solution to problem 10757, generalized quotients of continued fractions. *American Mathematical Monthly* **108** (2001), 875.

Q192. Problem 10913, related transpositions with different periods. *American Mathematical Monthly* **108** (2001), 977; solution in **110** (2003), 844–845. [CP 17–18]

Q193. Knuth comments on code. *Byte* **21**, 9 (September 1996), 40.

Q194. Der Perfektionist (interview by Harald Bögeholz and Andreas Stiller). *c't magazin für computer technik* *2002*, 5 (25 February–10 March 2002), 190–193.

Q195. 'Geleitwort' to *Das MMIX-Buch* by Heidi Anlauff, Axel Böttcher, and Martin Ruckert (Berlin: Springer, 2002), v–vi.

Q196. U.K. TUG, Oxford, Sunday, 12 September 1999, question & answer session with Donald Knuth. *TUGboat* **22** (2001), 15–19. Reprinted in *TEX's 2^5 Anniversary: A Commemorative Collection*, edited by Karl Berry and David Walden (Portland, Oregon: TEX Users Group, 2010), 12–19.

Q197. All questions answered. [Transcript of a lecture at the University of Oslo, 30 August 2002.] *TUGboat* **23** (2002), 249–261.

Q198. Solution to problem 10825, a Fibonacci–Lucas extremum. *American Mathematical Monthly* **109** (2002), 762–763.

Q199. Problem 10985, some Bernstein polynomials. *American Mathematical Monthly* **110** (2003), 58; solution in **111** (2004), 447, 922. [CP 18]

Q200. Problem 11021, a modular triple. *American Mathematical Monthly* **110** (2003), 542, 963; solution in **112** (2005), 279–280. [CP 18]

Q201. Robert W Floyd, in memoriam. *SIGACT News* **34**, 4 (December 2003), 3–13. Reprinted in *IEEE Annals of the History of Computing* **26**, 2 (April–June 2004), 75–83. [DA 1–18]

Q202. (with David S. Johnson and Zvi Galil)   Changes at the *Journal of Algorithms*. *SIGACT News* **35**, 1 (March 2004), 85.

Q203. Problem 11078, cube-free sums. *American Mathematical Monthly* **111** (2004), 361; solution in **113** (2006), 368–369. [CP 18]

Q204. Three Catalan bijections. Report No. 04, 2004/2005, spring (Djursholm: Institut Mittag-Leffler, The Royal Swedish Academy of Sciences, 2005), i + 19 pages. *Available online and worth a look.*

Q205. Problem 11142, largest weighted Stirling numbers. *American Mathematical Monthly* **112** (2005), 273–274; solution in **114** (2007), 361–362. [CP 18]

Q206. Problem 11151, partitions of a circular set. *American Mathematical Monthly* **112** (2005), 367; solution in **114** (2007), 265–266. [CP 18]

Q207. Problem 1721, Fibonacci graphs. *Mathematics Magazine* **78** (2005), 239; solution in **79** (2006), 219–220. [CP 18–19]

Q208. Searching graphs (a brainteaser). *ACM Transactions on Algorithms* **1** (2005), 158–159; solution in **2** (2006), 132–133. [CP 19]

Q209. Alphametic 2621: Table setting. *Journal of Recreational Mathematics* **33** (2004–2005), 67; solution in **34** (2005–2006), 59–60. [CP 19]

Q210. Mathematical vanity plates. Excerpted in *The Mathematical Intelligencer* **33**, 1 (Spring 2011), 33–45. *What license plate should I choose for my car?* [FG 121–160]

Q211. Problem 11243, perfect parity patterns. *American Mathematical Monthly* **113** (2006), 759; solution in **115** (2008), 668–670. [CP 20]

Q212. Problem 11264, d-swaps. *American Mathematical Monthly* **114** (2007), 77; solution in **116** (2009), 277–278. [CP 20]

Q213. Problem 11274, binomial coefficients and powers of 2. *American Mathematical Monthly* **114** (2007), 165; solution in **116** (2009), 548–549. [CP 20]

Q214. TEX's infinite glue is projective. *TUGboat* **28** (2007), 4.

Q215. The 'Art' of being Donald Knuth (extracted from the oral history transcripts at the Computer History Museum by Len Shustek). *Communications of the ACM* **51**, 7 (July 2008), 35–39.

Q216. Donald Knuth: A life's work interrupted (extracted from the oral history transcripts at the Computer History Museum by Len Shustek). *Communications of the ACM* **51**, 8 (August 2008), 31–35.

Q217. Problem 11320, a recurrence involving maxima. *American Mathematical Monthly* **114** (2007), 835; solution in **116** (2009), 649. [CP 20]

Q218. Problem 11336, near-deBruijn cycles. *American Mathematical Monthly* **115** (2008), 71; solution in **116** (2009), 848–849. [CP 21]

Q219. Problem 11369, an exponential inequality. *American Mathematical Monthly* **115** (2008), 567; solution in **117** (2010), 377. [CP 21]

Q220. The TEX tuneup of 2008. *TUGboat* **29** (2008), 233–238. Reprinted in *TEX's 2⁵ Anniversary: A Commemorative Collection*, edited by Karl Berry and David Walden (Portland, Oregon: TEX Users Group, 2010), 20–29.

Q221. Alphametic 2651: Two ways to eighteen. *Journal of Recreational Mathematics* **33** (2004–2005), 221; solution in **34** (2005–2006), 218. [CP 21]

Q222. Alphametic 2683: Spice of life. *Journal of Recreational Mathematics* **34** (2005–2006), 141; solution in **35** (2006), 152. [CP 21]

Q223. Move it or lose it (with commentary by John Beasley). *Variant Chess* **8** (2009), 96. [FG 231–234]

Q224. Latin square word puzzles. *Word Ways* **42** (2009), 248; solutions in **43** (2010), 14. [FG 431–432]

Q225. Donald Knuth: Geek of the Week (interview by Richard Morris, 26 November 2009: `http://www.simple-talk.com/opinion/geek-of-the-week/donald-knuth-geek-of-the-week/`).

Q226. Problem 11452, permutation flipping. *American Mathematical Monthly* **116** (2009), 648; solution in **118** (2011), 657. [CP 21]

Q227. An earthshaking announcement. *TUGboat* **31** (2010), 121–124. *This paper is sort of a right parenthesis that closes what I opened in P1.* [FG 707–715]

Q228. Memories of Martin Gardner. *Notices of the American Mathematical Society* **58**, 3 (March 2011), 419–420. [FG 705–706]

Q229. The father of geekdom (an interview by Dave Wieczorek). *Think: The Magazine of Case Western Reserve University* (Fall/Winter 2010), 22–23.

Q230. Comment on problem 2680. *Journal of Recreational Mathematics* **35** (2006), 161.

Q231. (with David Fuchs, John Hobby, Frank Liang, Oren Patashnik, Michael Plass, Tom Rokicki, Luis Trabb Pardo, Howard Trickey, and Joe Weening) TUG 2010 panel discussion, moderated by David Walden. *TUGboat* **31** (2010), 125–137.

Q232. Interview with Donald E. Knuth (by Gianluca Pignalberi). *Free Software Magazine*, Issue 7 (August 2005), 13–15. Reprinted in *TUGboat* **26** (2005), 183–185. Italian translation in *ArsTEXnica* **1** (2006), 5–7.

Q233. (by James Buchanan) Interview with Donald Knuth. *Linux User & Developer*, issue 77 (March 2008), 38–45.

Q234. (by Andrew Binstock) Interview with Donald Knuth for the informIT website (April 2008) = [`http://www.informit.com/article/article.aspx?p=1193856`]. Chinese translation by 赵健平 [Zhao Jianping] in *Programmer* (July 2008), 99–101 = [`http://blog.csdn.net/programmer_editor/archive/2008/07/10/2631316.aspx`].

Q235. (by 赵健平 [Zhao Jianping], in Chinese) Eight questions answered by Donald Knuth. *Programmer* (November 2008), 108–110 = [`http://blog.csdn.net/programmer_editor/archive/2008/12/11/3501111.aspx`].

Q236. Problem 1868, dominoes in a frame. *Mathematics Magazine* **84** (2011), 150; solution to appear. [CP 21]

Q237. Problem 2808, a pentomino tour. *Journal of Recreational Mathematics* **36** (2007), 166–167. Solution to appear.

$$- * - * - * - * - * - * - * - * - * - * - * -$$

R1. Tic Tac Toe on the 650. Case Computing Center (Cleveland, Ohio: 1957), 8 pages.

R2. Case Soap III. Case Computing Center, series IV, **1** (Cleveland, Ohio: February 1958), 28 pages.

R3. Runcible I. Case Computing Center, series V, **1** (Cleveland, Ohio: March 1959), 67 pages.

R4. (Editor) *Engineering and Science Review*. Case Institute of Technology, vol. 2, no. 1, 3, 4 (1959). Associate Editor, vol. 3 (1960). Article: "The revolutionary potrzebie" (November 1958), 18–20. Features: "Th$_5$E$_4$ CH$_3$EmIC$_2$Al$_2$ Ca$_3$P$_4$Er" (March 1959), page 32; "The plot thickens," (November 1959), page 45; "Math ace," (May 1960), page 24. [CP 35–36, FG 19–26, 59–62, 401–404]

R5. (Editor) *Case Handbook*. Case Institute of Technology, 1959.

R6. SuperSoap. Case Computing Center, series IV, **2** (Cleveland, Ohio: August 1959), 55 pages.

R7. The internals of Algol 205. Burroughs Corporation, 1960. 30 pages.

R8. Balgol 220 (annotations on listing). Burroughs Corporation, 1960.

R9. mth powers of algebraic roots. California Institute of Technology, Mathematics Department (Pasadena, California: April 1961). 7 pages.

R10. Burroughs Algebraic Compiler for the 205. Burroughs Corporation publication no. 205-21003-D (Detroit, Michigan: October 1961), 30 pages.

R11. FORTRAN II for the Univac Solid State computers. UNIVAC Division Sperry Rand (Bluebell, Pennsylvania; October 1962), 85 pages.

R12. (with William C. Lynch) QADAAD (Quick And Dirty Assembler And Documentor), an assembly system for the Solid State II. Internal memorandum (August 1962).

R13. (with William C. Lynch) FORTRAN II Routine Block Chart (Annotated). UNIVAC Division Sperry Rand, publication no. UP-3843.1 (Bluebell, Pennsylvania: 1963), 50 pages.

R14. A good scrambling function suitable for hardware. Burroughs Corporation Electrodata Division, Engineering Technical Memorandum 234 (Pasadena, California: October 1963), 22 pages.

R15. *Textbook of Combinatorial Mathematics*, a partial translation of the second edition (1927) of E. Netto's *Lehrbuch der Combinatorik*. Deposited in the California Institute of Technology Library (Pasadena, California: 1963); approximately 150 pages.

R16. Finite semifields and projective planes. Ph.D. thesis, California Institute of Technology (Pasadena, California: 1963), 70 pages.

R17. Computer languages. California Institute of Technology, Seminar series on computer applications to biology (Pasadena, California: February 1963), 15 pages; (December 1964), 12 pages.

R18. Notes on Chebyshev approximation theory. California Institute of Technology, Mathematics Department (Pasadena, California: 1964). 7 pages.

R19. Lectures in software design. Burroughs Corporation Electrodata Division (Pasadena, California: 1964), approximately 200 pages.

R20. Notes on complex variable theory. California Institute of Technology, Mathematics Department (Pasadena, California: 1965), 36 pages.

R21. The Thue–Siegel–Roth theorem. California Institute of Technology, Mathematics Department (Pasadena, California: 1966). 41 pages.

R22. Exploration of the direct product (Kronecker product, tensor product) of matrices: Results of Math 5B class project. California Institute of Technology, Mathematics Department (Pasadena, California: March 1966), 10 pages.

R23. Estimating the running time of BACKTRACK programs. IDA-CRD Working Paper No. 279 (Princeton, New Jersey: November 1969), 42 pages.

R24. The Art of Computer Programming — errata et addenda. Stanford Computer Science Report 194 (Stanford, California: January 1971), 28 pages

R25. (with R. L. Sites) MIX/360 User's Guide. Stanford Computer Science Report 197 (Stanford, California: March 1971), 11 pages.

R26. The analysis of algorithms. In *The Teaching of Programming at University Level*, edited by B. Shaw (Newcastle upon Tyne: The University of Newcastle upon Tyne Computing Laboratory, 1971), 49–62.

R27. (with V. Chvátal and D. A. Klarner) Selected combinatorial research problems. Stanford Computer Science Report 292 (Stanford, California: June 1972), 29 pages.

R28. Matroid partitioning. Stanford Computer Science Report 342 (Stanford, California: 1973), 12 pages. [DA 235–243]

R29. Selected topics in Computer Science. Lecture Note Series, Matematisk institutt, Universitetet i Oslo (Oslo, Norway: 1973), Nr. 1 and Nr. 2. [Notes by Ole Amble, Ole-Johan Dahl, Erik Holbæk-Hanssen, Arne Jonassen, Torvald Kjeldaas, Stein Krogdahl, Åmund Lunde, Arne Maus, and Arne Wang. Part 1 contains: analysis of quicksort; dynamic storage allocation; flowcharts and Kirchhoff's first law; theory of matroids; complexity analysis of equivalence algorithms. Part 2 contains: strong components; hard problems; backtracking algorithms; pattern matching in strings; generation of combinatorial patterns.]

R30. A review of *Structured Programming*. Stanford Computer Science Report 371 (Stanford, California: June 1973).

R31. "Stable marriage" — problemet og samanhangen med hashing og "coupon collecting" (in Norwegian). University of Bergen (Bergen, Norway: June 1973), 20 pages.

R32. Sorting and Searching — errata and addenda. Stanford Computer Science Report 392 (Stanford, California: October 1973), 35 pages.

R33. The State of *The Art of Computer Programming*. Stanford Computer Science Report 551 (Stanford, California: June 1976), 57 pages.

R34. (with Michael J. Clancy*) A programming and problem-solving seminar. Stanford Computer Science Report 606 (Stanford, California: April 1977), 99 pages.

R35. Tau Epsilon Chi, a system for technical text. Stanford Computer Science Report 675 (Stanford, California: September 1978), 198 pages. Reprinted with corrections as part 2 of TEX and METAFONT (see Chapter 19).

R36. (with Chris Van Wyk*) A programming and problem-solving seminar. Stanford Computer Science Report 707 (Stanford, California: January 1979), 83 pages.

R37. The errata of computer programming. Stanford Computer Science Report 712 (Stanford, California: January 1979), 57 pages. Reprinted in *Dr. Dobb's Journal of Computer Calisthenics & Orthodontia* **5**, 6 (June 1980), 27–39.

R38. METAFONT, a system for alphabet design. Stanford Computer Science Report 762 (Stanford, California: September 1979), 105 pages. Reprinted with corrections as part 3 of TEX and METAFONT (see Chapter 19).

R39. The Computer Modern family of typefaces. Stanford Computer Science Report 780 (Stanford, California: January 1980), 406 pages.

R40. (with Allan A. Miller*) A programming and problem-solving seminar. Stanford Computer Science Report 863 (Stanford, California: June 1981), 81 pages.

R41. The last whole errata catalog. Stanford Computer Science Report 868 (Stanford, California: July 1981), 41 pages.

R42. The WEB system of structured documentation. Stanford Computer Science Report 980 (Stanford, California: September 1983), 206 pages. Most of this report has been reprinted in *Weaving a Program: Literate Programming in WEB* by Wayne Sewell (New York: Van Nostrand Reinhold, 1989), 271–434.

R43. (with David R. Fuchs) TEXware. Stanford Computer Science Report 1097 (Stanford, California: April 1986), 10 + 30 + 53 + 53 pages.

R44. A torture test for TEX. Stanford Computer Science Report 1027 (Stanford, California: November 1984), 142 pages.

R45. (with Joseph S. Weening*) A programming and problem-solving seminar. Stanford Computer Science Report 989 (Stanford, California: December 1983), ii+91 pages.

R46. (with John D. Hobby*) A programming and problem-solving seminar. Stanford Computer Science Report 990 (Stanford, California: December 1983), 61 pages.

R47. (with Ramsey W. Haddad*) A programming and problem-solving seminar. Stanford Computer Science Report 1055 (Stanford, California: June 1985), 103 pages.

R48. A torture test for METAFONT. Stanford Computer Science Report 1095 (Stanford, California: January 1986), 78 pages.

R49. (with Tomas G. Rokicki*) A programming and problem-solving seminar. Stanford Computer Science Report 1154 (Stanford, California: April 1987), 89 pages.

R50. (with Tracy Larrabee* and Paul M. Roberts*) Mathematical writing. Stanford Computer Science Report 1193 (Stanford, California: January 1988), 117 pages. Reprinted with corrections by the Mathematical Association of America (see Chapter 19). Japanese translation by 有澤誠 [Makoto Arisawa], with additional illustrations and notes by the translator, *Kunuusu Sensei no Dokyumento Sampō* (see Chapter 19).

R51. 3:16, an approach to Bible study. In *A Sixth Conference on Mathematics from a Christian Perspective*, edited by Robert L. Brabenec (proceedings of a conference at Calvin College, May 1987, sponsored by the Association of Christians in the Mathematical Sciences), 3–25.

R52. (with Tomas G. Rokicki and Arthur L. Samuel) METAFONTware. Stanford Computer Science Report 1255 (Stanford, California: April 1989), 30 + 42 + 87 + 48 pages. Reprinted in *TEXniques* **13** (1990).

R53. (with Silvio Levy) The CWEB system of structured documentation. Stanford Computer Science Report 1336 (Stanford, California: October 1990), 200 pages. Also issued as University of Minnesota Supercomputer Institute Research Report UMSI 91/56 (Minneapolis, Minnesota, February 1991). Also published as a book (see Chapter 19).

R54. (interview translated into French by Philippe Gabrini) La foi d'un scientifique. *La Vie Chrétienne*, Journal de l'Église Presbytérienne au Canada (October–November 1991), 11–12.

R55. (with Kenneth A. Ross*) A programming and problem-solving seminar. Stanford Computer Science Report 1269 (Stanford, California: July 1989), 87 pages.

R56. Stable husbands (extended abstract). In *25th International Seminar on the Teaching of Computing Science at University Level*, edited by B. Randell (Newcastle upon Tyne: University of Newcastle Department of Computing Science, 1992), III.1–III.7.

R57. The Stanford GraphBase: A platform for combinatorial computing (extended abstract). In *25th International Seminar on the Teaching of Computing Science at University Level*, edited by B. Randell (Newcastle upon Tyne: University of Newcastle Department of Computing Science, 1992), III.8–III.14.

R58. (interview by Dan Doernberg) Donald E. Knuth: Programming for a human being instead of a computer. *New Book Bulletin*, Computer Literacy Bookshops (Spring 1994), 4–5 = (Summer 1994), 4–5 = [http://nowcomment.com/documents/1472/]. Czech translation by Jiří Zlatuška, *ÚVT MU Zprovodaj* **6**, 1 (1995), 1–4; **6**, 2 (1995), 15–20.

R59. Digital typography. *Kyoto Prizes 1996* (Kyoto: Inamori Foundation, 1997), 82–109. Russian translation by O. A. Маховая in *Компьютерная Типография* (see Chapter 19), 19–35. [DT 1–18]

R60. (oral history conducted by Philip L. Frana) An interview with Donald E. Knuth. OH 332 (Minneapolis, Minnesota: Charles Babbage Institute, 8 November 2001), 27 pages.

R61. (by Wolfgang Stieler, in German) Freude, die ein Maler empfindet. *Technology Review*, German edition (25 November 2005). Reprinted in *Die TEXnische Komödie* **18**, 1 (2006), 6–10.

Chapter 21

Alphabetical Index of Titles

Each entry below shows the title of a paper or other work, followed in most cases by the number of that paper in the master lists of Chapter 20, and by the page numbers where the archival form of that paper has been reprinted. Page numbers are preceded by a two-letter code to indicate the relevant volume:

> AA = *Selected Papers on Analysis of Algorithms*;
>
> CL = *Selected Papers on Computer Languages*;
>
> CP = *Companion to the Papers of Donald Knuth*;
>
> CS = *Selected Papers on Computer Science*;
>
> DA = *Selected Papers on Design of Algorithms*;
>
> DM = *Selected Papers on Discrete Mathematics*;
>
> DT = *Digital Typography*;
>
> FG = *Selected Papers on Fun and Games*;
>
> LP = *Literate Programming*.

A notation such as '#Q14 ↝ #P29' means that paper Q14 was subsumed by the paper P29, a later publication. Similarly, the notation '#Q22 ↝ *TAOCP* §4.1' means that paper Q22 was subsumed by Section 4.1 of *The Art of Computer Programming*. Many papers of the Q series are indicated only by a generic title such as '*Foreword*' or '*Interview*' or '*Solution*'. Papers of the R series are omitted entirely from this index, unless they've been reprinted in one of the volumes listed above or have special significance for some other reason.

3:16 Bible Texts Illuminated. CP 219
5 × 5 × 5 word cubes by computer. #Q131, FG 433–436
A bijection for ordered factorizations. #P128
A carol for Advent. FG 189–191

An almost linear recurrence. #P25, DM 525–535
An analysis of alpha-beta pruning. #P70, AA 105–147
An analysis of optimum caching. #P104, AA 235–255
An earthshaking announcement. #Q227, FG 707–715
An empirical study of FORTRAN programs. #P47, CL 507–543
An exact analysis of stable allocation. #P149, AA 415–427
An example of CWEB. LP 341–348
An experiment in optimal sorting. #P52, AA 495–500
An imaginary number system. #P3, DM 271–276
Analysis of a simple factorization algorithm. #P78, AA 303–339
Analysis of algorithms. #P44, AA 27–34
Analysis of algorithms, mathematical. #P46, AA 1–18
Analysis of Algorithms, Mathematics for the. CP 216
Analysis of Algorithms, Selected Papers on. CP 215
Analysis of alpha-beta pruning. #P70, AA 105–147
Analysis of optimum caching. #P104, AA 235–255
Analysis of the subtractive algorithm for greatest common divi-
    sors. #P76, AA 195–204
Ancient Babylonian algorithms. #P53, CS 185–203
Andrei Ershov, memories of. #Q115, CP 37–38
Another enumeration of trees. #P33, DM 209–219
Arc digraph, oriented subtrees of an. #P26, DM 203–208
Are toy problems useful? #Q46, CS 169–183
Arithmetik. CP 210
Art and science, the difference between. #Q97
Art of Computer Programming. CP 207–213
Arta programării calculatoarelor. CP 208, 210, 211
Arte de programar ordenadores. CP 207, 210, 211
Artistic programming. #Q133, CS 241–242
Asymptotic number of geometries. #P62, DM 425–427
Attribute grammars, the genesis of. #Q114, CL 423–438
Automata, programming languages for. #P28, CL 237–262
Average height of planted plane trees. #P51, AA 215–223
Average time for carry propagation. #P90, AA 467–471
Avoiding 'go to' statements, notes on. #P42, CL 495–505
Axioms and Hulls. CP 219
Aztec diamonds, checkerboard graphs, and spanning trees. #P150,
    DM 187–192
Babylonian algorithms, ancient. #P53, CS 185–203
Backtrack programs, estimating the efficiency of. #P69, AA 55–75
Backus Normal Form versus Backus Naur Form. #Q11, CL 95–97

The asymptotic number of geometries. #P62, DM 425–427
The average height of planted plane trees. #P51, AA 215–223
The average time for carry propagation. #P90, AA 467–471
The birth of the giant component. #P140, DM 643–792
The Bose–Nelson sorting problem. #P55, DA 19–30
The calculation of Easter. #Q3 ⤳ *TAOCP* exercise 1.3.2–14
The chemical caper. #R4, FG 401–404
The Chinese domino challenge. #Q142, CP 12–13
The complexity of nonuniform random number generation. #P80, AA 545–603
The complexity of songs. #Q48, FG 33–39
The computer as Master Mind. #P81, FG 219–229
The concept of a meta-font. #P100, DT 289–314
The *CWEB* System of Structured Documentation. CP 219
The dangers of computer science theory. #P56, AA 19–26
The difference between art and science. #Q97
The distribution of continued fraction approximations. #P106, AA 181–187
The early development of programming languages. #P83, CL 1–94
The error log of TEX. LP 293–339
The errors of TEX. #P124, LP 243–339
The expected linearity of a simple equivalence algorithm. #P88, AA 341–389
The final errors of TEX. DT 655–662
The first cycles in an evolving graph. #P122, DM 585–642
The future of TEX and METAFONT. #Q118, DT 571–572
The Gamov–Stern elevator problem. #P35, FG 79–86
The genesis of attribute grammars. #Q114, CL 423–438
The history of sorting. #Q31 ⤳ *TAOCP* §5.5
The IBM 650: An appreciation from the field. #P112, CS 227–239
The initial reception of *Concrete Mathematics.* #Q149
The Knowlton–Graham partition problem. #P154, DM 439–443
The letter S. #P96, DT 263–284
The *METAFONT book.* CP 214–215
The new versions of TEX and METAFONT. #Q112, DT 563–570
The orchestra song. FG 179–184
The plot thickens. #R4, FG 59–60
The potrzebie system, official tables of. FG 9–18
The potrzebie system of weights and measures. #P1, FG 1–8
The power of a prime that divides a generalized binomial coefficient. #P121, DM 515–524

Combined Index

The index entries below list the relevant page numbers from the present companion volume together with all relevant page numbers from the eight individual volumes of Donald E. Knuth's collected works:

AA = *Selected Papers on Analysis of Algorithms*;

CL = *Selected Papers on Computer Languages*;

CS = *Selected Papers on Computer Science*;

DA = *Selected Papers on Design of Algorithms*;

DM = *Selected Papers on Discrete Mathematics*;

DT = *Digital Typography*;

FG = *Selected Papers on Fun and Games*;

LP = *Literate Programming*.

conversion of fractions, binary to
decimal, DA 157–165.
decimal to binary, DA 155–157.
floating point, DA 165, 346.
rational to decimal, DA 164.
convex combination, DM 95–96.
convex corner, DM 160.
convex function, DM 538–539.
convolution family, DM 225–227.
convolution matrix, DM 234, 238.
convolution minimization, DM 538.
convolution polynomials,
DM 225–256, 569.
Conway, John Horton, 252, CS 116,
121, 170, DA 326, 328, DM 304,
FG 72, 119, 140, 450, 452, 455,
465, 706.
Conway, Melvin Edward, CL 285,
325, 545–546, 573, CS 236.
Cook, Curtis, LP 356.
Cook, Matthew Makonnen, AA 75.
Cook, Stephen Arthur, AA 23, 485,
488–491, 493–494, CL 262,
DA 118, 119, 132.
Cook, William John, FG 570.
Cool, Anastasia, FG 402.
Cool, Cynthia, FG 401–402.
Cooper, David Charles, CL 505,
LP 38, 51, 83.
Cooper, Frank James "Gary", 127,
141.
Cooper, Patrick Ian, DT 138–139,
142, 150–152.
cooperating processes, DA xi, 9,
175–180.
copernicium, FG 403.
Copi, Irving Marmer, CL 79.
Copits, Lou, CL 492.
Coppersmith, Don, DM 438.
coproduct of graphs, DM 147.
copy editing, DT 28.
Cora system, 62, 68, DT 482, 506,
539.

Corasick, Margaret John, DA 108,
131.
Coray, Giovanni, 240, DT 154.
Corbis Corporation, 47.
Cordero Brana, Minerva, DM 344.
Cordes, David W., LP 350–351.
core allocation, AA 415–416.
core of a multigraph, DM 678.
core storage, DA 407, 409.
Corless, Robert Malcolm, 246, 262,
DM 256.
Cormack, Gordon Villy, DA 69.
Cormen, Thomas H., AA 494.
Cornell, Brian Clinton, FG 178.
Cornell University, 96–97, 185–186,
CL 426, 428, 432, 542, DA 7.
Cornuejols, Jean, FG 484.
coroutines, CL xii, 179, 197,
545–574, DA 192–194, LP 62.
initialization of, CL 566.
optimization of, CL xii, 569.
recursive, 8, 14, 17, CL 545–574,
DA 5–6.
correctness of programs, DA xi, 2,
9, 13, 90, 103, 134, 141–173,
436; see also invariant
relations.
correspondence problem, CL 284,
296, 345.
coset, DM 359.
cost of a vector, DM 127.
cotrees, DM 191.
Coueignoux, Philippe Jean-Marie,
DT 61, 309–310.
counters, CL 416.
counting, units of, FG xiii, 20, 22.
counting binary ones, CL 440.
coupling, AA xii, 457.
coupon collecting, AA 238, 242,
442, DM 57.
Cousquer, Alain, 257, DT 662.
covering problem, 130–131.
covering relation, DM 180, 407.
coverlet, FG 665–667.

declarations, CL 121–122, 194, 218–219, 244.

declarative language, CL 65–66.
versus imperative, CL 415–416, 424, DT 318, 320, 581.

decompilation, CL 449, 459, 463–464.

decomposable matrix, DM 97.

DECsystem KL-10, CS 180.

Dedekind, Julius Wilhelm Richard, AA 149, 180.
sums, AA 149–180, CS 116.

dedication page, AA v, CL v, CS v, DA v, 14, DM v, DT v, FG v, LP vii.

deep cutoffs, AA 112, 116–117, 138.

Defense Advanced Research Projects Agency, CS 56.

deferred decisions, AA 432.

deficiency of a multigraph, DM 646–647, 714, 729, 735, 740, 753.

deficiency of a string, CL 265.

define, LP 182.

degrees of operators, DA 277.

Dejon, Bruno, CS 261.

Deken, Joseph Gerard, DT 544.

Dekker, Theodorus Jozef, DA 347.

Dekking, Frederik Michel, FG 606–613.

Dektar, Joan, FG 155.

Del Corso, Gianna Maria, AA 531.

Delange, Hubert, AA 338.

Delaunay, Boris Nikolaevich, 243.

deletions, AA 257–264, 279, 283–302.

delimiters, CL 239, 252, 287, DT 633, 643.

Della Valle, Vincent Angelo, CL 78.

Dellac, Hippolyte, AA 2, 17, 503.

Delorme, M. R., 239.

Delsarte, Philippe, DM 176.

demand paging, 4, CL 541, DA 181.

demerits, DT 79–80, 107, 111–112, 119, 154.

DeMillo, Richard Allan, AA 529, 530, LP xiii, 39, 46, 86.

demons, 193.

DemoTEX, DT 212, 221–223.

Dempster, John Robert Hugh, 223, CL 115.

Demuth, Howard B., AA 2, 17, 20–21, 25.

Dénes, József, CS 55.

Denise, Alain, 217.

Denning, Peter James, CS 29, LP 78, 351.

density functions, AA 262, 337, 577.

dependency graph, CL 301.

depth-first search, CS 160–161, FG 225, 438, 441, 697.

deque, LP 93.

derangements, 11.

Deransart, Pierre, CL 435, 436.

DeRemer, Franklin Lewis, CL 360.

derivative anomalies, AA 582.

derived function, AA 393, 396–397, 412.

Derr, John Irving, CL 94.

Dershowitz, Nachum, DA 314.

Desargues, Girard, DM 317.
projective plane, DM 8–9, 333.

Désarménien, Jacques Robert Jean, 246, DM 105, 481–482, DT 390, LP 334.

Descartes, René du Perron, DT 266.

descenders of letters, DT 293–294, 298, 300.

design, LP 138, 288.

design by committee, CL xi, 115, 127, 155–156, 232, 429, DT 352, 354, 599–600, 621.

design motifs, FG 482, 485–486, 488, 509, 521–523.

design of algorithms, DA 1–436.

design of books, DT 369–371, 374–375, 545.

Gibbons, Jeremy, DT 573, 593, 598–599.
Gibbs, Josiah Willard, DT 24.
Lecture, 70, 202, DT x, 19, 24, 608.
Gibbs, Norman Edgar, AA 528, 529.
GIER computer, CL 125.
Gilbarg, David, CS 262.
Gilbert, Edgar Nelson, AA 343, 379, DA 38, 48, 118, 119, 132.
Gilbert, John Russell, FG 300, LP 352.
Gilboa, Itzhak, 241.
Gill, G. W., FG 224, 229.
Gill, John Thomas, III, DA 17.
Gill, Philip Edward, DT 539.
Gill, Stanley, CL 40, 41, 70–71, 86, 90, LP 52, 84.
Gillies, Donald Bruce, 202.
Gillogly, James John, AA 123, 141, 142.
Gillon, Paul N., CS 207.
Gilstad, Russell Leif, AA 21, 25, 214.
Gingerich, Owen Jay, CS 197, 202.
Ginibre, Jean, DM 789.
Ginsburg, Seymour, 244, CL 236, 238, 253, 261, 279, 284, 333, 348–349, 359, 361, 362, 372–373, 375, CS 28.
Gioconda, *see* Mona Lisa.
girlfriends, 80, 117–119.
Girou, Denis, DT 581.
Giustiniani, Agostino, DT 129–130, 132, 134, 152.
Gladstein, David Steven, CS 111.
Glaisher, James Whitbread Lee, DA 373, 380.
Glaser, Anton, 253, DM xiv, 41.
Glassey, Charles Roger, DM 382, 385.
Gleason, Andrew Mattei, 188.
Glennan, Thomas Keith, 121.

Glennie, Alick Edwards, CL 35–42, 45, 52, 76, 79, 83, 285, 325.
glitches, FG 198, 619, 683–684, 714.
global analysis of algorithms, AA x, xii, 28, 485–603.
global data structures, FG 438.
global optimization, CL 455, 521.
global quantities, CL 408.
global variables, CL 158, 179, 191–192, 197–198.
glue, 265, DT 29–31, 70–71, 75, 483, 489–490, 507, 513–515, 662.
Gnebbishland, FG 185–188.
Gnewt, Ursula Nom-de-Plume, DM 44.
GNU Emacs editor, LP 354.
go to statements, AA 5, 10, 114, 599, CL 12, 22–23, 25, 30, 37, 51, 105–108, 112, 119, 162–163, 169, 171, 201, 233, 495–506, 510–513, CS 252, DT 243, FG 54, 236, LP 17, 97, 128, 138, 153, 186, 248, 275, 298.
goals for a programming language, CL 231–236.
God, 118, 193, 202.
Goddijn, Franciscus Theodorus Hendrik, DT 627, 635, 637.
Godfrey, Michael DeWitt, CS 225.
Godsil, Christopher David, DM 192–195, 202.
Goemans, Michel Xavier, FG 144, 153, 156.
Goetz, Martin Alvin, CL 492.
going configurations, DM 622, 758.
Goldbach, Christian, DA 5.
Goldberg, Andrew Vladislav, DA 97, 230, 233.
Goldberg, Karl, DM 25.
Goldberg, Richard, CL 79, 84.
Goldberg, Samuel, DT 541.
golden ratio (ϕ), AA 144, 173, 175, 184, 487, DA 109, 144,

Kielland, Susanne Sophie Caroline
   Gustava Blom, FG 646, 648.
Kilgour, Donald Marc, FG 218.
Killgrove, Raymond Bruce, DM 10,
   11.
Kim, Scott Edward, 205, DT 317,
   348, 350, 352–353, 356–358,
   364, 540.
Kinder, Franz, 251.
Kindersley, David Guy Barnabas,
   DT 18, 62, 310, FG 619.
Kindler, Guy, AA 603.
King, Frank Haydon, FG 224.
King, James Cornelius, DA 6, 17.
King James Bible, FG 423–425,
   428.
Kingman, John Frank Charles,
   AA 336.
Kinnaman, Clarissa J., CL 491.
Kinzler, Henry, CL 85.
Kiong, Derek, LP 358.
Kirchhoff, Gustav Robert, law, 269,
   AA 5, 44, 47, 60, DA 33.
Kirschenhofer, Peter, DM 641.
Kirwan, Richard, LP 15.
Kishi, Nobuko, 253, 261.
Kislitsyn, Sergei Sergeevich, AA 14.
kite shape, FG 499, 643.
Kjeldaas, Torvald, 269.
Klamkin, Murray Seymour, DM 40.
Klammerausdrücke, CL 76.
Klarner, David Anthony, 238, 252,
   269, DA 11, DT 539, FG xv,
   xvi, 103, 411.
Kleber, Michael Steven, AA 75.
Kleene, Stephen Cole, CL 64,
   CS 101, 112, LP 38, 85.
Klees, Robert E., FG 127.
Klein, Christian Felix, AA 180.
Kleinfeld, Erwin, DM 9, 11, 306,
   335, 341–343.
Kleitman, Daniel J (Isaiah
   Solomon), 231, AA 531, 616,

DA 245–246, 249, 251, 269,
   272, DM 385, 421, 429, 432.
Klensch, Richard Joseph, DT 470.
Klimenko, S. V., 214.
Kloks, Antonius (= Ton) Jacobus
   Johannes, AA 531, 532.
Kloper, Kenneth, FG 216–217.
KMP (Knuth–Morris–Pratt)
   algorithm, DA 99–115,
   117–119, 133.
knight graphs, FG 511, 541.
Knight's Page, 55–56, 78.
knight's tour mosaics, FG 491, 553,
   554, 557, 559, 570, 657.
knight's tours, 12, AA 69–70, 73,
   DT 226, FG xiii, 477–570.
   $3 \times n$, FG 478–479, 481, 485–486,
   508–539.
   Celtic, FG 489–509, 700–701.
   geometrically distinct, FG 479,
   492, 516, 536, 537.
knitting, FG 668–669.
knockout tournament, 7.
Knopp, Konrad Hermann Theodor,
   DA 374, 381, DM 535.
Knott, Gary Don, 204,
   AA 258–260, 279–281, 287,
   299, 301, 302.
Knowlton, Kenneth Charles,
   DM 439, 443, DT 431, 447.
Knuth, Carter John, CL xvi,
   FG 189.
Knuth, Donald Ervin, xiii, 4, 6, 23,
   25, 34, 41, 197, 221, AA iv, xiii,
   5, 17–18, 26, 33, 53, 73, 74, 99,
   103, 117, 142, 180, 187, 189,
   192, 202, 205, 223, 233, 236,
   254, 257, 281, 287, 299, 302,
   335, 379, 385, 396, 413, 414,
   425–427, 444, 466, 471, 481,
   482, 500, 503, 543, 602, CL iv,
   ix–x, xiv, 2, 78, 83, 85–87,
   89, 97, 122, 125, 173, 187,
   204, 236, 325, 375, 398, 422,

Lins, Charles A., LP 355.
Lint, Jacobus Hendricus van, 374,
    DM 104.
Linux® operating system, FG 151,
    160.
lions and lionesses, DT 549, 552,
    562, 627–628.
Liouville, Joseph, FG 99, 101.
    numbers, FG 99–100.
LIPED editor, LP 352.
Lipitakis, Elias A., 263.
Lippel, Bernard, DT 471.
Lipscomb, William Nunn, Jr., 184.
Lipton, Richard Jay, AA 529, 530,
    LP xiii, 39, 46, 86.
Lisina, Marina Vladilenovna, 214,
    DT 18.
LISP language, 167, 192, 244,
    AA 116, 396, 404, 413, CL 65,
    168, 538, DT 483, 507, FG 149,
    LP 55, 101, 356.
list heads, DA 59.
list notation, CL 23–24.
list procedure, CL xi, 138, 145–146,
    151, 154.
list processing, 153, 167, CL 32.
list structures, CL 10.
Listing, Johann Benedict, FG 668.
liter, FG 17–19.
literals, DA 91.
literate programming, 141–142,
    164, 200, 215, 246, DA 13,
    DM 422, DT 225, 247, 545,
    560–561, 649–652, FG xii,
    235–394, 465, 684, 712,
    LP 99–358.
  examples of, DA 245–274,
    DT 114–122, 145–150,
    166–173, 197–223, 241–245,
    250–261, 434–446, FG 235–394,
    LP 102–116, 144–167, 185–233,
    341–348.
  history of, DT 613–615.
little-endian convention, FG 53.

little-oh notation, 33, AA 35–40,
    532, FG 137.
little-omega notation, AA 37, 532.
Littlewood, Dudley Ernest,
    DM 463, 464, 477–478, 481.
Littlewood, John Edensor,
    AA 36–38, 40, 142, 155.
Litwin, David Ari, FG 658.
Liu, Chung Laung, 249.
Lïubimskiĭ, Éduard Zinov'evich,
    CL 54, 76, 85.
living, 134.
lizards, DT 144.
LL(1) grammar, CL 318–322.
LL(k) grammar, 194–195, CL 314,
    316–317, 322–323, 430.
LL(k) language, CL 319, 322.
Lloyd, Edward Keith, DM 104.
Lloyd, Norman, FG 38.
Lloyd, Stuart Phinney, AA 329,
    335.
Lluis i Biset, Joan, 207.
LOAD, CL 442.
load-and-go compiler, CL 452.
load factor, AA 81.
load-store motion, CL 521.
local analysis of algorithms, AA x,
    28, 43–483.
local optimization, CL 451, 468,
    521.
local probability, AA 434.
local variables, CL 179, 192, 197.
Lochbaum, Carol, DT 63.
Lochs, Gustav, AA 34, 193–194.
Lockhart, Brooks Javins, CS 206.
Lockheed Missiles and Space
    Corporation, CL 510–513, 539.
Lóczi, Lajos, 212.
Lodi, Ed, DT 541.
Loeb, Henry Leon, DA 413, 433.
log (logarithm to unspecified base),
    AA 441.
log books, LP 244, 261.

random function generation versus
random number generation,
DA xi, 329.
random graph process, DM 587,
647.
random graphs, AA 342–343,
532–533, DA 256, 258,
DM xii–xiii, 52, 585–792.
Random House Dictionary,
FG 398–399.
random integers, AA 322.
random mappings, AA 103, 245,
249–250, 388.
random multigraph process,
DM 587, 647.
random number distributions,
CL 195.
random number generation,
AA 19–20, 545–603, CL 109,
525, DA 329, 349, FG 358,
LP 144–145.
random objects, DM 4, 406, 414.
random paths, CS 39–43, 102.
random permutations, DA 4, 34.
random polynomials, AA 330.
random real numbers, AA 565.
random sampling, CS 39–43, 96,
179, FG 128; *see also* Monte
Carlo method.
random variables, 1.
random walks, AA 216, 226–227,
DM 727.
randomized algorithms, AA 86,
145–147, 532, DT 57–59,
286–287, 324–325, 386,
391–396.
randomness, FG 193–198, 282, 617,
673.
defined, DM 265.
Randrianarimanana, Bruno,
AA 302.
Raney, George Neal, DM 209, 219,
223–224.
range checks, LP 30.

rank and file, FG 541.
rank in a matroid, DM 411, 416.
rank of apparition, DM 518.
Ranucci, Ernest Raymond, FG 632.
Rao, Gururaj Seshagiri, 234,
AA xiii, 101, 254, 379.
Raphael, Bertram, CL 66.
Rapoport, Anatol, AA 103–104.
raster, DT 6, 34–35, 52–56, 307,
419, 449.
Ratfor, LP 354.
Rathmell, Edward Cary, FG 134.
rational numbers, 17.
Raymond, Eric Steven, FG 57, 58.
Raymond, François Henri, DT 136,
151.
Read, Ronald Cedric, 230, AA xv,
215, CS 28.
read-backward polyphase merge,
AA 211.
readability, CL 472, DT 133, 292,
308, 371, 636, LP 126.
reader's manual, LP 179.
reading a program, LP 137.
reading a **WEB**, DT 197.
Reagan, Ronald Wilson, FG 44,
126–127.
real number representations,
AA 561–566.
real numbers, 16, CS 105–108,
DA 137, FG 141–144, 583,
598–599; *see also* fundamental
constants.
extended, DA 209.
real part, DM 598, 693.
real-time algorithms, DA 53, 56,
68, 109, 119.
Rearrangement Device, AA 15–16,
18.
Reasons, George, FG 125, 159.
Rebozo, Charles Gregory "Bebe",
FG 126.
recipes, DT 177–180, 190–193.
reciprocals, CS 186, 197–200, 203.

Winograd, Terry Allen, DT 540,
    619, FG 430, LP 263, 308.
Winston, Patrick Henry, 59–60,
    DT 544, 558, FG 468, LP 249,
    291.
wire recorder, 78.
wires, identifying, DM 439.
Wirsing, Eduard, AA 183, 187.
Wirth, Nani, 97.
Wirth, Niklaus Emil, 97, 186, 254,
    CL 322, 323, 326, 395–396, 398,
    430, 504, CS 113, 250, 260,
    DA 42, 48, DM 422, DT 152,
    505, LP 21, 36, 48, 49, 67, 78,
    84, 88–89, 131, 248.
Wis-SOAP II assembly program,
    DA 400.
Wischmeyer Ehlert, Clara Louise,
    FG 630.
Wisconsin Academy of Sciences,
    Arts and Letters, Junior
    division, FG 1, 9, 17.
Wise, Richard B., CL 67.
Wiseman, Neil Ernest, DT 150,
    310, 577.
Witt, Perry Odd, FG 281.
Woeginger, Gerhard Johannes,
    FG 92.
Woehr, Jack, 260.
Wolder, David, DT 154.
Wolf, Hans, 57–58, 86, DT 59, 562,
    620.
Wolf, Kurt Bernardo, DT 544.
Wolfe, Philip Starr, DA 433.
Wolfram|Alpha™, FG 26.
Wolontis, Vidar Michael, CS 239,
    DA 433, 436.
Woltman, George Frederick,
    FG 160.
Wolverton, Basil Barnbrain, FG 4,
    10.
Wong, Eugene, DA 38, 48.
Wood, David Edward, AA 143.

Wood, Wallace Allan, 222, FG 1–8,
    10, 17, 19, 21.
Woodall, Herbert J., DM 303.
Woodbridge, George Charles,
    FG 30.
Woodcock, Jim C. P., 247, FG xvi,
    437.
Woodger, Michael, CL 90, 91, 97,
    173, LP 78.
Woodrow Wilson Foundation, 123,
    152, 200.
Woods, Donald Roy, CL 236,
    FG xii, 41, 43, 57, 58, 235–236,
    240, 289, 292, 296, 380,
    LP 291.
Woods Berners-Lee, Mary Lee,
    CL 80.
Woolf, William Blauvelt, DT 352.
word count, LP 151, 341.
word cubes, FG 433–436.
word golf, FG 416.
word ladders, FG 415–427.
word links, FG 416.
word play, FG ix, xii–xiv, 395–436.
word problems, DA 7, 275–314.
    defined, DA 286.
word processing, DT 26, 145.
word puzzles, FG 27–30, 415–419,
    421, 423–425, 431.
word squares, FG 425, 428,
    435–436, 464.
words (well-formed formulas),
    DA 277.
work habits, 127–129, 133, 135–138.
workaholic, CL 426, 482.
working outdoors, 128–129, 153,
    235, CL 432.
working storage, CL 42–44, 55–56,
    449, 462.
Worlton, William Jack, FG 467.
Worsley, Beatrice Helen, CL 76,
    91–92.
worst case of dot diffusion, DT 454.